Shaking Up the Schoolhouse

Phillip C. Schlechty

Shaking Up the Schoolhouse

How to Support and Sustain Educational Innovation

 JOSSEY-BASS
A Wiley Company
San Francisco

Jossey-Bass books and products are available through most bookstores. To contact Jossey-Bass directly, call (888) 378-2537, fax to (800) 605-2665, or visit our website at www.josseybass.com.

Substantial discounts on bulk quantities of Jossey-Bass books are available to corporations, professional associations, and other organizations. For details and discount information, contact the special sales department at Jossey-Bass.

TCF Manufactured in the United States of America on Lyons Falls Turin Book. This paper is acid-free and 100 percent totally chlorine-free.

Library of Congress Cataloging-in-Publication Data
Schlechty, Phillip C.
  Shaking up the schoolhouse : how to support and sustain educational innovation / Phillip C. Schlechty.— 1st ed.
      p. cm. — (The Jossey-Bass education series)
  Includes bibliographical references and index.
  ISBN 0-7879-5540-X
  1. School improvement programs—United States.   2. Curriculum change—United States.   I. Title.   II. Series.
  LB2822.82 .S34 2000
  371.2'00973—dc21

                                                                    00-009570

FIRST EDITION
HB Printing   10 9 8 7 6 5 4 3 2 1

The Jossey-Bass Education Series

Contents

Preface

The pace of change in American society is far outstripping the capacity of schools to keep up. The consequence is that more and more influential persons are seeking alternatives to the public schools. I am convinced, in fact, that the entire edifice of public education in the United States, which is an essential part of the institutions that support our democracy, is more threatened now than it ever was in the past. Yet I remain hopeful that with the right leadership these threats can be transformed into opportunities and that the weaknesses of the schools can be overcome by the strengths these institutions possess.

For these leaders to do their jobs it is essential first to acknowledge that in spite of numerous waves of reform U.S. schools are not much different—either for good or ill—than they were fifty years ago. Certainly there have been changes, but for the most part they have been fragmented, episodic, multidirectional, and lacking in coordination and persistence. School systems are change prone, but they are not good at transforming change into improved performance. School leaders introduce one innovation after another, yet things stay pretty much as they were before the innovation was introduced.

In this book I shed light on why this is the case and what might be done about it. My basic argument is that the social systems that make up schools and the context in which schools exist must be changed in ways that make schools more adept at selecting, installing, and maintaining innovative programs and projects. In brief, if public schools in the United States are to continue to play a vital role in the education of our children, educational leaders must learn how to create schools and school systems that are adept at supporting and sustaining innovations while introducing new practices into the system.

The first step in this process is for those who lead the schools to become clear about and agree on the nature of the business they are in. Currently we have such a jumble of nominees for the real purpose of schools, it is little wonder that change is fickle and episodic. As the

Cheshire Cat long ago pointed out to Alice in *Alice in Wonderland,* if you don't know where you are going, "Then it doesn't matter which way you go."

Is learning the business of schools? Is teaching the business of schools? Or is it both? Is providing the economy with a world-class workforce the business of schools? Or is that business creating a culturally literate citizenry committed to lifelong learning and democratic citizenship, or perhaps endowing students with the capacity for critical thought and the skills and attitudes needed to live in a society characterized by diversity?

Recently some leaders have adopted the habit of inviting various stakeholder groups to help them "discover" the purpose of schools and establish learning standards. This approach is justified by the view that in a democracy, it is the right and duty of the citizenry to assert what the ends of education should be. However, exercises such as these sometimes confuse the ends of education and the purpose of schools. The ends of education and the purpose of schools are distinct objectives. The *ends of education* have to do with such things as providing the society with a culturally literate citizenry, a world-class workforce, people who can think and reason and use their minds well, and so on. The *purpose of schools* is to provide students with experiences that ensure that these educational ends are attained for all, or nearly all, children.

To answer properly the question, What is our business? organizational leaders must concentrate attention on *what the organization does to produce results* rather than on the results themselves; namely, they must focus on the organization's purpose. For example, the business of Ford Motor Company is to produce an automobile that people will buy at a price that will keep the company in business and provide company stockholders with a decent return on their investment. Providing the stockholders with a decent return on their investment is not the business of Ford Motor Company. A return on investment that meets the needs of the stockholder (who is also a customer of Ford) is what happens when Ford does its business well.

Education, like return on investment, is the result of schools doing their business. Education is not, however, the business of schools any more than making a profit is the business of the Ford Motor Company. Ford strives to provide affordable, reliable transportation to individual car owners. Profit is a result of Ford doing its business. Schools strive to provide students with tasks, assignments, and other experiences that engage students. The end result is that students learn things valued by their parents, themselves, and the society at large.

Statements of the aims of education are important to all of us, because we are all in some way dependent on the schools to meet some need: the world-class workforce, the culturally literate citizenry that has those skills, attitudes, and habits of mind that are most likely to lead to happy and productive lives in a democracy typified by diversity. However, as the number and diversity of those invited into the conversation about the ends of education have broadened, educators are discovering, as business leaders have discovered, that a wide range of values come to bear on what various constituencies expect the schools to "produce." Reconciling these competing claims and determining which to respond to and which will receive priority are among the most difficult decisions leaders make. Business leaders and school leaders alike are finding it necessary to redefine the purpose of their business and the customers their business serves.

Consider, for example, the case of IBM, which for many years focused primarily on corporate customers who were in a position to buy large mainframe computers and who valued service above all. IBM became highly successful at producing what these customers valued. With the advent of the PC, what customers valued changed, and what IBM produced no longer made the company so successful. Bringing about the changes needed to address this new condition has tested and continues to test the adeptness of IBM in supporting and sustaining wrenching changes.

The public schools are facing a similar but much greater test. For years they have taken as their primary customers those students who come to school with the backgrounds, incentives, and work habits that lead them to desire to engage in academic pursuits. Most statements about the purpose of education have emphasized the intention of the schools to provide all students with the "opportunity to learn." What the schools have promised to do as their business has been to provide work for students that, as long as they are willing to do it and do it with enthusiasm, will result in the students' learning what they need to learn to be educated.

As academic institutions, the schools of America have worked well for students who have needed only access and opportunity in order to succeed. Moreover, as long as there have been no substantial social or economic penalties for those who have not fully availed themselves of the educational opportunities schools provide, society has been able to ignore the fact that the schools have not been serving all their customers well. As long as a youngster can drop out of school and get a well-paying job, for example, the relationship between academic education and the economy will not be seen as critically important.

Today's demand is that the schools serve a wider range of students than they did in the past and that they cause all, or nearly all, of these students to undertake tasks that result in substantial academic learning. In addition, the standards all students are now expected to meet are standards that just a generation ago only a relatively few students—mainly the college bound—were expected to meet. The business of schools as it was defined in the past cannot meet this demand.

Producing educated citizens is an important result of schooling, but it is not the business of school. Rather, the business of school is to provide students with intellectual tasks that they will do because they find these tasks to be meaningful, challenging, and satisfying to themselves and others. These tasks and activities must be designed in such a way that students will not only engage in the tasks assigned, but they will also persist with these tasks when they experience difficulty. Finally, doing the tasks assigned must produce in students a sense of accomplishment and pride, for it is pride more than any other factor that leads to the pursuit of high standards. Serving this purpose well is what schools and those who work in them should "busy" themselves with, for that is their "busy-ness."

In this book, as in all my other books, I have applied what C. Wright Mills has called the "sociological imagination" to the problems of education. Furthermore, I agree with Mills when he says that in this age of facts it is not facts that are needed. What is needed are ideas for making sense of the facts we already have, ideas that allow us to summarize what we are experiencing in terms that are understandable and in phrases that can be shared. Without such understanding, facts overwhelm us.[1]

The reader who is seeking new facts about the condition of our schools is likely to be disappointed. Rather than present more facts, this book provides those whose decisions will determine the destiny of public education with ideas that will organize and discipline the facts they now have. I hope that, armed with these understandings, these leaders in education will seize the moment and act to ensure the preservation of public education in America, for the demise of public education will almost certainly be a harbinger of the demise of American democracy.

OVERVIEW OF THE CONTENTS

Part One (Chapters One and Two) offers an overview of the current situation in U.S. public schools, looking especially at changes in society and technology that are changing needs and expectations, and outlining the characteristics of change-adept organizations. It also introduces the idea of systemic change; our schools will not succeed in making the kind of changes they must make to meet the expectations of politicians, parents, employers, and citizens in general until school leaders cause systems that now support the status quo to support change instead.

Part Two (Chapters Three through Seven) is intended to be especially useful to teachers and administrators, though any reader who wishes to view the world of education from an educator's perspective will find these chapters of value. They present a framework I have found useful for helping teachers come to grips with the problems associated with improving the quality of the experiences they provide for students.

Beginning with the idea of managing by results (Chapter Three), this section then moves into a discussion of the core business of schooling (Chapter Four). Chapter Five (initially titled "Lessons Learned in an Allentown Bar") demonstrates how the habit of studying the competition leads to a better understanding of what one needs to do to succeed (and schools today experience a great deal of competition for students' attention). Chapter Six describes the Working on the Work framework for assessing the quality of schoolwork and a number of standards and indicators for that assessment. Chapter Seven discusses several ways to use this framework in developing schools that meet today's expectations.

Part Three (Chapters Eight through Ten) is specifically directed to those who occupy positions of formal authority in the leadership structure of schools: teacher leaders, principals, superintendents, and boards of education. Chapters Eight and Nine offer many specific steps leaders can take and issues they can address to bring about successful structural and cultural change. Chapter Ten responds to the many people who have asked me what is the best way to get started in bringing about or supporting a major change effort. It offers some specific initial actions for each of the major groups involved in school reform, from boards of education to members of the community at large.

The Epilogue offers a scenario of the future we may face if we cannot succeed in making public schools experts in systemic change and continuous improvement, and some words of encouragement.

Overall, I have tried to address a broad readership. Our schools should matter to us all, and one of the major ideas underlying this book is that a strong sense of community is critical to strong and effective schools. It is imperative that schools develop the capacity to build communities as well as to serve them. It is also imperative that those outside the schools and those who have no children understand that they have a role to play in the education of the country's children. I hope that this book will be a valuable tool for all who engage in the struggle for better schools.

ACKNOWLEDGMENTS

This book, as everything I do in education, has benefited much from insights and suggestions provided by others. I will not attempt to list all of those to whom I owe so much. I do, however, want to thank some people who have made direct and immediate contributions to the production of this book. First and foremost, I want to thank Tena Lutz, who has worked with me for sixteen years and seen me through several books. Without her help, none of the books would have been completed. Similarly, I owe a continuing debt to Hugh Cassell, who always gives me good editorial advice. Other CLSR staff who have been especially supportive of my efforts are Ron Barber, Dennis Boswell, Don Dyck, Jack Edwards, Tammy Hatcher, Lennie Hay, Marilyn Hohmann, Tom Johnson, Bob Nolte, Niki Piccione, Shanna Rucker, Darlene Settles, George Thompson, Bobbi Vogel, and Joan Wimsatt. A special thank you goes to Judy Hummel, who helped me think through issues related to leadership and leadership development.

I would like to thank all the teachers, principals, and superintendents who have taken the time to talk with me about my ideas and helped me think more clearly about the issues I address in this book. I especially want to thank Roland Chevalier, Janice Davis, Ann Denlinger, Carlos Hick, Jim Jenkins, and Jane Kendrick, each of whom is an outstanding superintendent and each of whom spent much time with me reacting to an earlier version of the manuscript that resulted in this book. I am sure that because of their input the book is better than it would otherwise have been. Dennis Sparks, executive director of National Staff Development Council, also made a number of suggestions that I know improved the book.

The encouragement and support I have received from the editorial staff at Jossey-Bass during an especially trying time made this book possible. I especially want to thank Lesley Iura, who has worked with me on three books and has always encouraged me even when I have been about to give up. Others I would like to thank are Alice Morrow Rowan and Elspeth McHattie, who helped me turn this manuscript into what it has become.

Writing a book always takes a toll on family life and I could not have completed this book, or the others I have written, had my wife Shelia not given me the support she has throughout my career. Thanks again, dear wife.

Near the end of my work on this book I was informed of the death of Jay Robinson, former superintendent of the Charlotte-Mecklenburg Schools, vice president of the University of North Carolina, and chairperson of the North Carolina State Board of Education. Those who know me know of the debt I owe to Jay. He taught me many lessons about leadership and what leaders do. He provided me with many stories to tell and retell. His passing is a loss to all who care about public education in America. To dedicate a book is to inflate the importance of the book beyond what it might deserve, but to the extent that this book is deserving of any honor, it is dedicated to Jay Robinson, a friend, mentor, and guide. Much that I write he taught me. Clearly many of us owe much to Jay, as do many children yet to be born.

Louisville, Kentucky   Phillip C. Schlechty
September 2000

The Author

Phillip C. Schlechty is founder and CEO of the Center for Leadership in School Reform and the author of *Reform in Teacher Education: A Sociological View* (1989), *Schools for the 21st Century: Leadership Imperatives for Educational Reform* (1990), and *Inventing Better Schools: An Action Plan for Educational Reform* (1997), as well as numerous other publications. Formerly a professor at the University of North Carolina at Chapel Hill and executive director of the Jefferson County Public Schools/Gheens Professional Development Academy, an organization he conceived and instituted, he serves as adviser to many school districts in the United States and Canada and conducts seminars and training sessions for superintendents, school board members, union leaders, principals, teachers, and parent groups.

Schlechty is one of the nation's most sought-after speakers on topics related to school reform. Business groups as well as educators find his perspective useful and understandable.

He received his B.S., M.A., and Ph.D. degrees from the Ohio State University.

Born near Rossburg, Ohio, Schlechty has two daughters, and he and his wife reside in Louisville, Kentucky.

Shaking Up the Schoolhouse

PART ONE

Understanding the System

When the rate of change outside an organization is greater than the rate of change inside, the continuing existence of that organization is threatened. American society, the external environment for U.S. schools, has been experiencing dramatic shifts in structure over the past half century. The effect on schools is compounded by the fact that some of the most profound shifts have been in the core technologies of schooling, more specifically, shifts in the means by which information is stored, retrieved, transmitted, and processed. These shifts require school leaders to respond with dramatic and powerful changes in the way schools go about doing their business and perhaps even with a redefinition of the nature of the business they do.

To date, however, the response has been slow. Most efforts to bring about improvement in school performance have met at best with only modest success, and what success there has been has largely taken the form of turning truly terrible schools into mediocre ones. There has been less success in making mediocre schools excellent and in driving excellent schools to excel even more.

The reason this is so has little to do with the will or intelligence of educators. If all it took to improve schools were bright leaders who had the will to change our schools, those schools would already be performing at much higher levels than they are now. The reason schools have not improved is that they have changed so much and so often with so little effect that leaders seem baffled about what to do next.

To change a system, leaders must control that system and feel that they are in control. Today many educational leaders—policymakers, administrators, and teachers—feel powerless and feel that the systems they lead are out of control or beyond their control. If educational leaders are to improve these systems, however, they must learn to control them; for without control there can be no systematic improvement. Any improvement that might occur will be more attributable to chance than to leadership.

To improve the systems they lead leaders must first understand those systems. The chapters in Part One present the background material necessary to an understanding of the systems that can support change.

CHAPTER ONE

Introduction

Social Change and School Reform

I n the early 1980s, school reformers were full of hope. Many believed that U.S. schools in the twenty-first century would differ dramatically from the schools of the 1970s. Student achievement would be up; dropout rates would be down. The public schools would be viewed with pride by all American citizens. America's schools would be, as the saying goes, world-class.

The twenty-first century is now upon us. The public schools of America in the year 2000 are not that much different from the schools of the 1970s. The pace of public school change and improvement has been slow, so slow that increasing numbers of serious men and women have begun to doubt that real improvement in the American system of education is likely.

I have written this book because I believe that to give up on our ideals for universal public education is to give up on our democratic way of life and because I believe that real improvement is possible. Schools can improve when their leaders turn them into organizations where change is embraced as an opportunity rather than coped with as a problem.[1] Improvement must be continuous and must be embedded in all systems a school comprises. Schools can improve when school leaders learn how to build a supportive community, respecting diversity but healing divisiveness. Schools can improve when school leaders focus on their business and have properly understood the nature of that business. In this book I describe how school leaders, including teachers, can improve their schools in all these ways. In this introductory chapter, I sketch the world of public criticism, social change, and technological challenge in which schools must become change adept, build community, and become expert at the business of creating engaging work for students.

THE CLIMATE OF COMPLAINT

It is not an exaggeration to say that the history of school reform is a history of complaint. Though Americans long held public schools in high regard, they also always complained about them.[2] Historically, however, most of those who complained about the schools as *academic* institutions were members of the academy (university presidents, college deans, and so on) or members of the cultural and educational elite (such as journalists, editors, and professional social critics). In recent years such criticism has become much more widespread. Governors and presidents, members of Congress, and state legislators too are critical of the schools, as are increasing numbers of local mayors. These critics have focused particularly on the failure of the schools to produce students with sufficient academic skills to ensure a *world-class workforce* within the context of an economy that requires *knowledge work* as its primary mode of increasing productivity. Many business leaders are now echoing this complaint as are increasing numbers of parents.

Business leaders of the past tended to focus on the schools' role in vocational training. Today those leaders say that schools do not develop the academic skills students will need to engage in continuous, purposeful learning as employees. These leaders are equally concerned that the schools are not developing or enforcing the moral standards and work habits that they see as necessary for a world-class workforce. One poll has shown that after nearly twenty years of active involvement by business leaders in efforts to improve America's schools, 78 percent of the American business leaders surveyed viewed education as either the number one or number two barrier to the success of their organization.[3]

And of course the number of citizens, parents and nonparents, prepared to be critical of schools' academic quality has expanded. The parents most likely to be concerned have always been those who plan on college for their children. More Americans than ever before are enrolling in colleges and universities. Indeed, the present generation of adult Americans contains a larger proportion of high school and college graduates than any generation before. Furthermore, there is some evidence that better-educated individuals are more likely to see the schools as lacking in academic standards, and these people also have the verbal and organizational skills to make their complaints heard. There is a certain irony in the possibility that the past successes of America's public schools are making today's schools more likely to be subjected to criticism, especially criticism of their academic programs.

For example, a recent Phi Delta Kappa/Gallup poll asked respondents this question: "As you look on your own elementary and high school education, is it your impression that children today get a better—or worse—education than you did?" Forty-one percent of all respondents in both 1979 and 1998 perceived the schools to be better. The percentage that perceived the schools to be worse rose from 42 percent in 1979 to 48 percent in 1998.[4] This may not seem a large gain in negative assessments. However, a more fine-grained analysis is revealing. According to Rose and Gallup: "Groups more likely to believe children are receiving a worse education include the West (27% better, 59% worse), political independents (33% better, 52% worse), college graduates (31% better, 51% worse), those with incomes of $50,000 and over (34% better, 55% worse), and professionals and business people (33% better, 55% worse). Groups likely to feel children are getting a better education include nonwhites (53% better, 40% worse), Democrats (47% better, 42% worse), those in the South (49% better, 43% worse), and public school parents (49% better, 43% worse)."[5] It is reasonable to speculate that those most likely to see the schools as worse than they used to be are also those who may have benefited most from the schools of the past (for example, professionals and businesspeople and those with incomes above $50,000); whereas those who see the schools as better are also those for whom the schools of the past may have been less effective (Southerners and nonwhites).

At the same time, many educators believe that the criticisms they are now receiving from all parts of society are unjustified. As a result they often respond with expressions of hurt, bewilderment, and anger. Some go so far as to claim that the biggest problem the public schools have is a public relations problem. Bad news sells. Good news does not sell. The press prefers bad news to good news, so the good news about the schools does not get to the public.

Some of the criticism of the schools is valid, but there is also considerable justification for the claim that educators too often receive unfair and misguided criticism, and it is important that we sort out the valid from the unfounded complaints. Indeed, America's schools are far better than many critics say,[6] and many American citizens are terribly ignorant about the public schools. Not only do they underestimate present performance, they overestimate the performance of schools in the past. Their criticism too often assumes there was a time when America's schools were more productive, a time when all students could read, high school dropouts were few, and all parents were supportive. For example, *A Nation at Risk,* the report that many credit with initiating the present reform movement, described the performance of America's schools as "a rising tide of mediocrity."[7] The image was one of an eroding system that had once been great. The goal was to restore America's schools to their former greatness.

Yet judged as academic institutions America's public schools have always been suspect.[8] In the not-too-distant past, schools were judged as much on social productivity as on academic productivity. The primary mission of the schools, functionally speaking, was to select and sort students according to the talents they brought to the schools and to "Americanize" the children of immigrants. Today, the assumption is that the talents once thought to be inherent in the individual, especially academic talents and skills, can be developed by the schools. Therefore a school judged successful in the past would not meet our expectations today.

Critics of America's schools lament the current dropout rate but never acknowledge that it is substantially lower than in the past. In 1970, for example, 52.2 percent of Americans above the age of twenty-five had attended four years of high school. Today that number is in excess of 85 percent.

When it comes to criticism of students' geographical illiteracy, scientific illiteracy, and historical illiteracy we should remember the curriculum projects of the 1960s designed to eradicate such illiteracies and make our scientists competitive with other countries' scientists. If the schools of the past were so effective, why are we hearing the same criticisms four decades later? It *is* disgraceful that some of the young soldiers who fought in the Gulf War probably could not find Saudi Arabia on the map if given two continents to spare. It is also a shame that young soldiers going to Bosnia may not know who the Archduke Ferdinand was or why he was important to the world. But are they all that different from the young men who joined the Army in 1941 who did not know where Pearl Harbor was?

In the not-too-distant past a significant number of Americans were literally illiterate in that they could not decode words on the written page. Today, 99 percent of all adult Americans can read in the sense that they can decode words.[9] The illiteracy rate that concerns us today is the *functional* illiteracy rate. Nearly half of adult Americans are functionally illiterate; they cannot read well enough to manage daily living and employment tasks that require reading skills beyond a basic level. Literal illiteracy has been eradicated. What remains to be eradicated is functional illiteracy, which represents a newer, higher standard.

Taking a romantic view of the past in relation to the present often translates into misguided policies and acerbic commentary, summed up in the battle cry "back to the basics." But how, it should be asked, can we go back to where we have never been?

Yet educators cannot take comfort from the fact that complaint about the schools is an ongoing and even traditional process in America. To make this mistake is to foreordain the demise of our system of public education. Instead, once we have weeded out the criticisms based on myths about the past, we must look at the very real differences in the nature of past and present criticisms and there we will find concerns that must be addressed if public schools are to survive as a vital force in American life.

First, as described earlier, many more people, from politicians to businesspeople to taxpayers to parents, are criticizing the schools today. Second, their criticisms are increasingly focused on academic standards. There are many forces at play that make the academic quality of schools of growing importance. For example, there is the concern mentioned previously about developing a more effective workforce of individuals prepared to perform knowledge work and prepared to function well in multinational companies. There is the concern about preparing young people to carry out their responsibilities as citizens in an environment in which people are bombarded twenty-four hours a day with raw data and unprocessed information. In the past it was adequate if one could critically analyze the interpretations of others such as journalists, ministers, newspaper editors, and authors. Nowadays, the ability to synthesize facts and to give meaning to these facts is as much a necessary tool for citizenship as it is a skill needed to work in the modern workplace. Further, when interpretations are offered, they are likely to come not from known quantities in the local community, with known agendas and biases, but from sources outside the community and outside the context of community values. Under such conditions the survival of American democracy may well depend on the ability of citizens to think for themselves and not just choose among preprocessed ideas handed to them by competing talk show hosts and nationally oriented publications.

Given the changing demands placed on schools and, as I discuss later in this chapter, the changing context in which those demands are being made, it is not surprising that many Americans are becoming convinced that the present education system is sick, without direction or standards, and unable to repair itself. It is also understandable that more and more Americans are willing to consider options to public education such as vouchers and charter schools that would have been rejected outright by the majority of American citizens a generation ago. According to the Phi Delta Kappa/Gallup poll, for example, 44 percent of those surveyed favored tax-based support for private education and vouchers in 1998, up from 24 percent just five years previously. In 1998, 48 percent of public school parents and 59 percent of blacks favored tax proposals for private schools as well.[10]

Are such measures called for? Perhaps. If nothing else results, the threat that many educators see in charter schools and vouchers may be a spur to change in the way public schools go about their business, creating a sense of urgency that is too often lacking today. Yet there are also many problems inherent in voucher and charter school programs, including the likelihood that nonparent taxpayers will want some control over the ways their money can be spent in such programs, and the very real possibility that careless implementation could destroy public schools without improving the quality of education in America.

We will probably do better to focus our energies on taking action to improve our existing schools, but too many educators today feel powerless to do so. If they have not dismissed as unfounded the shrill, mean-spirited, and accusatory criticism they hear, they have often dislocated problems from the schools and insisted that the solutions lie elsewhere—for example with parents or the larger society.[11] Such a view places the problems of the schools beyond the control of educators, which produces feelings of powerlessness. Feelings of powerlessness turn into feelings of hopelessness and despair. Hopelessness and despair encourage inaction. Legislators and critics insist that "something" needs to be done and that educators need to be "accountable."

In the face of apparent inaction, this desire for action gets transformed into threats and intimidation. Threats and intimidation produce fear and panic. Fear and panic produce frenetic activity—activity that is without clear direction, activity that has little prospect of correcting the conditions that give rise to the threat in the first place, though it consumes considerable energy and gives the illusion that "something" is being done. The upshot is that in spite of great effort, little improvement occurs and the criticism goes on.

If America's system of public education is to be preserved and revitalized, its leaders must take purposeful and persistent action. *Such powerful action will come about only when educators accept the fact that as good as America's schools are, they are nowhere near reaching the level of productivity that is required for them to continue to survive—let alone to thrive—in the twenty-first century.*

Moreover, because public schools have no history of producing an entire population of academically well grounded citizens, despite the persistent myth of a golden age of education, *if the schools of America are to survive and thrive, American educators must be prepared to do things that have never been done, under conditions that have no precedents in our history.* To achieve powerful action and make schools thrive, educators must first understand the tremendous social shifts and technological changes they are confronting and the expectations these conditions impose on them.

SEISMIC SHIFTS

School leaders, like leaders in other organizations, have implicit and explicit assumptions about the environment in which the organizations they lead exist, and these assumptions are the basis on which schools are organized, rules and norms are developed, roles are assigned, and relationships are established. Over the past fifty years there have been major shifts in the structure of the larger society in which the schools are embedded, and these shifts are challenging the assumptions on which the schools are based. These changes are of such a magnitude that they may well be compared to seismic shifts. And like seismic shifts, they can lead to the destruction of the smaller structures that depend on the larger structure for support.

Which shifts are most significant in shaping the problems that confront school reformers? I nominate the following eight for the consideration of all concerned with the future of our schools.

Every Child an Academic Success

Shift 1: From a society in which only the culturally elite and the intellectually gifted were expected to achieve high levels of academic competence to a society in which nearly all students are expected to perform at levels once assumed to be the purview of a few.

It is now commonplace for educators to assert that every child can learn at high levels. There was a time when such a belief would have been viewed as absurd, when it was argued that academic learning was not for everyone. Today it is assumed that academic learning is for everyone and that to fail to ensure literacy in the basic subjects (especially science and mathematics) is to fail utterly. Just fifty years ago, for example, high school algebra was a part of the college preparatory curriculum and reserved for those few who would be attending college. Today many states and local school systems have made algebra a graduation requirement.

Schools are failing to meet this expectation that all students can learn, and it is all too common for educators to blame parents or students for this lack of performance. It is certainly the case that some students lack ambition, are careless about their performance, and are unwilling to expend more energy than is essential just to get by. And certainly individual students should assume responsibility for their own performance. Parents as well as schools should teach such values and standards as those contained in words and phrases like *duty, obligation,* and *respect for legitimate authority.* Persistence and working hard remain essential notions to anyone interested in pursuing excellence in any field of endeavor. However, sloth and laziness, short attention spans, and poor work habits do not explain why so many children are not learning more. *The reason America's schoolchildren are not learning what we want them to learn is that in too many instances they are being asked to do things they do not see as worth doing in order to learn things adults want them to learn. If educators want students to work hard and be persistent, they must find ways of designing work that students believe to be worth doing.*

Currently, our schools offer students a limited range of experiences through which to develop, apply, and refine academic skills and concepts. When students are not prepared to participate fully in these experiences that reflect the norms, values, and work styles of the academy, they have no alternative means of learning. There is, after all, an anti-intellectual streak running throughout America's social landscape.[12] Americans, especially in the working classes and the business classes, show a strong preference for the practical over the theoretical and the applied over the abstract. Such distrust of the "merely" theoretical and the nonpragmatic is not limited to the less schooled. Teachers who disavow theory as a guide to practice are evidencing the same distrust of ideas that the business leader evidences when he or she states, "Those that can, do; those that can't, teach," or that Archie Bunker shows when he refers to his educated son-in-law as "Meathead." Thus, despite the demand for academic skills, people do not want to gain these skills through traditional academic methods.

In many other nations, especially Germany and Japan, it is recognized that the ways of the academy are not the only ways through which one can develop academic skills and understandings. In much of Europe and Asia vocational education is a mechanism for teaching not only vocational skills but also academic skills. In fact, it is reasonable to speculate that broadly conceived vocational education offering intellectually challenging experiences is one of the reasons European students with middling academic talent perform better on academic tests than their American peers do.

Yet these techniques are probably not importable to the United States. When American schools do provide optional ways of learning academic content or developing academic skills, these options often become stigmatized as programs for inferior students who are incapable of doing high-quality academic work. This has happened to various vocational education and apprenticeship programs, and there is no reason to believe that newer efforts, such as the school-to-work initiative, will enjoy a happier fate. Indeed, as one proponent of more investment in vocational education has sardonically observed, "Most parents would rather say their child flunked out of the University of Georgia than that he attended a technical school."[13]

Most Europeans are neither shocked nor dismayed when they observe that those who gain entry to high-quality academic programs come disproportionately from families that have attended these same kinds of programs. Although meritocratic principles permit some social mobility and ensure that the system of education valued in Europe can be rationalized as consistent with the idea of democracy, for the most part education in Europe and also Japan reflects clear social class biases, and these biases are in the main accepted as legitimate.

In America—where it is assumed that upward mobility is a more desirable state than social class stability and that academic education is a prime driver of this upward mobility, which has historically shaped the so-called American dream—similar patterns of enrollment lead people to assume the programs involved are exclusionary, antidemocratic, and fraught with difficulties that must be addressed through positive social action. Conversely, when a program seems to have too many children from families that have no history of great academic success (usually disproportionately the poor, including poor minorities), it is typically attacked as racist or as designed to keep poor kids in their place. In America academic education is preferred because it bestows and confirms status. College-educated Americans may want better vocational education for the children of other people, but for their own offspring, a sound academic program is what is desired.

The upshot of all of this is that in America it will not do to make vocational studies more academic, for vocational studies will still be stigmatized studies. Instead, American educators need to figure out what it is about vocational studies that makes them engaging to students and then ensure that academic studies reflect the values embedded in these less academically oriented efforts.

Such lessons are more likely to be learned if educators come to understand and embrace the notion that academic work is simply a special kind of work, what Peter Drucker refers to as knowledge work.[14] Work, after all, is nothing more or less than purposeful activity that has a clear end in view. Intellectual work (and schoolwork should be intellectual work) is no less work than is work that calls for the application of muscle and sinew. Knowledge work is nothing more or less than the disciplined application of the mind and the creation and application of the products of this effort. Therefore it should be possible to describe what leads youngsters to do work (to engage in purposeful activity) and then to design work that leads to academic skills in ways that are responsive to the motivational frameworks students bring to their tasks.[15]

Parents as a Shrinking Minority

Shift 2: From a society in which parents were in the majority and the ethnic and racial composition of that majority was clear and understood to a society in which parents are in the minority and majority status is no longer so clear.

Educators are generally aware of the implications of such important demographic shifts as changes in the racial and ethnic composition of student populations. Yet equally important though less well recognized demographic shifts are occurring as well. For example, as a result of better contraceptive devices and the increasing desire of young women to pursue careers, well-educated women are tending to have their first child at an average age well beyond the average age of fifty years ago. The result is that the range in age and educational experience among parents who are sending their first child to school is generally much wider than it was in the "good old days." In nearly every school there will be the children whose mothers are barely out of childhood themselves and the children whose mothers decided to have children only after finishing a Ph.D., M.B.A., or M.D. degree. It is unlikely that these two mothers will have basically the same needs and require the same things from schools.

Another unrecognized—or at least not commonly acknowledged—demographic fact is that less well educated parents send proportionately more children to school than do the more well educated. Furthermore, the children of the poor are more likely than are the children of the affluent to come from families where there is only one parent.

Yet another often overlooked fact is that many more Americans than in the past are choosing to have no children at all and that those who make this choice are more likely to come from among the more well educated (and presumably more influential) segments of the communities in which they live.

Such unrecognized demographic shifts may mean that policies and changes in practices advocated by reformers may worsen rather than ameliorate overall educational problems. For example, much of the rhetoric surrounding the voucher movement is based on "the rights of parents to choose." What is overlooked is that when the right of parents to unfettered choice is guaranteed then the nonparents, who now pay the majority of the taxes, lose even the semblance of control over the way their money is to be spent. Education under these circumstances becomes an entitlement and a private right rather than a civic duty and a public good. In the full-blown voucher system some are proposing, the only involvement nonparents will have in the conduct of the schools is to pay for them. It will be up to a minority (parents) to determine how the money of the majority of the taxpayers will be spent. In the long run, this condition can serve only to further estrange senior citizens and nonparent taxpayers from the schools.

Similar effects can be expected from efforts to decentralize school systems by assigning much of the decision-making authority to teams of teachers, parents, and school administrators rather than to elected boards of education. Ineffective though many are, boards of education do much to maintain at least the semblance of community and citizen control of schools and, with appropriate reform, may even provide the last best hope for realizing this local influence.[16]

Educational reformers and leaders who are concerned about revitalizing schools must find some way to integrate into the life of schools nonparent taxpayers, those who pay for schools but have no direct and concrete stake in them.[17] For example, educators can examine the way they communicate with the community about matters related to schools. Sending messages home with children no longer suffices when a majority in the community are nonparents. At the very least, educators and policymakers should take care not to endorse policies and practices that increase the already wide chasm between nonparent taxpayers and the schools.

Government Schools

Shift 3: From schools positioned as local institutions central to the life of the community to schools positioned as government agencies controlled and directed by state and national interests and forces.

Schools, like churches, were once perceived as focal points of community activity. Moreover, part of the bargain struck between taxpayers and parents has been that in exchange for receiving for their children an education paid for either wholly or in part by tax dollars, parents have yielded some control of the child's education to the community. So long as the schools were viewed as community agencies, this did not constitute a serious problem for most parents. They too were a part of the community, and they had a voice in the direction set by the community.

As schools have increasingly come to be seen as government agencies rather than community agencies, this bargain has become suspect. Critics of the public schools see, for example, religious freedom translated into religious indifference rather than religious neutrality. They see the valuing of pluralism and diversity translated into what they consider a value-free and therefore valueless curriculum. This is happening at the same time that the trust citizens have for government agencies and government leaders is eroding. The consequence is increasing estrangement from the schools and growing distrust of school leaders (whom the most distrustful sometimes refer to as "educrats").

It is technically correct to say that schooling in America is and has been for over two hundred years a function of state governments. All state constitutions attest to this fact. In the not-too-distant past, however, it was up to the local community to decide what should be transmitted from one generation to the next. The state could advise, but local control of local schools has long been a sacred icon in American education. Local control encouraged the citizenry to see the schools as local community institutions. Now, increased state and federal activism in the areas of educational policy and programming has dramatically altered this view. Prior to the late 1950s, the presence of the federal government in the life of public schools was almost nil, limited primarily to a linkage between the Department of Agriculture and vocational agriculture programs. But beginning in the mid-1950s and accelerating in the 1960s and 1970s, the federal government became deeply involved in life in the local schools. Federal activism first appeared when the government, through the Office of the President, used the military to enforce court desegregation orders. In 1957, the same year that troops were first used to obtain compliance with such court decisions, the launch of Sputnik and the linkage political leaders made between the "missile gap" and what they saw as the failure of America's schools to turn out enough scientists served to legitimize increased federal activism in educational policy as witnessed by such developments as the National Defense Education Act and the National Science Foundation curricula and teacher training programs.

In making these observations about increased government intervention, I do not want to be misunderstood. Local control of schools is not now nor has it ever been an unmixed blessing. Given the diversity of American society, the values expressed in local communities can sometimes be at odds with the values that guide the larger society as these values are expressed in such documents as the Constitution of the United States or as they are expressed in more cosmopolitan and well educated circles. Such differences are what the culture wars that surround the schools are mostly about. This is why *Brown* v. *Board of Education* was deemed necessary to bring about desegregation, and it is the reason Public Law 94-142 was passed by Congress to ensure the rights of the handicapped.

The clash between local preferences and more general values in the areas of civil rights and civil liberties has been played out in the federal courts and the halls of Congress. In order to act as they have acted, the courts had first to assert that the schools are first and foremost government agencies and only secondarily community institutions. For example, in order to force the issue of desegregation, it was necessary for lawyers to sue states or to emphasize the fact that local school districts are creatures of the state and that the will of local communities and local elites is necessarily subservient to the will of larger government units that represent the common good.

Again, I do not want to be misunderstood. This is not to say that *Brown* v. *Board of Education* was misguided. Clearly, not all students were being equally or well served by the schools that existed at the time of the Brown decision. That there was an obligation to do something about this matter and that the courts behaved properly in undertaking that action seems now generally accepted. Indeed, as many Southern educators and civic leaders now attest, integration has turned out to be not a necessary evil imposed by an interventionist federal government but a positive good, appealing to communities' better instincts rather than to the unlovely and antidemocratic passions that racist policies arouse.

Nevertheless, one of the unintended consequences of this set of actions has been to give support to subtle shifts in people's minds about what the schools are and whom the schools should serve. The federal troops at Central High School in Little Rock allowed desegregation to proceed, but they also symbolized for some a stronger government role in schools thought of as community schools—even though in excluding African-American youngsters they had clearly excluded a large portion of the total community.

Battles over civil liberties as well as civil rights have further reinforced the increasing public perception that the schools are creatures of some distant government rather than institutions reflecting local community values and preferences. Supreme Court decisions on school prayer, for example, which argued that local communities could not use a state agency to promulgate religious practices, were and are continuing to be sources of citizens' estrangement from the public schools. The arguments regarding the separation of church and state have clearly positioned the schools as creatures of the state.

The federal government has also emerged as one of the chief advocates for equity generally and the rights of the handicapped in particular. And again, much that is good has happened that would not have happened without federal intervention. Adult Americans today are surely more understanding of handicapping conditions and the needs of the learning disabled than were parents in the days when a character named Denny Dimwit dominated the comic pages and Mortimer Snerd and Cauliflower McPugg were regulars on radio and later television. However, parents whose children have no special needs often see federal advocacy for disabled students, especially those with behavioral difficulties, as nothing more or less than a government ploy to force their children to interact on a daily basis with children who are "bad and disruptive."

Words like *inclusion* do not resonate with many of these parents. For example, in the Phi Delta Kappa/Gallup poll mentioned previously only 10 percent of nonpublic school parents and 29 percent of public school parents said they believed that students with learning problems should be taught in the same classrooms with other students.[18] Moreover, fighting and violence and lack of discipline and control were the top two issues of concern among all those polled. Given such views, there seems to be quite a disparity between what local community leaders want and the world envisioned by the regulations and laws developed in response to advocates for students with special needs. The disparity is only made worse by the fact that many federally funded initiatives are presented in the most bureaucratic, jargon-laden language imaginable, further estranging local citizens used to their traditional terms. Rather than speaking of *schoolhouses* and *teachers,* federal agencies refer to *local educational agencies* and *professional employees.* Euphemisms like *at-risk* (usually applied to poor youngsters who lack the supports assumed necessary to succeed in school) and *urban* (usually applied to schools serving large numbers of racial and ethnic minorities) often conceal as much as they reveal. To be sure, such language protects some of the weakest and most vulnerable among us from needless hurt and pain. Yet it sometimes also discourages the kind of straightforward conversations we all need to engage in if we are to change public schools in ways that build our communities rather than destroy them.

A final fact that must be considered when attempting to understand the repositioning of the schools in the public perception as government rather than core community agencies is that in addition to federal intervention, state activism in education and educational policy has increased dramatically, and it seems unlikely to abate in the near future. Much of this state activism is spurred by economic development interests, specifically the desire for a world-class workforce to attract and retain industry. Another spur has been the court decisions holding that the schools are creatures of the state and that it is in the state constitution rather than in the local community that schools find their reason for being. When local resources are unequally distributed, it becomes the legal obligation of the state to address these issues, thus the recent emergence of a plethora of financial equity lawsuits.

One consequence of this activism, however, is that local boards of education are coming to see themselves as losing control of their schools, and local administrators are finding themselves increasingly accountable to the state rather than to the local school board. *The upshot of all this is that schools are increasingly positioned (to borrow a marketing term) as cold, bureaucratic government agencies where once they were viewed as a special kind of house—a schoolhouse.* As a result the crisis in public confidence that confronts government agencies in general is affecting schools as well.

Nevertheless, the public still has more confidence in the public schools than in many other institutions, including some whose leaders are most eager to offer scolding and advice to educators. For example, 42 percent of all respondents to the poll mentioned earlier said they had some or quite a lot of confidence in the public schools.[19] Though not a resounding endorsement, this was better than the expression of confidence given to local government (37 percent), state government (36 percent), big business (31 percent), the national government (30 percent), and organized labor (26 percent). Such findings have not discouraged mayors from taking over schools or state governments from mandating specific school reforms. They have not discouraged the national government from directing local school districts on the best ways to solve their problems. Nor have they discouraged leaders of big business from asserting that the schools need to be run more as businesses are run. But what educators really must do if America's schools are to be saved is to figure out ways to ensure that the schools are once again central to the life of the community. And they must do these things in the face of the growing public cynicism toward institutions and especially toward government institutions. Perhaps viewing the schools as agencies intended to build communities rather than as agencies intended to serve communities, often in places where a sense of community no longer exists, is a means to this end.

The Loss of Community

Shift 4: From a society in which the place where one lived and one's sense of community were highly correlated to a society in which

one's sense of community is determined more by the interest groups
to which one belongs, the place one works, and one's racial and ethnic identity.

Numerous books and articles have been written about Americans'
increasing loss of a sense of community. Sometimes these authors also
point with justifiable distress to the apparently growing lack of civility
in public dialogue, the declining willingness of individuals to put
themselves at risk on behalf of others, and the general feeling of isolation and estrangement. It is also my view that our society's very idea
of community is substantially different from what it was when the
American system of public education was being built. Such ideas are
usually based in myth as well as fact, but it is the change in belief that
matters here. As initially conceived, the purpose of the schools was to
serve the community, and it was assumed there was a community
to serve. Today, serious writers can raise the question, Is there a public for public schools?[20] This contrasts starkly with a time (1932) when
George S. Counts's question, "Dare the school build a new social
order?"[21] was taken seriously because schools were assumed to have
such power.

One need look no further than the dynamics of many local school
boards to see the harmful effects of the loss of a traditional sense of
community and the rising influence of interest groups and factions.
School board meetings too often become nothing more or less than
formalized bargaining sessions among interest groups seeking their
own advantage. At these meetings, interest group politics, value
clashes, and factionalism bear directly on the formulation of school
goals and procedures. Rather than serving as builders of the community and creators of a common vision, rather than serving the interests of students and the interests of the future, too many boards
symbolize and exacerbate the many ways communities are torn and
divided against themselves.[22]

Rather than serving *the* community, modern educators must serve
many communities, factions, interest groups, and organized lobbies—
each of which is in a position to make demands and assert expectations. Rather than asking, How can we best serve the common good?
educational leaders increasingly feel compelled to ask, How can we
satisfy competing interests enough that they will permit us to survive?
It is becoming abundantly clear that for public schools to survive the
culture wars that surround them, school leaders, including boards of

education, must find ways of building and leading community as well as ways of representing and responding to the diverse interests and beliefs that characterize so many local school districts. Skill in building communities and skill in creating a sense of the common good is what is now needed in schools. It is difficult to serve the community when there is no clearly defined community to serve.

A Tribe Apart

Shift 5: From a society in which adolescents were integrated into the life of the community to a society in which the young are increasingly segregated from the more vital aspects of adult community life and are led to establish a life almost totally lacking in meaningful interaction with adults.

As Patricia Hersch argues so convincingly, the world of the young and the world of adults have grown further and further away from each other.[23] Indeed, she calls today's young "a tribe apart." This shift has come about not only because the level of meaningful interaction between adults and children has declined in terms of both the numbers of adults who interact with each child and the depth of those interactions that do occur but also because adults increasingly tend to create conditions of anonymity and separation for the teenage crowd through such devices as special teen clubs and gathering places. Of course such special places can have a desirable function; nevertheless, there is a vast difference in the patterns of interaction that occur at a teen-oriented site and those that occur, for example, on a slow-pitch softball team that includes both adults and adolescents.

In addition, compared to previous generations the present generation of students has much more access to information totally free of adult censorship. The "liberation" of America's youth began with the invention of the portable recorder and the car radio, which made it possible for young people to listen to Elvis Presley and other "forbidden music" beyond the hearing of parents (the living room Victrola was hard to take to the beach). The increasing availability of paperback books and inexpensive magazines made it possible for youngsters to bypass adult censors and to read what they wanted to read, whether or not their parents, their teachers, or the librarian approved.

Finally, the rise of the Internet and electronic technologies for storing, distributing, analyzing, and communicating verbal, pictorial, and symbolic information has helped turn local groups into national audiences and has created a world for adolescents that transcends the boundaries of families and locales. The institutions that have historically been the primary agencies of socialization (the family, the religious institution, and the school) are finding it difficult, if not impossible, to compete with the masters of media, mass entertainment, and mass communication for the attention of children and youths.

The electronic revolution has also been instrumental in the erosion of traditional authority. Schools work on the assumption that children are obliged to obey their elders, that teachers stand in the place of parents (*in loco parentis*), and that adults are generally in agreement about what should be expected of children. In what must surely be one of the most penetrating descriptions of the internal life of schools, Willard Waller describes the school as

> a despotism threatened from within and exposed to regulation and interference from without. It is a despotism capable of being overturned in a moment, exposed to the instant loss of its stability and its prestige. It is a despotism demanded by the community of parents, but specifically limited by them as to the techniques which it may use for the maintenance of a stable social order. It is a despotism resting upon children, at once the most tractable and the most unstable members of the community. . . .
>
> To understand the political structure of the school, we must know that the school is organized on the authority principle and that that authority is constantly threatened. The authority of the school executives and the teachers is in unremitting danger from: (1) the students, (2) parents, (3) the school board, (4) each other, (5) hangers on and marginal members of the group, and (6) alumni. . . . The difficulties of the teacher or school executive in maintaining authority are greatly increased by the low social standing of the teaching profession and its general disrepute in the community at large.[24]

The list of threats Waller generated in 1932 only hints at the threats to the authority of the schools today. Not only is the authority of the schools threatened but so also is the authority of parents. Indeed, in some cases parents themselves seem to accept the legitimacy of the view that the young, especially adolescents, are legitimately a "tribe apart."

In the not-too-distant past, adolescents had a difficult time gaining access to information that had not undergone censorship by adults who were generally known to them and to each other. Teenagers could assert their distinctiveness (as bobby-soxers, for example), but they could not establish the kind of anonymity required to emerge as a distinct subculture. Although adults have lamented the foibles of the young and worried about the moral character of the next generation throughout recorded history, the idea of an *adolescent culture* did not begin to take shape until the mid to late 1950s,[25] and the idea of a *generation gap* did not emerge until the 1960s. The advent of the individually controlled electronic media and the accompanying democratization of access to information have made a qualitative difference in the relationship between children and adults as well as in the relationships among adults themselves. This difference is a difference in kind rather than degree. It is a mutation rather than a transformation.

Put as directly as I know how to put the matter, up until the 1950s, if one knew what parents, teachers, and religious leaders were teaching the young, one could be relatively confident that one knew, in a general way, what the youngsters knew. This is no longer true. Much of what the young know today comes from forces and sources totally outside local community ken or control. Among the more powerful of these forces and sources is the adolescent society itself.

The erosion of adult authority is compounded when the schools function as though youngsters' access to information were still restricted. Waller commented in 1932 that "communities in general, perhaps especially American communities, have chosen to use the schools as repositories for certain ideals. . . . The belief is abroad that young people ought to be trained to think the world a little more beautiful and much more just than it is, as they ought to think men more honest and women more virtuous than they are. A high school student must learn that honesty is always the best policy. . . ."[26] Nowadays, even though there is little information adults have access to that children cannot also access if they have a mind to, parents and others in the community often insist that schools continue to function as museums of virtue. This causes those who teach to be less than candid about what they know their students know and students to be less than candid with their teachers. The upshot is that the confidence of students in the adult authorities in their school lives is further eroded.[27]

Despite all this, schools, more than any other institution, have the potential to reintegrate the young into the world of adults. Educators are more likely to achieve this end if they learn to view the school as a workplace. Each day 2.5 million teachers show up for work. An even greater number of support persons show up for work. All these people get paid for what they do, just as the physician gets paid, the computer programmer gets paid, and the person who hauls the garbage gets paid. They keep schedules, they solve problems and work in teams to do so, and they produce products and provide services. Moreover, the kind of work done in school is predominantly the kind of work that is becoming increasingly commonplace in the world beyond the school. It is knowledge work—work that involves the acquisition, development, and application of intellectual skills, concepts, theories, and problem-solving strategies as opposed to the application of muscle and sinew.

Knowledge work is what schools are about. Armed with this understanding, teachers can begin to see themselves differently. They can see themselves as leaders and inventors of knowledge work rather than as performers for students or even as educational diagnosticians and clinicians. They can serve not only as instructors and coaches and guides but also as master knowledge workers to students who are their apprentices.[28] They can see their primary role as demonstrating to the young how the knowledge work of the twenty-first century is to be done. They can require students to do such work and assist students in this work. They can become more self-conscious, reflective, and public about what they do and how they go about doing it and then share the results of these reflections and refinements with students and with each other.

Teachers need to develop and nourish rich intellectual lives, and students, especially older students, need to be brought into those intellectual lives. One part of this intellectual life must surely be serious consideration of the motives students bring to the school and the ways schoolwork can be designed to effectively address and capitalize on these motives.

The Eclipse of the Traditional Family

Shift 6: From the two-parent family to the single-parent family and blended families.

Shifts in the structure of the American system of sex, marriage, family, and kinship are so important to school life and some of the effects of the changes so apparent that we sometimes look past the subtleties and fasten on to obvious. The obvious is important but so are the subtleties. I will not endeavor to trace the causes of these shifts here other than to observe that the development of the birth control pill; the loosening of family bonds, largely due to social conditions during World War II; the rapid development of the mass media; and such things as the women's liberation movement must surely have had some impact.

Prior to the 1950s, divorce was a relatively uncommon occurrence, and out-of-wedlock births were relatively few. Nowadays, out-of-wedlock births are common and divorce even more common. The single-parent family was a rarity in most schools; it is now commonplace.

These are obvious changes. Less obvious is the fact that many schoolchildren are participating in *blended families,* families that result from what some sociologists refer to as serial polygamy (the marrying of several mates, though never more than one at a time). After one or both of their birth parents remarries, perhaps more than once, these children may have three, four, or sometimes six or more adults who are affecting—or endeavoring to affect—their lives in ways available only to parents. In education, the blended family has received less attention than has the single-parent family, but its importance in students' lives should not escape the attention of serious educators.

For example, a court injunction denying a noncustodial parent access to his or her children without the explicit consent of the custodial parent can be upheld only if school personnel join in to enforce it. Yet a noncustodial parent with an ex-spouse who is punitive cannot keep reasonable track of the educational progress of his or her child unless school personnel find ways to communicate effectively with both parents.

Such situations are not easy to deal with; furthermore, they are wrapped in legal issues of liability and fault. This leads to a great deal of timidity among educators when it comes to discussions of the special circumstances presented to schools by a rising divorce rate. Educators prefer to view divorce primarily as a child-care issue and to see their role as making counselors and supportive services available for the children (and sometimes the adults) who are undergoing the trauma of divorce. Certainly, such services are needed but so are clear policies and understandable practices for school personnel who must relate to and communicate with noncustodial parents, grandparents, and so on. New relationships between schools and the courts need to be forged and maintained.

The increased incidence of out-of-wedlock births also presents not-so-obvious problems to schools. It is now commonplace for schools to provide special programs for teenage parents. In the not-too-distant past a teenage girl "in trouble" was expected to leave school in some disgrace, and the boy who had fathered her child was "expected" to marry her. "Bastard" children were stigmatized just as their mothers (and sometimes fathers) were. It may be that the responses of earlier generations to the teenage sexuality and unwed mothers in their midst were misguided and harmful, but today's more thoughtful and humane approaches require schools to do things that many Americans, especially senior citizens and religious conservatives, persist in viewing as permissive and as shameful and disgusting.

What must be recognized is that changes in the family structure are a part of the larger set of changes in Americans' attitudes toward sex, marriage, family, and kinship. Fundamental transitions are occurring, and no one fully understands their dimensions. Is a child born out of wedlock an "illegitimate" child? Is the individual who engages in unprotected sex with multiple partners "promiscuous" or simply a "practitioner of unsafe sex"? When the school promotes discussions of safe sex is it confirming that sex with multiple partners or at least premarital sex is acceptable? What is the effect of discussions of "alternative lifestyles," by which is usually meant gay lifestyles? Issues such as these take up considerable organizational energy in schools and on school boards. They also stir up public passions that become focused on the schools even though the transitions that make them issues are located in the larger society. The fact is that when it comes to matters of sex, marriage, family, and kinship in America, the norms are not clear and what can and cannot be expected from parents and families is not easy to ascertain.

Realities such as these lead many educators to the sometimes comforting but always erroneous conclusion that whatever is wrong with the schools is beyond the control of the schools. Until families are stabilized and parents once again engage in appropriate child-rearing practices, there is little hope of significant improvement in student performance—or so some argue. Yet there is little prospect that the so-called traditional family will reemerge as the dominant form of home life for most children. In addition to the changes brought about by changing patterns of sexual relationships, there is the fact that more and more women are working outside the home and spending less time with their children. It seems likely that women are going to continue to pursue careers and that men are not going to stay home to substitute for them. The demands of the workplace will continue to compete with the demands of family life, if for no other reason than the separation of the place of work from the place where one rears one's family.[28]

Therefore educators cannot turn away from these changes. Instead they must develop skills in identifying the diversity of views relating to family life, and school leaders—especially boards of education— must become more adept than they now are at reconciling these competing views.

One additional shift that may have profound implications for what occurs in the classroom is a fundamental alteration in the structure of the two-parent family itself. The birthrate in America is declining, and one effect of this is that there are now proportionately more firstborn and firstborn–only-born children entering school than at any time in the past. Moreover, these children are likely to be from comparatively affluent homes.

Though the current research on birth order effects is less than instructive, it is safe to say that whatever effects birth order has will be magnified in the present entering student body and will be magnified further in the future. In addition, the change in the structure of two-parent families has numerous implications, most of which are unexplored by educators and reform advocates. Among the more important are the following.

First, parents of firstborn and firstborn–only-born children are more likely than other parents to be college educated. Their expectations about the kind of education they want for their children are also likely to be different from the expectations of parents who are less well educated. Parents of firstborn–only-born children and small families, affluent as they are, are well positioned to leave the public schools, since they have more money and fewer children to support. According to the Phi Delta Kappa/Gallup poll mentioned earlier, 39 percent of all public school parents would place their children in a private or parochial school if the government paid the tuition.[30] Those who have fewer children and are more affluent are less in need of supplemental support than are those with more children and fewer resources, therefore parents of firstborn and only-born children are more likely than other parents to be able to take advantage of generalized voucher plans and tuition tax credits in order to take their children out of the public schools.

Second, cross-age interaction has long been recognized as a powerful mechanism in support of education and socialization. Larger families with multiple children born at relatively short intervals have many more opportunities for such interactions than do single-child families or families with relatively wide ranges in age among their children. It is probably safe to say that there has never been a society in which age segregation is so well developed as it is in the affluent suburbs of America. Our graded school system once operated in a social context where family structures militated against age segregation; now it operates in a social context in which segregation by age is a common phenomenon. Consider, for example, the increasing numbers of housing developments for retired citizens that exclude children or at least discourage their presence. Schools must find ways to encourage cross-age interactions among students and also to reintegrate the young and the old.

Finally, it is sometimes unrecognized that the children of affluent and well-educated parents are almost always overrepresented in any parent group. Why? Because the single child in a two-parent family is represented by two parents, whereas the poor child's single mother may be representing the interests of three or four children. More than that, the affluent and well-educated parents are usually better equipped than the poorer and less educated parents to achieve positions of leadership among parents. Any school efforts to gain the support of parents must take such factors into account.

The New Competitors

Shift 7: From a society in which schools had little competition for the hearts and minds of children to a society in which powerful commercial interests are seeking to attract students to their wares, even at the expense of distracting students from schoolwork.

In the not-too-distant past, the family, the religious institution, and the school were the primary sources of intellectual, moral, and aesthetic experiences for children. This is no longer so.

One of the consequences of the emergence of the information society, especially the revolution in publishing and in electronic communication, is that schools, parents, and religious organizations now must compete with the entertainment industry, the electronic gaming industry, and others for the attention and commitments of children and youths. Information considered inappropriate for discussion in a high school civics class is now openly discussed on television talk shows. What children and youths know today is no longer largely prescribed and proscribed by the intentions and desires of families, schools, and religious organizations. Rather, much of what students know and learn is presented to them by persons who view them as a market segment to be served, a set of customers to be attracted. And as each report appears that shows that youngsters watch a great deal of television and invest innumerable hours in playing computer games of little educational relevance and questionable moral content, educators, parents, and religious leaders lament the findings, but many do not know what action to take and simply throw up their hands in despair.

Unless educators learn to compete in this new environment, however, schools both public and private are likely to forfeit more and more of students' attention and their interest in learning to the educative (and miseducative) forces and sources that are emerging outside the context of schools, families, and religious institutions. What purveyors of entertainment like Disney and computer game makers understand and accept is that the children who use their goods and services are volunteers. Conversely, even though families, religious leaders, and school leaders have not always been in agreement about what and how children should learn, they have all subscribed to the belief that children should be subject to adult preferences in learning and consequently, as discussed earlier, have offered narrowly defined routes to academic learning. The mass media and the Internet have not submitted to the discipline of this myth. The consequence is that the traditional sources for the socialization of the young are increasingly impotent in the face of those who understand the young as customers.

In this competitive world, where traditional adult authority is suspect and options abound, students can be compelled to attend school, but they cannot be compelled to be attentive while they are there. Students can be compelled to comply and do enough to get by, but they cannot be compelled to be committed, self-directed, and self-controlled.[31]

This is not to say that students should decide what they need to learn. Rather it is to say that teachers and other school leaders could benefit from taking something like the attitude expressed by Sony cofounder Akio Morita when he wrote: "It is our plan to lead the public with new products rather than ask them what kind of products they want. The public does not know what is possible, but we do."[32] Applied to education this statement might read, "It is our plan to lead students to new forms of schoolwork that they will find engaging and from which they will learn that which adults consider to be important for them to learn."

To be student centered is not to cater to student whims. Rather, it is to understand the students and the things that motivate them better than the students understand themselves and their motivations. It is also to understand how schoolwork, which I will define later as the primary product of the schools, can be designed to appeal to these motives and to push the limits of the possible so that this work is increasingly attractive and compelling to all students.

Mass Customization

Shift 8: From a society in which efficiency and standardization were greatly valued to a society in which quality, choice, and customization are core values.

The U.S. automobile business grew to greatness through standardization. Levittown offered few housing choices. However, in a shift beginning in the 1960s and accelerating during the 1980s and 1990s, Americans have become more concerned with quality, uniqueness, and customization than with standardization. Even McDonald's hamburgers, the original model of fast-food standardization, can now be customized. *Mass customization* is a new buzz word among business consultants and the authors of books for business leaders.

Much of the current drive for vouchers and for charter schools derives from the assumption that education can and should be customized as well. Furthermore, as schools are now organized, those schools that appear to be the most successful (suburban schools) are standardized to fit the needs of a group of children and families, the majority of whom share the same customs. However, such standardization does little to address the academic needs of those outside the majority, such as the children from nonacademically oriented families and the children of affluence whose parents are particularly ambitious for them.

On the one hand the conditions of democracy require that diversity be accommodated and responded to. On the other hand democracies require a commitment to a common set of values and a body of common experience that make it possible for this diversity to serve as a positive good rather than to lead to rancorous struggles that end in the worst cases in Balkanization, civil strife, and figurative if not literal "ethnic cleansing."

The mission of the schools as promulgators of a common democratic culture is not much talked about nowadays. Rather, the conversation

is about education and its link to the economy or about the school as
a cure for various social ills. Yet the American school system was initially established to define and communicate to the young a common
culture. It is time for educators to revisit this original intent. Because
the quest for a common culture can—as our history shows—also lead
to cultural imperialism, in which the values of the dominant group
become the yardstick by which each member of the community is
measured, the question educators should investigate is this: How
might the schools promote a common culture as they also create a
value system that treats diversity as a common good? In answering this
question, educators will not only address the issues associated with
the demand for customization but will also address many of the issues arising as a result of the other shifts that are occurring in the social infrastructure on which our schools are based.

THE CHANGING TECHNOLOGIES OF EDUCATION

In addition to the implications of these eight seismic social shifts, educators need to understand the implications of the new technology.
Just as social shifts require us to reconceive the organizations embedded in our society, technological changes should also spur structural
changes in these organizations. The alternative is to allow our organizations to expel the technology or modify it so that it does not intrude
into an organization's habitual life. For example, it is commonplace
for schools to use computers as though they were typewriters, pro-
grammed textbooks, or calculators. It is, unfortunately, less common
for schools to use computers to develop new forms of intellectual activity for students. One of the most important differences between organizations that continuously improve and those that do not is the
way they respond to changes in the core technology that affect the way
they do their core business. In the case of schools, once again, this
business is to design work that students believe to be worth doing.

Tools, Processes, and Skills

The first point it is useful to understand about any technology is that
knowledge is affected by technology. Knowledge is based on and derives from information. Knowledge is information that has been
processed in a way that gives the information meaning, coherence, and

propositional qualities (that is, it can be used to explain and perhaps to predict and control). When prediction and control are required, scientific knowledge is to be preferred, but scientific knowledge is not the only form of knowledge of significance to humankind. Revealed knowledge, or knowledge believed to be revealed, has had at least as much impact on human history as has scientific knowledge. Craft knowledge transmitted from master to apprentice is often not codified, but it is important knowledge nonetheless, as are aesthetic knowledge regarding the beautiful and the ugly and moral knowledge regarding what is good and bad and what is right and wrong.

New information causes these forms of knowledge to change and evolve. For example, as the ability to extend human biological functions beyond the life of the brain increases, the question of when death occurs is much more than theological. It also a scientific question and a broad moral and ethical question whose answer must draw upon the great traditions—including religious traditions—that shape our culture and our thought.

Given the centrality of information to the knowledge work process and given the centrality of knowledge work to the conduct of the core business of schools, it is apparent that the technologies most important in the lives of schools are those that have to do with communicating, storing, retrieving, and processing information. Although educators now tend to use the word *technology* as a synonym for *electronic* means of communicating, storing, retrieving, and processing information, technology has a much broader meaning. *Technology is the means of doing the job, whatever the means and whatever the job may be.*[33]

Schooling as an organized activity has existed for thousands of years, and it has used technologies since its inception. Those who work in contemporary schools employ technologies that have a long and distinguished history. The oldest technologies of teaching are storytelling, the dialogue, and the monologue (lecture). The invention of the technology of writing led to such advanced tools as the handwritten manuscript, which in turn required more skill (the ability to read) on the part of both teacher and student. The effectiveness of these technologies was highly dependent on the skill of the teacher and of the person turning out the technological tools. There were good storytellers, and there were bad ones. There were teachers who used dialogue to stimulate inquiry, and there were others who turned dialogues into inquisitions. There were scribes who were thorough, accurate, and diligent as they copied manuscripts, and there were others that were less so.

The invention of the printing press represented a basic shift in the technology of education and made it reasonable to contemplate overcoming two of the most intractable problems confronting educators—limited access to knowledge and variability in the quality of knowledge. Though purchasing a book or a pamphlet was still out of reach for most people, books were clearly more accessible and more widespread than were master storytellers or tutors. Furthermore, careful proofreading could reduce the random errors that were a feature of handwritten manuscripts. The printed word opened the possibility of universal education. Once the hardware (books, pamphlets, tracts, and printed lectures) was in place, two tasks remained. One was finding ways to ensure access to this hardware. The community lending library, the paperback revolution, and the explosive growth of magazines are all illustrations of efforts to increase access. The other was to find ways to ensure that teachers possess the skills needed both to use the established technologies of schooling and to explore innovative ways of using the printed word for educational purposes. The creation of the graded reader like the graded school was, after all, a fundamental innovation in education. The encyclopedia, the textbook, and the infamous workbook are all technological innovations using the printed word.

Now we are facing a technological shift that seems destined to have effects on schooling even more profound than the effects of the printing press. Like the printing press, this technology is not simply an extension of or an improvement on existing technologies. It is different in kind, rather than in degree. This technology is the ability to electronically transmit, receive, store, and process information. Although this revolution has been underway for nearly a century in the form of radio and then of television and recording technologies, it is only now—with the arrival of such tools as computers, the Internet, portable and compact electronic audio and video recorders, and fiber optics—that educators are beginning to appreciate the implications of this technological revolution for the conduct of schools' core business. Moreover, it is becoming clear that if public schools do not have new tools based on this technology available, if processes to access these tools are not available, and if teachers are not skilled in using these tools, alternative organizations will arise that do have these tools, processes, and skills.

In short, technology is not *a* thing; technology involves three things: tools, processes, and skills. When tools are available but processes are not in place to make them available or the skills are not present to use them effectively, then the technology is not present. For example, there are many schools where the overhead projectors go unused because no one has thought to create a process for replacing burned-out bulbs quickly and efficiently, that is, for having available both the bulbs and someone who knows how to replace them. Operationally speaking, a school does not have an overhead projector until it has processes and skills in place to make it work. Similarly, in schools where textbooks are available but many students cannot read them, the textbooks are effectively not available to these students. Even the Internet is unavailable to such students because very little on the Net is useful to those who cannot read. Simply choosing links to follow requires a reasonable level of literacy.

Frozen in Time

When the printing press was invented, it was first used to reproduce the old manuscripts that had formerly been laboriously reproduced by hand. It took some time for people to realize the printing press could also produce newspapers, pamphlets, tracts, and books newly written for popular consumption. When any new technology comes on the scene, it is generally the case that people first use it to do old work in new ways. It is only after considerable experience that the potential of the new technology for creating new forms of work and producing new and different products is explored.

Moreover, established organizations are usually among the last to explore the possibilities of new technologies, especially when these technologies affect the way their core business is conducted. The consequence is that when there is a major technological revolution that goes to the heart of an industry or enterprise, it is likely that new organizations will arise to exploit the technology, especially when the existing industry is typified by ineptness in leading and managing change.

In the modern school, the printed word, in the form of books (especially textbooks) is assumed to be the core technology that must be mastered, both by the teacher and by students. It goes without saying that students who do not develop the skills necessary to master this technology (that is, those who do not learn to read) have real difficulty in benefiting fully from their experience in school. They will also have difficulty in later life, for the keys to access to the most important technologies in advanced societies are the skills associated with reading. That is why reading is viewed as a *basic skill.*

Television, computers, video recording, radio, and CD-ROMs all make available to educators new forms of technology that go directly to the core business of schooling. Yet past efforts by educators to use radio and television for educational purposes illustrate how existing organizations are likely to misuse or underexploit new technology. Certainly, a person who delivers mediocre lectures in the lecture hall will do no better or be any less boring on the television screen. Even recording and storing a lecture that is excellent in the classroom setting given the interaction between students and teacher and making it available via an electronic medium is not an adequate use of the new technology. What those who use electronic media with effect understand is that when the one-on-one relationships through which students can become engaged with the instructor as well as the subject of instruction are lacking, one must find other values that will lead to students' engagement with the subject. It is for this reason that the Discovery Channel attends to entertainment values whereas many educational channels offer little more than talking heads. Indeed, educational uses of television, especially in classrooms, have frequently been so unimaginative that the term *educational television* has come to be associated with words like *boring, unexciting,* and *humdrum.*

It can be argued with some justification that the reason schools and teachers do not use television as it might be used is that schools do not have the resources to do so. Yet, having observed that student television productions often manage to have many of the communication values contained in the best of commercial television, I have come to the conclusion that the problem with introducing new information-processing technologies into the schools is more than a hardware, or tool, problem. Rather, the problem is that schools lack a sufficient number of people with the skills needed to use the tools imaginatively, and those who do have the needed skills are seldom in a position to employ their skills in ways that benefit students most. For example, although school district media specialists are often capable of providing well-done television productions to support presentations the superintendent wishes to make to school boards and communities, I have seldom seen such support made routinely available to teachers. Neither have I often found these talented producers working directly with students to aid them in developing their skills at communicating with the new technology. Even those students who are already skilled in the use of computers and television, and there are many of them, seldom work with their teachers as they are learning content to produce quality presentations about that learning for later use.

The result is that the de facto education of children is moving from the classroom to the production centers of cable television channels and recording studios and to those who are bent on exploiting the entertainment values of the new technologies rather than their educational values.

For schools to exploit new technologies properly and recapture the attention and commitment of students, old systems must change. New systems must be prepared to change the way time, people, and space are organized and the way information and power are distributed. The rules, roles, and relationships shaping organizational behavior that were appropriate to schools in which lectures and books were the prime technologies must be changed to rules, roles, and relationships that can also fully exploit the new technologies that are emerging. To change these rules, roles, and relationships (to restructure) leaders must also change the system of shared beliefs, meanings, values, traditions, and lore (in short, the culture) in which these structures are embedded. It is the failure to appreciate the linkage between structure and technology and the linkage between systems and programs that leads to the failure of change efforts in schools, just as it does in business.

Among the primary tasks of leaders are to identify the technologies that are essential to the organization's core business, and to endeavor to provide the tools, processes, and skills needed to employ these technologies. That means it is the task of leaders to see to the development, control, and continuous improvement of the processes associated with the effective use of these technologies and to develop in themselves and in others the skills needed to control these processes and to use the tools effectively. The key to continuous improvement is that teachers have the skills to use a variety of technologies and therefore the ability to choose among competing technologies. Knowing the conditions that define a particular educational situation and understanding the business of schools, they should be able to determine the most effective and efficient means of doing the job they need to do. Leaders must ensure that these means are available and accessible.

To accomplish these tasks, educational leaders, like leaders in business and industry, must also develop new understandings. The understanding they most need is that which emerges from endeavoring to answer the questions: What is our business, and what must we do to do this business well?

CONCLUSION

American society has, over the past fifty years, undergone a "great mutation."[34] The world of the year 2000 is less like the world of 1950 than the world of 1950 was like the world of 1850. Indeed, it was the seemingly placid 1950s that put in place many of the revolutionary forms that have shaped our present context.[35] The portable phonograph was created, television became commonplace, the suburbs began to emerge, and race-based urban ghettos became increasingly common features in the life of America's cities.

In addition, federal activism in school programs and policies began. Then, inspired by the need for economic development in their states, governors in the Southeastern United States, governors like Bill Clinton of Arkansas, Richard Riley of South Carolina, Lamar Alexander of Tennessee, and William Winter of Mississippi, placed education and school reform high on the agenda of state legislators. All of this has occurred in a context where the mass culture, supported by the entertainment industry, has become increasingly focused on the so-called youth market and increasingly effective at competing for the time and attention of children and youths. The diversion of the Mickey Mouse Club has evolved into the Disney empire and the relatively harmless wiggles and squiggles of Elvis Presley on the *Ed Sullivan Show* have evolved into nihilistic hard rock and rap music that celebrates violence. Mickey Mouse has become Beavis and Ward Cleaver has become Bart Simpson.

It is in this dramatically altered context that educators must now work, and the work they do must produce more and different results than have ever before been expected of America's public schools. Moreover, the students who attend America's high schools today are generally further from meeting citizen and employer expectations than was the case for students fifty years ago, even though today's students in general are probably academically more well prepared than were past generations. This leads to increasing dissatisfaction with the schools. And this dissatisfaction must be of urgent concern to educators.

Although the public expects it, no school district has yet been able to ensure that nearly all students learn to read with comprehension, compute swiftly and accurately, and write well, let alone master algebra, chemistry, physics, and a second language. Until these expectations can be met, or demonstrable progress is made toward meeting them, public disaffection with the schools is likely to grow. To meet such expectations, the public education system must undertake changes much more radical than called for by those who would "break the mold." Indeed, compared to the needed changes, most efforts to "break the mold" have done little more than crack some china.

School leaders must begin working to meet these expectations. They must also confront the bewilderment and lack of a sense of urgency that typify much of the in-house conversation among teachers and school leaders regarding the troubles that beset the schools. They must confront the perception of many educators that they are helpless and misunderstood victims and help them see that they must become leaders of a crusade to save public education in America. They must confront the loss of community and recognize that schools are the one institution that is positioned to build the communities we so desperately need if our civic and cultural life is to be enriched and our economy is to be sustained. In a world where religious conservatives demand that the value of abstinence be taught and liberals in the health care community want condoms distributed in the high schools, it is sometimes difficult to remember that schools were established to promote a common culture. In a world where parents of children with learning disabilities have successfully lobbied to have their children fully integrated into the classroom but nearly two-thirds of parents with children in public schools and 70 percent of parents with children in private schools disagree with this policy, it is difficult to remember that the public schools owe their existence to the assumption that all citizens have a common interest in the well-being of all children, not just their own children or children like them.

As a person who has labored for nearly forty years in the effort to reform America's system of education, I find it painful to write an appraisal like the one I have presented here. Yet I and others who still believe that public schools are vital to the survival of American democracy and the fulfillment of the American dream must acknowledge that schools do have many real problems and that public perceptions about the schools are also real in their consequences. In the following chapters, I provide educators with some tools they may use to change perceptions and to address problems caused by new demands on the schools, seismic social shifts, and the technological revolution.

To fail to rise to this challenge is to lose public education—and perhaps our democratic way of life as well. To look to forces beyond the control of educators as excuses for the failure to respond is defeatist. What is needed in this time are educational leaders of nearly Churchillian stature, men and women who, when confronted with seemingly overwhelming odds, believe and can inspire others to believe that this can be American educators' "finest hour." My hope is that this book offers the support and encouragement school leaders need to achieve not only their finest hour but their day and their century.

CHAPTER TWO

Characteristics of Change-Adept Organizations

I t is often asserted that public schools are change resistant. This is not so. There is in fact so much change occurring in schools that teachers and school administrators rightly feel overwhelmed by it. However, this change is seldom accompanied by clear improvements in performance. Schools are change prone, but they are also change inept.

School leaders seem to be unable to focus the changes they introduce to improve the performance of the systems they lead. Instead, the focus is typically on a specific project or program. Consequently, each time a new wave of "reform" threatens, teachers and principals retreat, waiting for it to pass over so they can get about doing what they "were hired to do." "This too shall pass" is among the most commonly heard phrases in the faculty lounge of a school where the newest reform fad is being introduced. As some of the more cynical and jaded teachers are prone to say, schools too often seem to engage in change for the sake of change.

Compared to sustaining change, starting change is relatively easy. That is why there are so many more changes initiated in schools than are sustained. Individual men and women can start a change process, sometimes even without the support of the systems of which they are a part. It is sustaining change that is the challenge.

Two things sustain change: one is a leader or leadership group that acts as a change agent; the other is a system, or group of systems, that supports change. When changes are started in systems that are without the capacity to sustain them, the changes are unlikely to outlast the tenure of the change agent and may indeed hasten his or her departure. I view the world through a sociological lens. I am therefore much more interested in how systems shape behavior and performance than I am in studying the personalities of leaders. This is not to say that the personal characteristics of leaders are unimportant. Rather, it is to say that systems as well as people make a difference. It is to argue that social structure as well as self determines what is likely to be done and to what effect. It is to conclude that history as well as biographies must be taken into account when attempting to discover what is going on and why things are the way they are.

Before we can make not just change but improvement the goal of school reform, school leaders must gain a firmer understanding of those organizational features that contribute to and detract from the capacity of the schools they lead to support and sustain change. With such an understanding, those who lead can create systems that can sustain change. Today, too many policymakers and members of the public believe the key question in school reform is, Why are schools so change resistant? Some are then concluding that because schools are change resistant they should be abandoned. Their question, and thus their conclusion, is wrong. The key questions for reform leaders are: What qualities make an organization change adept? and, How do we ensure that school systems and communities possess these qualities?

The first step in such an understanding is to define the nature of systemic change and to examine some examples of change failure to see where systemic change would have made a difference. Subsequent steps involve identifying the specific characteristics of change-adept organizations and then recognizing how change can be supported by driving the core business of schools throughout the organization.

PROJECTS, PROGRAMS, AND SYSTEMS

It is perhaps easiest to understand change that is focused on the systemic properties of the organization undergoing change if we contrast it to change that is project focused and change that is program focused. Rosabeth Moss Kanter distinguishes these three different change efforts this way:

> *Change projects:* discrete, specific streams of action designed to address a particular problem or need. These can succeed in the short-term, especially if they are focused, results-oriented, and do not depart much from company tradition. But if they are merely discrete, stand-alone projects, they will often have no long-term impact, memory of them will fade, and later generations will discover the same need.
>
> *Change programs:* interrelated projects designed to have major cumulative organizational impact. Here success often depends less on the quality of the plan or tool itself than on the way each project links to other streams of action in the company. Change programs often fail because they are isolated from ongoing business activities, contain too many projects that don't fit well together, or are carried out by an elite of converts who expect everyone else to stop what they are doing and join the cult.
>
> *Change-adept organizations:* investments that create the capability for continuous innovation and improvement, for embracing change as an internally desired opportunity before it becomes an externally driven threat, by mobilizing many people in the organization to contribute. Success with efforts of this kind depends on whether the conditions necessary to make the organization change-friendly exist, so that change can occur continuously and feels natural.[1]

Viewing the scene in American public education today, it is clear that educators have had quite a bit of experience in leading and managing change projects. They have also had experiences with program initiatives. What are lacking are serious efforts to create systems that are supportive of change and that can sustain new programs and new projects over time.

The primary reason this is so, I believe, is that change leaders, funding agencies, and policy makers too often overlook or look past creating in school systems conditions that are supportive of change and instead fasten on programs and projects that promise to have immediate results. In a word, efforts to improve schools usually attend more to the introduction of projects and programs than to the systems in which these programs and projects are to be implemented.

There are many factors that encourage not only school leaders but also other reform leaders, policymakers, and funding agencies to avoid systemic reform and to concentrate instead on programs and projects. Programs and projects are usually relatively concrete and observable. Systems are abstract and can be seen only in their effects. Program and project change can be viewed linearly. The dimensions of change are known and relatively easily understood. Systemic reform is messy and uncertain, and its direct impact is hard to assess. In addition, educators sometimes confuse program-oriented changes with systemic reform. Comprehensive program changes often require a wide range of interrelated changes and may be quite complex, involving whole schools and all the parents of students in those schools. Such large-scale program efforts do present very different leadership challenges than project-oriented reform efforts do. But program reform, no matter how comprehensive and no matter how complex, is not systemic reform.

Finally, educators have traditionally thought in terms of people and programs; systemic change requires them to think primarily in terms of social structures and culture. A social structure consists of the system of rules, roles, and relationships that give direction to behavior within a social system, such as a group or organization. Social structures are sustained and given meaning by interlocking sets of beliefs, values, physical artifacts, lore, and tradition. Such beliefs, values, physical artifacts, lore, and tradition constitute the culture in which the social structure is embedded. *Systemic reform has to do with changing social structures and the culture in which these structures are embedded.* Systemic reform of an organization does not simply attempt to bring about temporary changes in the behavior of the individual men and women and boys and girls who live out a substantial part of their biographies in the organization; it focuses instead on changing the patterned regularities that characterize the organization and that shape behavior within the organization more generally.

Therefore, so long as the procedures and technologies that a program or project must introduce into the organization do not require a radical departure from tradition, systemic change is not necessary. However, systemic change is essential when programs and projects require procedural and technological changes that are so far out of the prevailing tradition that they cannot be supported by the existing structure and culture.

Such changes are by definition *radical* in that they "go to the root" of the system. They require not only that new programs and projects be installed but also that new structures be installed to support these programs and projects and that the organization's basic system of belief and meaning be adjusted to accommodate the new ideas and practices. Leaders engaged in systems reform cannot stop at installing a new way of doing business in one part of a particular subsystem, such as an individual school, and expect that new program or project to thrive. They must attend as well to bringing about supportive changes in the larger system in which the new program is embedded or in which the new project will function.

Consider the lesson contained in the following examples from the annals of school reform.

SOME ILLUSTRATIVE CASES

I have long been an activist in the area of school reform. Indeed, I have been somehow involved in every wave of reform that has swept over America's schools for the past forty years. I have learned important lessons from these experiences, as much from failures as from successes. I would like to look at the lessons from a few failures here (some better news is presented later in the book). Because I have been involved in the first two of these cases, I make no claim to absolute objectivity, but I do believe I have learned a few things of value.

Curriculum Reform 1960s Style

The sense of fickleness and fads that permeates educational change today stems from the fact that so many changes in education are project focused, with little attention given to the need to change systems so that they support needed projects. The result is that each new project is initiated only to be abandoned, with another, newer project put in its place. The fate of the curriculum reform efforts of the 1960s illustrates this problem very well.

Immediately following the launching of Sputnik I in 1957, there was much interest in reforming schools so that America could compete more effectively with the well-educated engineers in the USSR. Influenced by the thinking of Jerome Bruner,[2] there grew up in America a group of men and women who became convinced that the best way to improve education was to develop new and sophisticated curriculum materials that reflected the "structure of the disciplines." It was Bruner's contention that, properly engaged, any student could learn at some level of sophistication what was known by scholars in the various disciplines. It was the obligation of scholars in the disciplines to identify the structures of those disciplines so that curricula could be organized in ways that were accessible to students at different levels of sophistication and were also consistent with current scholarship. Moreover, curricula were designed to foster active learning and inquiry. Students were not only to learn real science but also to do real science; they were not only to learn real geography but also to learn to do what geographers do.

Out of such thinking grew a wide range of curriculum projects, dealing first with science (for example, the Biological Sciences Curriculum Study) and later the social sciences (for example, the High School Geography project). It was a heady time. It was a time when members of academic departments on university campuses took seriously the notion that they needed to collaborate with their colleagues in the department of education for the purpose of developing curriculum materials that were academically sound and pedagogically sophisticated.

As these projects began to mature, sponsoring agencies such as the National Science Foundation turned their attention to implementation. Millions of dollars were spent in bringing teachers to university campuses to be "updated and upgraded" in their understanding of the subjects they were teaching and to be trained in the use of these new curriculum materials. (For nearly a decade, I led some of the summer institutes for teachers funded by the National Science Foundation.) Despite the soundness of the materials, the enthusiasm of many teachers, and the training programs, it eventually became clear that the materials were not being taught as intended or used as extensively as anticipated.[3] After a brief flurry of effort to alter the way they went about their business, most teachers abandoned the new materials in favor of more conventional and more pedantic approaches. At the same time, some conservative parents and politicians began objecting to materials developed for the project *Man: A Course of Study.* The consequence of all of these events was that government funding agencies began to withdraw support from these curriculum reform projects, and efforts to disseminate the materials disappeared.

Thus Kanter's description of the typical fate of change projects certainly applies to the curriculum reforms of the 1960s. Because they were discrete stand-alone projects, they had no impact, and the memory of them faded though the need remained. Reformers today are calling again for more hands-on science, increased attention to learning as an active process, greater student engagement, and so on. Even now, various private groups are developing and marketing curriculum materials designed to respond to this need—and are presenting these materials and this need as new.

Few seem to remember the curriculum reform efforts of the 1960s and the two lessons we ought to have learned from them. Recently, I summarized those lessons this way:

> The reason curriculum reform did not work is because the structure of schools could not, and cannot, support new technologies and new work for students. Radically different curriculum designs are not accommodated by the existing structure of schools. . . .
>
> The reason structural change has not worked is that efforts to change the structures of schools proceeded without real attention to the reasons such changes were needed. The consequence has been that in spite of many structural changes, for example, teaming in middle schools, the emergence of site-based councils, and decentralization, little has happened that necessarily affects the quality of the work provided to students. *Until restructuring is coupled with improving the quality of work provided to students and curriculum reform is coupled with providing students with access to profound knowledge through work that is engaging, compelling, and satisfying, there is little chance that either restructuring and "recurriculuming" the schools will produce the results for students, teachers, parents, or communities that they promise to deliver* [emphasis in original].[4]

School Reform in the 1980s

In the late 1970s and early 1980s, as a special assistant to the superintendent of the Charlotte-Mecklenburg Schools (CMS) of North Carolina, I led an effort to create and implement a program designed to alter the career structure of the teaching occupation in Charlotte. This project, the Charlotte-Mecklenburg Teacher Career Development Plan, later became known as one of the early forerunners of the *career ladder* movement popular for a brief period in the 1980s. However, the intent of the CMS initiative was much more comprehensive than simply providing a new pay-for-performance scheme or a master teacher program in disguise.[5] It aspired to nothing less than a fundamental change in the structure of the teaching occupation and the way teachers are inducted into that occupation.[6] Its goal was to provide career options for teachers that would make it possible for them to remain in the classroom and still enjoy the advantages of a progressively rewarding career.

Career ladder initiatives outside of Charlotte, including many that were purportedly based on the CMS model, were in fact less grandiose in their intentions. What most other career ladder initiatives were about was more accountability, better evaluation systems for teachers, and an improved system of merit pay. Changing the structure of the teaching occupation had little to do with the thinking of many advocates of career ladders. But in Charlotte, in the early days of the project, changing the ways teachers were recruited, inducted, and sustained was the primary focus of the project. Issues of evaluation, accountability, and pay, although important, were secondary.

The CMS program was designed to give all teachers rewards and incentives for excellence in performance, and it included a staff development system. It was assumed that anyone who reached Career Level I would, by definition, be a master teacher. Career Level II teachers were expected to develop the skills needed to provide in-school leadership in such areas as curriculum development, staff development, and the assessment of instructional programs. They were also expected to be willing to be assigned duties in the school (in addition to their teaching duties) that called on them to use these skills while maintaining excellence in their own classrooms. Career Level III teachers were to be persons willing to employ their skills on behalf of the entire school system. For example, a Career Level III teacher was expected to be willing to accept an administrative transfer to a troubled school and would have the skills needed to provide leadership that would produce improved results in that school. Rather than promoting teachers out of the classroom, then, the idea was to promote them in the classroom. Rather than paying teachers for being barely adequate, fair, and excellent, the CMS plan assumed all who reached Level I would be excellent as teachers, or they should not be afforded career status.

Other plans were different. In Tennessee, for example, a statewide career ladder program was established that was simply a merit pay system. Career Level II teachers were teachers whose teaching skills were supposed to be demonstrably superior to Career Level I teachers, and only Career Level III teachers were to be master teachers. Although some language of the CMS plan was adopted in publicizing the Tennessee plan, its primary purpose was to ensure that good teachers were paid better than mediocre ones. Changing the way teachers were recruited, inducted, and sustained was secondary. That is, the Tennessee plan assumed that it was normal and acceptable to have some teachers performing at a lower level of effectiveness relative to their stellar peers so long as the stars were paid more. The CMS plan, in contrast, assumed that students should not have to suffer minimally competent teachers.

Once the Tennessee plan become operational, it began claiming the attention of those interested in school reform, and when North Carolina adopted a statewide career ladder plan, that plan was based largely on the Tennessee model. Legislators assumed that any differences between the Tennessee plan and the Charlotte plan were minor. But they were wrong. The state plan was more a merit pay system and less a career development system. In effect, the CMS idea was revised until it fit into the traditions of the larger system in which it was embedded.

Thus one of the lessons here is that projects and programs that depart dramatically from tradition cannot be implemented successfully until and unless the systems in which they are embedded are changed so as to support to them. Environmental forces beyond the direct control of program designers and program leaders are continuously pushing to reformulate new programs and projects so they will fit existing structures, including traditional public and political perceptions and beliefs. If these programs and projects cannot be altered, they will be expelled or suppressed. The CMS case illustrates this point well.

The CMS case also illustrates the importance of another systems issue, continuity in leadership. For reasons totally unrelated to the CMS career development ladder, both the superintendent and I left the Charlotte-Mecklenburg Schools prior to the full implementation of the program. We had provided much of the leadership needed to keep the program on track in the early stages and thought it had enough strength to stand on its own and that new school leaders could carry it through. We were wrong. We failed to create a CMS leadership structure that could sustain the necessary effort.

John Kotter calls such a structure a *guiding coalition,* a group of persons empowered to lead and manage the change process.[7] A guiding coalition is essential when program changes are underway that require systemic changes as well. The members of this coalition must be persons who have power in the organization: persons who occupy positions of authority and who therefore have the ability to make things happen when the time for action is upon the group. A fair number of recognized leaders must be a part of the group. Indeed, I would argue that anyone who is likely to be looked to as a provider of leadership in the cutting-edge activities that will provide direction to the change should be not only a de facto member of the guiding coalition but a member of the leadership team within that coalition.

It is also important that some members of the group have technical competence in the area or areas that are the focus of the change. For example, if the change affects curriculum, it is critical to have persons skilled in the design of curriculum materials as members of the guiding coalition. They should be in a position to help the team assess whether difficulties experienced in the change process are attributable to flaws in the ideas and technologies that underpin the change or whether these difficulties have more to do with the ways and means of implementing the change.

Finally, it is critical that the group have members who have credibility with those who are most likely to be affected by the change in the early stages and credibility with those who are most likely to resist change at any point in the process.[8] Thus, if teachers are expected to participate in the change, it is critical to have persons on the guiding coalition whom teachers respect and trust and in whom they have confidence. These people need not be teachers, but they probably will be. Similarly, if initial efforts are going to place demands on parents, union leaders, principals, or any other identifiable group, then persons who have credibility with these groups need to be members of the guiding coalition.

The caveat here is that these credible persons need not be representative of the individuals and groups who will listen to them, nor is it always good that they be representative. What is needed are credible people who have empathetic understanding of the perspectives of affected groups. What is not needed are advocates for the interests of this or that group. Real change affects the real and perceived interests of all groups. Advocates too often protect these interests single-mindedly rather than seeking ways of harmonizing these interests with the new directions being set by the intended change.

The guiding coalition is also not the typical task force made up of representative stakeholders. Although the team may decide to create such representative stakeholder groups, the function of the guiding coalition is to provide overall direction to the change effort, to ensure the effort is sustained, and to provide a framework for deliberation and informed debate when problems arise. It is not nor should it be permitted to become an intentionally political body nor is it representative. It is a core team that can be depended on to get the job done and that can ensure that momentum is maintained.

Another way, then, to view the failure of the original intention of the CMS teacher career development program to survive is to understand that certain programs, unlike projects, have major cumulative organizational impacts.[9] It is sometimes difficult for any except those already well initiated in such a program to understand it well enough to lead and manage the change effort connected with it. Persistent, committed, and continuous leadership is essential to the success of such programs.

Rosabeth Moss Kanter observes:

> It is also too easy for managers to give up when the Big Idea does not produce results quickly enough—and to move on to the next potential blockbuster. Yet the difference between success and failure is often just a matter of time: staying with the project long enough to overcome the unexpected developments, political problems, or fatigue that can come between a great-sounding plan and actual results. A basic truth of management—if not of life—is that nearly everything looks like a failure in the middle. At the same time, of course, the next project always looks more attractive (because it is all promise, fresh and untried).[10]

Since abandonment of the CMS local career development program, several new big ideas have been tried, and even now new big ideas are being explored. In Charlotte, as in so many other school districts, willingness to change and to take risks is not the problem. The problem is creating systems that will sustain changes long enough to reap the benefits that are promised.

No change occurs in a vacuum. Many forces outside an organization affect change just as much as inside forces do. What change leaders must do is to put systems in place that permit them and their successors to give direction to the chaos and confusion introduced by these outside forces, so that the system can "thrive on chaos" rather than be overwhelmed by it.[11] They must communicate a clear vision of the future that will sustain the program even in the face of adversity.

There are many other instances of the inadequacy of nonsystemic approaches to changes requiring systemic reform. For example, one assumption of the Annenberg Challenge as it was originally conceived "was that by giving money to reformers on the ground, rather than to the school bureaucracy, the challenge could make public education work for poor and minority students and deepen existing grassroots efforts." That assumption now seems unworkable. And Barbara Cervone, Annenberg Challenge national coordinator, has said, "The reality is that there's no such thing as positioning yourself outside the district."[12]

And John Anderson, president of the New American Schools Corporation, sums up the situation this way:

> Two major streams of school reform are operating in America today. One, which has been dominant over the past decade, holds that reform primarily requires changes in the school governance system—standards, assessment, accountability, site-based management, charters, vouchers. The other emphasizes school-by-school, classroom-based change, where the improvement process is aided by national networks of trainers, well-designed materials, and extensive, detailed professional development.
>
> A growing body of evidence demonstrates that neither top-down system changes nor bottom-up school changes alone can lead to improvements in student achievement. What is needed is system change specifically targeted to support the improvement of classroom practice. Our experience at New American Schools bears this out and suggests that it is time we stop debating the approach, recognize that both kinds of action are necessary but not sufficient, and commit to work together to systematically apply what we know succeeds for large numbers of children in diverse communities.[13]

Systemic reform works at creating the conditions in schools that must be present for the schools and school system to be change adept. To paraphrase Kanter, it creates the conditions in schools that ensure that schools will embrace change as an internally desired opportunity before it becomes an externally driven threat, by mobilizing many people in the organization to contribute.

DEFINING CHANGE-ADEPT ORGANIZATIONS

Leaders in change-adept organizations use demands for change as the impetus to continue an already established pattern of improvement.

Furthermore, once changes are initiated they are persistently pursued and supported, even in the face of adversity.[14]

In change-inept organizations, each change is treated as an isolated and singular event. Leaders in change-inept organizations often appear paralyzed and helpless in the face of demands for fundamental change. Even when these leaders make serious efforts to move the system forward, they often find they cannot, for the organizations they lead do not have the characteristics required to support and sustain a serious change effort.[15]

In the private sector, change-inept organizations usually do not survive. They are replaced, either by competitors who can adjust quickly to changing demands or by new organizations that enter the field to meet a need that is not being met by existing organizations. Similarly, vouchers, privatization, and charter schools all contain the possibility that the public schools will be replaced by some alternative organizational form. It is also possible that a new system will emerge (for example, an electronically based educational environment) that will make both public and private schools unnecessary.[16]

From time to time, however, even organizations that are notably change inept are blessed with leaders who understand that they must attend to developing the capacity to change along with introducing projects and programs that promise to directly affect the quality of products and services provided to customers. Public education in America is in desperate need of such leaders, individuals who understand the need for change-adept schools and who are prepared to act in ways that create such organizations.

Here are the chief characteristics that leaders must work to produce and maintain. In change-adept organizations:

- The core business of the organization is understood, and leaders can communicate their understanding of that core business to employees, board members, peers, colleagues, and others whose support they depend on.

- Employees have access to the technologies that are most appropriate to the pursuit of the core business of the organization; leaders are continuously scanning the environment for new or different technologies that hold promise for improving the way the core business is conducted.

- Customer needs are at the center of all decisions, and the core business of the organization is conducted in a way that best promises to satisfy those needs.

- Systems are in place that permit leaders to communicate the need for change to others and to engage the support of others in the pursuit of solutions to the problems that give rise to the need for change.

- Leaders have and communicate to others a clear understanding of the beliefs that ought to guide decisions in the organization and of the vision that results from those beliefs; everyone in the organization has a clear conception of "who we are, what we do, and what we must do well to satisfy our customers."

- Participatory leadership and employee empowerment are the normal patterns of behavior.

- Policies, practices, and programs designed to support continuity of effort are in place (for example, change-adept organizations usually have clear leadership succession plans and programs for inducting new employees into the culture of the organization).

- Heavy investment is made in employee development, training, and support, including personal support.

- Incentives encourage innovation and provide the flexibility employees need to experiment and explore alternatives.

- Open and permeable boundaries are encouraged so that the organization can engage in a wide variety of collaborative undertakings advantageous to the pursuit of its core business.

It is not common for schools and school districts to manifest many of these attributes. It is, however, possible for every school system to develop these capacities. To do this, those who lead school reform must focus their attention on the properties of the systems they lead. Without attention to these properties, the endless round of change without improved results will continue. If lack of improvement continues, public education will cease to be a vital force in American life. And without the schools as a rallying point, it is unlikely that many communities will have the moral strength to resist what Arthur Schlesinger Jr. refers to as the "disuniting of America."[17]

GETTING THE BUSINESS RIGHT: THE KEY TO IT ALL

The first step in creating change-adept schools and the systems that support them is for those who lead the schools to understand the true business of schools. Most persons who write about life in organizations agree with Peter Drucker's often-cited observation that one of the most important contributions of a leader is to define the nature of the organization's business and to communicate this understanding to others.[18] When leaders do not understand the nature of the organization's business, systemic reform makes little sense and will have little impact.

Moreover, as I discussed in the Preface, the ends of education, the results that we expect from the schools, are different from the business of education. The business of education is what schools must do to obtain the results that are expected of them.

- The business of schools is to invent tasks, activities, and assignments that the students find engaging and that bring them into profound interactions with content and processes they will need to master to be judged well educated; what the term *well educated* means is a judgment made by the adult community, especially those such as colleges, universities, employers, and parents who set standards for student performance.

- The learning of skills, the creation of a world-class workforce, the development of a democratic citizenry, the ability to think, reason, and use one's mind well, and the various other nominees for the purpose of school (the purpose of education) are all results of the school doing this business well, that is, providing students with engaging tasks, assignments, and experiences that produce these results.

- The proper focus of the schools, then, is on the quality of the work provided students and the capacity of that work to engage students, to cause students to persist when they have difficulty, and to produce in students a sense of satisfaction and accomplishment. School leaders who clearly grasp the business of schools and who act to carry out that business are in a better position to make their schools change adept than are those leaders who see their business as achieving outcome goals, no matter how noble and lofty those goals may be.

The key questions for schools to focus on concern what students are expected to *do* in order to learn whatever it is expected they will learn. They also ask how students can be brought to do those things that are likely to result in their learning what is intended. These are the questions that bring one to the very heart of the core business of schools: that is *the invention of tasks, activities, and assignments that the students find to be engaging and that bring them into profound interactions with content and processes they will need to have mastered to be judged to be well educated.*

DRIVING THE CORE BUSINESS
THROUGH THE SYSTEM

Once top-level leaders are clear on the nature of the enterprise they are leading, the next step is to drive this understanding down through the system. The goal must be to ensure that all those in positions to influence action in schools, especially principals and teachers, have a shared understanding of the way the business of the schools is to be defined.

In later chapters I discuss in more detail what leaders do to pursue this goal. Here I will simply assert that what effective leaders do is spend most of their time communicating their view of the nature of the enterprise they are leading, reconceptualizing their views on the basis of feedback received, and once again communicating their understanding.

This may sound like a prescription for top-down management. It is not. But as numerous students of leadership in business have observed, participatory leadership does not mean those at the top abdicate their roles; one of the jobs of the leader is to lead. Nevertheless, those who lead cannot accomplish what they intend unless those whom they intend to lead feel empowered to act on their own. Kanter puts the matter this way:

> People tend to prefer bosses with "clout." When employees perceive their manager as influential upward and outward, their status is enhanced by association and they generally have high morale and feel less critical or resistant to their boss. More powerful leaders are also more likely to delegate (they are too busy to do it all themselves), to reward talent, and to build a team that places subordinates in significant positions.
>
> Powerlessness, in contrast, tends to breed bossiness rather than true leadership. . . . it is powerlessness that often creates ineffective, desultory management and petty, dictatorial, rules-minded managerial styles.[19]

The choice then is not between grassroots democracy on the one hand and dominance by an authoritarian leader on the other. Rather, the choice is between leaders who know how to engage the commitments of others and who thus greatly increase their power and leaders who know only how to gain compliance through the exercise of formal authority and the preservation of that authority and whose power is thus limited to that authority.

A leader needs more than formal authority to change a system successfully. One of the ways a leader gets the necessary power is by having a clear view about where he or she sees the enterprise headed and then communicating this view to others in ways that are compelling to them. That is why having a clear answer to the question what is our business is so critical to all leaders, including those who lead our schools.

SEEING THE WORK OF SCHOOLS AS KNOWLEDGE WORK

The business of schools is providing students with work they find to be engaging and from which they learn those things that are considered by parents and other adults to be important to them and to the future of the culture and the society. That is, schools provide students with knowledge work. For some, this emphasis on *work* (as opposed to thought, analysis, and the development of aesthetic sensibilities) may smack of anti-intellectualism and vocationalism. But consider the full meaning of the word *work* and the ways knowledge is developed and acquired.

Work is purposeful and directed (usually self-directed) activity. And this activity may be mental as well as physical. Knowledge work is nothing more than or less than putting ideas, symbols, theories, propositions, and other forms of knowledge to use in solving problems, creating products (an essay is a product, just as this book is a product), and generating more knowledge, as happens in research.[20]

The value of thinking of the schools as knowledge work organizations is that it focuses attention on the fact that learning is an active process. It focuses attention on the fact that to do academic work is to purposefully work with ideas, concepts, forms, shapes, symbols, purported facts, and so on. This concept of schools does not turn academic institutions into trade schools. However, it does require everyone involved with schools to accept that the business of the school is to invent knowledge work for students; the jobs this work requires students to do are knowledge work jobs.

CONCLUSION: THE FIRST TASK FOR LEADERS

Systems are defined by the structure of rules, roles, relationships, values, beliefs, and norms that prescribe and proscribe human action within the context of a group or an organization. Systems not only define what must be done, they define what can be done. To bring about dramatic improvements in the results a given system is producing, the structural properties of the system must be changed to accommodate the requirements of whatever new programs are to be introduced. To fail to make this structural change is to fail over the long term to manage change successfully.

Change-adept organizations are organizations that not only manage new programs and projects effectively and efficiently but also manage the structural changes needed to accommodate these innovations. Our school systems have not been adept at change. They possess few of the qualities and attributes of change-adept systems. The first challenge for change leaders in schools, therefore, is to develop a detailed understanding of the key components of change-adept systems and then to create those components in the schools, school districts, and communities whose destinies will be determined by what these leaders do or fail to do.

PART TWO

Creating Quality Learning Experiences

Effective leaders understand and can articulate to others the nature of the core business of the enterprise they are leading. They know their customers well and understand those customers' needs. They are also clear about the products and services they are trying to provide and have an understanding of the customer needs that gave rise to the products or services in the first place. Armed with this understanding, effective leaders focus on results associated with the creation of these products or services. They put in place a system of standards to ensure that these products and services meet the needs of customers. Finally, they understand their competition and are constantly asking and causing others to ask, What is our competition doing that we are not doing, that we should be doing, and that we can do as well or better than they can? The chapters in this section develop and elaborate on these themes.

CHAPTER THREE

Focusing on Results

C ritics of America's schools, especially critics from the business community, frequently argue that educators do not pay enough attention to the "bottom line." From the perspective of these critics, the bottom line in education is student learning.

In response to this sort of criticism, educators and policymakers have become especially attuned to the need to determine, as they say, what students need to know and what they should be able to do, and to developing standards and measures for assessing how well students are doing in learning these things. Most of all, they have become attuned to the idea that learning should be the focus of all school activity and of all assessments of the effects of that activity. This chapter looks more closely at what schools are about and the ways we might measure what schools actually must accomplish.

THE LEARNING-FOCUSED SCHOOL

From a marketing perspective, the idea of the *learning-focused school* has considerable appeal. After all, if students do not learn, then the schools are not doing what the community expects them to do. Using measures of learning to assess the effectiveness of schools is increasingly commonplace. To say that schools are focused on learning is to say that the schools are focused on what the stakeholders care about.

It is true that if students are not learning, there is reason to believe the schools are not going about their business well or that they are going about the wrong business. The downside to being primarily learning focused is that it sometimes distracts attention from the fact that learning is not what teachers and school leaders should be busying themselves about. Learning, by which I mean the acquisition and construction of knowledge and skills, is what students are expected to do. Intended or desired learning is what happens when schools and teachers design work that the students find engaging and that is the right work, that is, it contains the needed content and develops the intended skills. *What schools are about is designing work for students that students will do and from which students learn what it is intended they learn.* Educational leaders must focus on those things that result in learning, for it is only by focusing on these things that learning can be enhanced.

Just as business leaders in troubled businesses have had to learn to focus on customers and their needs, educators should learn to focus on students and their needs. Businesses that focus on profit rather than on the customer and product quality go bankrupt. Schools that fail to focus on students and the quality of the experiences provided to students do not inspire learning.

Yet many educators confronted with the demand for improved performance make the same mistake that many business leaders make when their enterprises are threatened. Under such a threat, many business leaders resort to hiring more accountants, producing short-term financial reports, and changing accounting standards; they hire more inspectors, and they increase the advertising budget. When confronted with similar difficulties, educators (especially state education agencies) hire more specialists in tests and testing, teachers give "practice tests," legislators insist on better and more rigorous tests, state central offices conduct more inspections and audits, and nearly every school district seeks public relations specialists.

Eventually business leaders come to understand that without customers there is no profit and without products that have the right qualities there are no customers. It is for this reason that businesses generally measure many things in addition to profit and loss. They measure such things as cycle time (the length of time from product conception to product delivery) and product reliability because they know these things are important to getting and keeping customers, and they know as well that getting and keeping customers is the bottom line of business.

Just as measures of profit and loss are important to businesses, measures of learning are important to schools. And just as businesses measure more than profit and loss, measures of learning should be just one set of facts that school leaders use to evaluate the progress and health of the organization they lead. They should identify as well the proximate causes of learning and develop measures for them. Among the causes I nominate as worthy of attention are these:

- Curriculum alignment
- Student engagement
- Student persistence
- Student satisfaction

Curriculum Alignment

It is common sense to argue that students are more likely to learn what is intended when the curriculum content is organized to ensure that students have the opportunity to experience that content and gain practice in the desired skills. Unfortunately, common sense is not always common practice.

One of the tools educators have invented to ensure that the content taught is the content that is valued is *curriculum alignment.* Curriculum alignment ensures that the content and processes that are embedded in the work students are assigned or encouraged to undertake are relevant to what the community expects students to learn. At present, the clearest expressions of these community expectations are found in the standardized tests required by state and local officials. The facts that these tests are usually multiple-choice tests and that multiple-choice tests, unless very carefully constructed, tend to fragment, trivialize, and decontextualize knowledge and facts cause some to fear that curriculum alignment is nothing more or less than "teaching to the test." It can be that, but it need not be.

Assessing whether the curriculum is aligned with the intended content requires judging five conditions:

1. The scope of the content covered.

2. The level of sophistication and complexity of the knowledge.

3. The sequence or order of presentation.

4. The richness of the content.

5. The texture of the content.

The first three of these five conditions are more commonly attended to in efforts to align curriculum than are the last two. It is this fact more than any other that gives rise to the complaint that aligning curriculum to what is tested leads to trivialization of content, and there is some basis for this concern. Curriculum alignment will trivialize what is taught if the only concerns are breadth of coverage, the sequence in which materials are presented, and the level of mastery required. In addition to these matters, educators need to be concerned with the *richness* and the *texture* of the content.

Without attention to richness and texture, students may learn to decode words, but they are also likely to learn that reading is boring. Without attention to richness and texture, students may learn to compute, but they are unlikely to learn to use mathematics as a part of their own reasoning processes. Without attention to richness and texture, students may be able to identify, for purposes of a test, a set of dates and events, but they will be unlikely to see the connections among these events, between history and biography, and between past events and their own experiences. More important, they will not remember what they "know" for very long.

Richness has to do with depth, subtlety, and connectedness. It is an aesthetic judgment as well as a technical one. It requires teachers to know the subjects they teach well enough that they appreciate the possibilities and limitations of various expressions of the content they hope to convey to students.

Discovering the romance and enchantment of science, the wonder of a butterfly and the mystery of a cocoon, are as important to scientific understanding as are precise understandings of the process of metamorphosis and the generalizations made about this process. Science as discovery is as important as is science as fact.

History as adventure is as important as is history as dates and events. Reading that is exciting and aesthetically satisfying can convey important facts just as readily as can bland textbooks made up of facts strung together, rather than connected, by words. Literary expression is as important as is literal description. Richness determines the presence of such qualities and such possibilities.

Texture has more to do with the way knowledge and information are organized and presented. Knowledge is almost always presented in an orderly and linear fashion in textbooks; this is efficient, but it is also usually uninteresting. Knowledge should sometimes be embedded in stories as well as in literal statements and in metaphors as well as in straightforward description.

In brief, texture has to do with the extent to which those in charge of instruction endeavor to "package" the information and knowledge they intend students to acquire, so each student has optimal access to that knowledge and is optimally attracted to the activity that will produce desired learning outcomes.

Richness and texture have aesthetic and affective dimensions as well as technical ones, and those who design curricula and materials should attend to these dimensions. Teachers too need to seek to ensure that the content they want students to learn is organized and packaged in ways that are aesthetically and emotionally appealing to students.

For example, a movie like *The Grapes of Wrath* may give students a sense of the reality of the Great Depression that cannot be gained from a scholarly treatise. Certainly, this movie cannot substitute for more scholarly study of the Great Depression or for reading the novel on which the movie is based. However, viewing such movies and *grappling*[1] with their content can do much to enrich a student's understanding of an era and of the worldview of those who lived at that time and place.

Similarly, structured interviews with scientists working in local laboratories and captured on videotape by a team of students can do much to enrich the curriculum for both the students who conduct the interviews and the students who are the audience for the tape. Richness and texture have to do with the extent to which those who design curriculum and those who teach seek out and employ such culturally significant resources.

Student Engagement

Students learn from what they do. The art and science of teaching is found in the ability of the teacher to invent things that students will do and from which they will learn those things teachers and other members of the adult world believe they need to learn. Teachers know they have been successful when students are attentive; they most certainly know they have achieved this end when students stick with tasks they have been assigned or encouraged to undertake.[2] Without engagement (and persistence, discussed later) there is little likelihood that students will learn that which it is intended they learn. It is therefore important that teachers become discerning and systematic in assessing the level of engagement in their classes. Given such measures, teachers can then focus their attention on producing activities with the qualities to which students are likely to respond in ways that show evidence of increased engagement. But first, measures of engagement must be developed.

Engagement is not directly observable, yet assessing it is not a new idea or a totally undeveloped art. Teachers do it all the time. For example, when a teacher instructs students to "pay attention," the teacher is saying that he or she has observed something in the students' behavior that leads to the inference that they are not as engaged as the teacher wants them to be. Similarly, when a teacher observes that students are careless and sloppy in their work, the teacher is commenting on his or her perception that the students do not attach enough significance to the work to attend to details.

In developing measures of engagement, however, it should be understood that engagement and time on task are not synonyms. Neither is engagement synonymous with entertainment. People who are engaged do tend to be on task, and sometimes they find these tasks to be entertaining. To be engaged, however, is to invest energy beyond that needed simply to get by. Engagement is active. It requires the student to be attentive as well as in attendance; it requires the student to be committed to the task and find some inherent value in what he or she is being asked to do. The engaged student not only does the task assigned but also does the task with enthusiasm and diligence. Moreover, the student performs the task because he or she perceives the task to be associated with a *near-term* end that he or she values.

This is not to deny the importance of delayed gratification, nor is it to downplay the significance of the need to do work that is sometimes boring and tedious. Schoolwork, like all other work, is sometimes tedious and boring, but it should never be without meaning.

When a student is highly engaged in a task, he or she is more likely to do the boring and tedious parts of the task with enthusiasm than he or she is when less engaged in the task. For example, when so-called rote learning is not related to something to which students attach meaning, they are not likely to find it engaging. When rote learning is attached to something in which students find meaning, they are more likely to attend to it and to learn what it is intended they learn (see Chapter Five for an expanded discussion of this point).

To aid teachers in assessing levels of engagement, I have devised a five-level schema for distinguishing the intensity of engagement. It proceeds from the assumption that a student who is engaged fully in a task not only does the task but also finds personal meaning and value in the task. When the student does the task assigned, sticks with the task when he or she experiences difficulty, and finds personal meaning in the task, then it is appropriate to say the student is authentically engaged.

There are, however, different levels and types of engagement. The levels I have identified are

- Authentic engagement
- Ritual engagement
- Passive compliance
- Retreatism
- Rebellion[3]

Students who are *authentically engaged* conform to expectations because they embrace the intended ends of the instruction as meeting needs that they have and can express. They also accept the approved means because they find these means responsive to their personal needs and values. Students who are authentically engaged in content that reflects the studies of the academy are highly prized in schools. Unfortunately (or perhaps fortunately), not all students are interested in the things that compel university professors. If these less interested students are to be authentically engaged in work that results in their learning what the teachers intend, teachers need to learn to create ends in addition to academic ends for these students to pursue.

Ritual engagement is a second type of adaptation to the demands placed on students. Ritualism involves doing what is required, but not for the meaning found in the activity itself. Students who are extremely compliant to authority and are confronted with a task that is meaningless to them will comply with expectations, but more from obedience than from commitment. They will do what is required, indeed they may even go beyond the requirements, but the reward they seek is not found in the work they are doing or even in the products of that work. Rather, the rewards are extrinsic to the tasks assigned.

For example, for some students, college admissions are the ultimate exercise of adult authority. Such students are usually quite compliant with the official expectations of their teachers and their school as long as they believe that what the teachers and the school are about is enhancing the students' prospects for college entry.

The third type of engagement is *passive compliance,* which involves doing the minimum required to get by. Students who are engaged in this way seldom attend to detail. They are more concerned with having work accepted than with getting that work right and having it respected.

Retreatism involves rejection of both the official goals and the official means of achieving those goals. Sometimes students retreat because they feel they cannot do what is being asked of them. Sometimes they retreat because they are uncertain about what is being asked of them. And sometimes they retreat from serious academic studies because neither they nor their parents see much that is relevant to their lives growing out of academic studies.

Because engagement can only be inferred from what can be observed, it is easy to confuse authentic engagement with ritual engagement and passive compliance. Similarly, the student who has found the topic of a group discussion sufficiently uninteresting that he or she engages in retreatist behavior often goes undetected. Thus, teachers probably tend to overestimate the level of engagement in their classrooms, especially engagement in the work assigned.

Rebellion has to do with rejecting both official means and ends and substituting new means and new ends in their place. For example, grades are officially thought of as symbols that communicate levels of attainment. Some students reject the notion that learning and grades should be related, and they substitute good grades for learning. They sometimes also seek alternative means of achieving the substitute end, by cheating or by encouraging their teachers to be less demanding.

Students who are rebels are not always bad students or misbehaving students, though they may be. Rebelling students simply reject the premises from which academic educators work and pursue their own goals (or at least goals that are not officially recognized and sanctioned) by means other than those valued by the system of which they are a part.

In Chapter One, I mentioned the anti-intellectual tendencies in American life. I know of no research that investigates the possible relationships between anti-intellectualism and the poor response of the masses of students to academic pursuits, yet surely the disrespect and disdain some Americans have for the life of the mind and the belief among many (including many businesspeople) that scholarly pursuits are for those who do not have important, practical things to do with their lives are among the root causes of many of the problems of twenty-first century American schools.

I also pointed out in Chapter One that the present is the first time in the history of America that it has been expected that all students should develop high levels of academic understandings and skill. Yet educators are still relying on the fortunate circumstance of having students who are interested in the subjects the schools teach or having students with parents who will cause them to engage the content ritually, even when the students are not interested in it.

There are two ways to deal with this issue. First, we can change the culture so that it is less anti-intellectual. Second, we can modify the work needed to learn academic subjects so that it has more of those qualities about it that appeal to those who are not academics. The second way appears to be something educators could do now, and as it is done, the culture will change. It seems unlikely that we can change the culture any other way, and we do not have the time to wait while we find out whether some other way might work.

In addition to engaging tasks, there are engaging teachers. Engaging teachers, by virtue of personality and style, inspire students to care about what the teachers care about and are viewed by some students as significant models of how to go about assigned tasks. Engaging teachers, like other charismatic leaders, should be valued. However, charisma is in short supply. If all or nearly all students are to have a high-quality academic experience in school, it is essential that educators redefine the term *master teacher* to mean a person who is a master at creating engaging work for students and then leading them to do that work. Too often, master teachers today are viewed as persons who are personally engaging, persons who give stellar and entertaining performances, persons who are especially gregarious, and so on.

Shifting the focus from the performance of the teacher to the work the teacher provides to students does not diminish the importance or significance of what the teacher does. It does, however, place the meaning of teacher performance in a different context. It suggests that teachers should view themselves as leaders rather than performers. And it suggests that teacher educators should concentrate as much on helping teachers design engaging work for students as they now concentrate on helping teachers give stellar performances. Once the view is accepted that the business of schools and teachers is to produce engaging work for students, the quest for an explanation for the lack of student engagement would have to examine the qualities and the attributes of the work the teacher provides to students rather than teacher performance and behavior.

As things now stand, it is too often the case that teachers who are personally engaging are also prone to overestimate the level of student engagement. Rather than being engaged, many students may simply be attentive because they are entertained by the tasks assigned by the teacher and the performances provided by the teacher. Engaging teachers quite often gain compliance from their students by meeting one of the greatest needs students have—relief from boredom. But authentic engagement requires more than compliance. It requires commitment as well. To assess engagement it is necessary to determine both the level of effort a student is expending and the meaning and significance the student attaches to the tasks he or she is assigned. The engaging teacher may or may not require commitment from students. Sometimes engaging teachers mistake appreciation, respect, and compliance with intellectual engagement, just as some of their less engaging colleagues will settle for docility and compliance.

Obviously, it would be preferable to have teachers who are personally engaging and who are also capable of producing engaging work for students. However, the demand for such persons far exceeds the supply. Perhaps it would be more reasonable to expect teachers to be well-informed, sensitive to the needs of others, good social observers, articulate, and especially skilled in designing work for students that students find interesting, challenging, and satisfying. To accomplish this end, teachers and administrators as well as curriculum designers and supervisors need to learn to *work on the work* they provide to students (see Chapter Six).

Student Persistence

Persistence is very much intertwined with engagement. People persist with tasks even when they experience difficulty because they believe in the ends to which the tasks are directed or they fear pain and reprisal if they fail. Fear of failure can gain minimal compliance, but it does not inspire excellence. Indeed, when students are so uncommitted to a task that the only way to get them engaged at all is to threaten punishments, such as low grades, public humiliation, or negative reports to parents, the tendency is for the students to negotiate the standards ("What do I have to do to get by?") rather than to increase their own level of commitment and diligence.

Coercion produces minimal performance. Work that responds to the needs of students produces optimal commitment and optimal performance. Persistence—the willingness to stick with a task until it is completed in a way that is up to standard—results from commitment. Mere compliance results in below-standard performance and below-standard expectations. Indeed, in many instances it results in compromises: the teacher acts as though the students have learned, and the students act as though the teacher has taught. Indeed, it is likely that the present accountability movement—with its heavy reliance on so-called objective tests and concern about grade inflation and social promotions—results at least in part from the perception that such compromises are already too widespread.

Assessing persistence involves determining whether a student is willing to stick with a task until the result of the work meets or exceeds the desired standard. However, just as there are various levels of engagement, there are levels of persistence. Students who persist out of fear of failure are less likely than are morally committed students (those who see meaning and value in the work assigned) to achieve high standards. Morally committed students are engaged students.[4]

Student Satisfaction

The fourth proximate cause of learning that we should be measuring is student satisfaction. *Satisfaction,* as I am using the term, means that as a result of completing the intellectual tasks assigned and encouraged by the teachers and other adults associated with the school, students experience a sense of accomplishment and pride. They feel they have truly done something important, and that importance is to be found not only in what the accomplishment portends for their future but in how they view themselves now.

The best demonstration I know of student satisfaction is a comment made by a student in a videotape entitled "Good Morning Miss Toliver," which features a teacher who is engaging but who also provides her students with engaging work. The student says, "We're smart, and Miss Toliver proves it." This student was one of a class of students who also reported running from their social studies class to get to Miss Toliver's math class.

A Few Cautions

Schools have never been highly successful in getting most students authentically engaged in academic work. This fact has long been implicitly recognized through devices such as tracking, which assumes that the college bound would find academic work engaging whereas the vocation bound would find hands-on training more engaging. Those placed in the *general track* were assumed, I suppose, to be likely to find nothing the school had to offer very engaging, so all that was expected of them was compliance and persistence or perhaps polite retreatism. The most negative rebels would have been expelled or encouraged to withdraw voluntarily. In 1970, after all, only 52.2 percent of Americans above the age of twenty-five had attended four years or more of high school.

America's schools have been very successful in getting more students to attend school and to persist in it than was the case in the past. The challenge now is to get all students engaged in intellectual tasks that result in the students' learning academic concepts and skills. Can the schools earn the attention of all these students, especially when that attention must be earned in areas that were heretofore largely reserved for the cultural elites and those destined to move among these elites? Equally important, can schools, private as well as public, design intellectual activities for students that are sufficiently compelling and engaging to compete with the products of sophisticated entrepreneurs who have control over a wide range of electronically based technologies and media and who are increasingly finding ways to distract students from their schoolwork?

To put these questions another way, in the face of modern demands that all students receive a high-quality academic education and in the face of competition for the attention of students from forces and sources that never before existed, can the schools get the customers they never got before (such as those students who in the past would have been ritualists or so disengaged they dropped out) and at the same time not lose the customers they have always had (such as the children of families in which academic learning is appreciated, supported, and valued)?

DEFINING QUALITY SCHOOLWORK

For schoolwork to be judged quality work, the tasks to be accomplished must be designed and presented in such a way as to be authentically engaging. More than that, quality schoolwork results in students' persisting with the tasks assigned until their work meets the desired standard. Further, when students successfully complete quality schoolwork, they experience a sense of satisfaction, accomplishment, pride, and sometimes delight. Finally, quality schoolwork results in students' learning those things they need to know to do well on the tests the adult community prescribes as means of assessing learning results.

Because this definition embraces the premise that one characteristic of quality schoolwork is that the work is designed to respond to the demand for high test scores, some may find it too narrow. Others, especially those who hold that test scores are the bottom line in education, may find it too broad. However, the reason I include improved test scores in the definition of quality schoolwork is straightforward.

Critical stakeholders in education, especially legislators and media commentators and editors, use test scores as a means of evaluating school performance. They believe these scores are important, and they act on what they believe. Complaints from educators about the tendency of an overemphasis on producing high standardized test scores to produce unimaginative and sterile teaching increasingly fall on deaf ears and are heard more as special pleading than as an honest response. For example, in making an argument for school vouchers, conservative columnist Cal Thomas observed that the Alexandria, Virginia, school system scored "below the state average on each of 27 new exams that will eventually determine who graduates and which schools are accredited." He then commented, "The school board chairman, Stephen J. Kenealy, blamed his district's disappointing performance on the large number of poor children, the precise target of school choice, which has been shown to improve test scores as well as behavior and attitudes wherever it is tried."[5] It is easy to challenge Thomas's assertion that vouchers have proved successful wherever they have been tried. Furthermore, it is easy to demonstrate that Thomas is not especially well informed about his subject. (For example, in the context of the article, he confuses percentile with percentage of right answers. He also overlooks the fact that when percentiles are used, 50 percent of all schools will be in the bottom half. The other 50 percent, of course, will be in the top half.) What Thomas is not wrong about is that too many students in too many schools are failing to learn what they need to learn to do well on tests, and this failure is one of the most potent weapons available to those who would bypass public education in America. Any effort to improve schools that does not address this issue is destined to failure. What is needed are some sensible and defensible ways that will satisfy the increasing demand for objective evidence that the schools are doing what they claim to be doing yet will not compromise the ability of schools and teachers to do what they need to do to satisfy the demand for improved learning.[6]

The reason for including engagement, persistence, and student satisfaction in the definition of quality work is equally straightforward. Those inside education are right who argue that a too heavy emphasis on test scores will distort education. Students who are compliant and who are prepared to engage in ritualistic performances can and often do perform quite well on tests, especially when they are from families in which the parents are themselves well-educated. Indeed, one of the classic complaints of teachers in schools where most students score well on tests is that students appear to engage in too much ritualistic behavior, doing what needs to be done in order to get the needed grade rather than to achieve some desired end more closely associated with the task at hand.

One way to combat the shallowness in curriculum that might be inspired by standardized tests is to ensure that students are authentically engaged in the tasks assigned and are not just being ritualists or polite retreatists. One way to do this is to make the work sufficiently compelling that students persist with it even when they have difficulty. And one way to increase the likelihood that students will become lifelong learners is to ensure that the things they do to learn in school are sources of a sense of satisfaction, accomplishment, delight, and pride.

Schoolwork that has qualities and characteristics that result in student engagement, persistence, and satisfaction and that produces continuously improving learning results is quality schoolwork. The problem for teachers is to be found in creating such work and then leading students in the conduct of that work.

MEASURING EVERYTHING THAT COUNTS

Discussions of good schools and bad schools generally center on the degree of success schools have in producing students who meet some explicitly stated or tacitly implied *learning* standards. When measurement is discussed, the focus is typically on the kinds of tests best suited to provide measures of learning.

Most parties to the dialogue on standards acknowledge some other standards that need to be attended to as well: for example, standards for teachers, school safety, and resources. The focus on measuring student learning has sometimes distracted attention from the need to develop measures relevant to these and yet other standards. However, until and unless school leaders can identify, measure, and control elements central to these other standards, it is unlikely schools will show much sustained improvement in student learning. For example, if teachers provide students with tasks that are without significance to the students, only the most compliant will do these tasks. The remainder will withdraw, invest minimal effort, or rebel and their learning will be at best minimal.

What then should be the standards by which the quality of the work assigned to students should be assessed, and how might these qualities be measured? We should consider three general categories of standards.

- *Input or contextual standards,* which have to do with such things as the number of books in the library, the educational attainments of teachers, safety, space requirements, and so on.

- *Process standards,* which have to do with the ability of the system to perform in ways that will produce desired and intended outputs. As numerous management experts have observed, outcomes cannot be controlled by any direct means. What can be controlled are processes, and processes can be controlled only when they are understood and when they are measured and assessed.

- *Outcome standards,* which have to do with the results desired by the end-users of the products provided by the schools.

Historically, most outside assessments of schools and school quality have centered on input measures. For example, it has until recent years been commonplace for regional and state accrediting agencies to emphasize such things as the number of books in libraries, the level of education of teachers, student-teacher ratios, and so on. Little if any attention was given to evidence of output—that is, evidence of student learning such as scores on state-mandated tests, dropout rates, and failure rates.

Beginning in the early 1980s, educational critics began to insist that schools should be evaluated primarily on the basis of outputs, or results. As a consequence of the demand for results, most regional accrediting agencies have moved or are moving toward some form of student performance–based accreditation. In addition, most states have moved or are moving toward a system for evaluating schools and teachers based primarily on assessment of student performance. Many business critics of schools have always had a pay-for-performance system high on their list of proposed changes or schools. It is now high on the list of proposed remedies coming from legislative halls as well.

Over the past decade the issue of standards for schools has become as much a political issue as a technical one. One of the unfortunate consequences is that much of educators' attention is now fastened on improving test scores, with too little attention being paid to how to ensure that students learn more. This is akin to business leaders' worrying about how to get profits up without worrying about the quality of the products they produce or the customers they serve. It also has turned debates about standards into debates over which tests to use and which test is best.

Concern with measures of learning is so great that in some states it is difficult to get any serious consideration of ways to improve student experiences precisely because teachers and administrators feel an urgent need to improve test scores regardless of what students actually learn. When a state like Kentucky, after eight years of serious effort to improve the quality of its schools and after becoming looked on by many as one of the leading states in comprehensive school reform, announces in July 1998 that it is *time to turn attention to teachers and what happens in classrooms as a means of improving schools,* it tells us that the focus all that time has not been on teachers and what happens in the classroom.

Kentucky is not alone. Throughout this nation, things that should be seen as interrelated parts of the same system—improved experiences for students, improved student learning, and improved test scores—have become dissociated in the minds of teachers, administrators, and policymakers. Instead, the primary activity of many faculty and school leaders has been figuring out what will be on the test and then ensuring that students are exposed to these things so that they can recall them. I have been in many schools where the primary strategy developed to improve test scores is a form of bribery. Students whose test scores improve or who score at a given level win a trip to a theme park.

In defense of such strategies, let me quickly add that it is also probably now the case in many low-performing schools that some students do not do as well as they could do on tests because they perceive the tests to be unimportant. Furthermore, some students have no concern for high-stakes academic consequences either, for they have long ago given up on being academically successful. In these circumstances, it is likely that the opportunity to go to a theme park will focus some students' attention on a test and doing as well as they can on it. What we should be concerned with in these schools, however, is what happens when students do take the tests seriously and it turns out they do not know what they need to know to do well. We should also be concerned about the students who already do well on tests yet find themselves spending days and weeks in preparation that they do not need and do not want.

In the politics of education reform, whether or not more students learn more is sometimes not as important as is ensuring that more students test well. Indeed, improving test-taking skills is sometimes touted as a powerful school reform strategy, because children who have these skills are more likely to show what they already know on tests than are those who lack these skills. There is a perverse logic to such thinking, but as a strategy for improving the educational experience and the learning of students, it is sheer nonsense.

This is not to say that test scores are unimportant or trivial. Neither is it to say that efforts at curriculum alignment are misguided. Tests are one of the means by which the citizenry can communicate what they believe students should learn. It is the obligation of the schools to endeavor to meet these expectations *by ensuring that the content, processes, and skills the citizens value are in fact taught.*

What policymakers also sometimes overlook is that achievement test scores are more useful in identifying the fact that something is amiss than they are in helping school leaders figure out what is amiss and what can be done to correct the situation. High test scores alone are not sufficient evidence that a school is healthy or doing a good job. Improving test scores do not necessarily mean the school is doing a better job than it was. And declining test scores do not mean the school is doing a worse job than it was. Low test scores do mean, however, that the job is not being done. The question is, Why is this so and what can be done about it? For answers to this question, we must consider processes, the measurement of processes, and efforts to bring critical processes under control.

When test scores go up or go down, educators must be in a position to determine whether or not the variance is attributable to processes and procedures employed in the school or to factors outside the control of the school. When the variation is attributable to factors under the control of school personnel (including boards of education), these factors should be identified and then measured, so that they can be brought under control. When the variation is negative and the primary causes are factors beyond the control of the school, such as a shift in student demographics, then school leaders must search for new processes to offset the effects of these uncontrollable events.

Currently, few educators and even fewer policymakers understand that processes can be measured, just as inputs and outputs can be measured. The consequence is that when changes in test scores occur, few educators are in a position to diagnose the causes correctly. The result is that they too often misdiagnose the causes. Frequently, this misdiagnosis rests on the tacit assumption that the primary determiner of the quality of education is to be found in the qualities of the students themselves. It is commonplace, for example, to hear that "the reason test scores are going down in our school is because our student population is changing, becoming more poor and minority." Such a misdiagnosis is harmful and results in defeatism. In contrast, Engelhard Elementary School, which was selected by the Disney Corporation as its spotlight school of the year, is an example of a historically low-performing school that over the past five years has increased test scores dramatically, improved attendance significantly, and increased parental involvement as well. The principal (with whom I and other staff at the Center for Leadership in School Reform have worked for many years), and her staff are not afraid to be held accountable, and they know that what they are about is increasing the level of student engagement in significant work by designing schoolwork that is engaging.

The task of teaching children to read when their parents do not read to them is different from the task of teaching children to read when their parents have the inclination, time, and skills to assist in this learning process. The children whose parents do not or cannot fulfill this tutorial function probably need a different approach to reading and language development than do children from homes where verbal facility is encouraged, admired, and rewarded. This does not mean, however, that the reason schools are failing to turn a proportion of nonreaders into readers is those students' family background. Rather, it means that given the family backgrounds of many low-performing children, the schools may not be doing the right things to teach them. What educators need to be about is figuring out how to provide experiences for these youngsters that will result in their learning to read (not to be confused with simply decoding words), rather than explaining away the present circumstances.

It is generally the case that the highest-performing schools in America (that is, the schools with the largest proportions of high-performing students) are in the more affluent suburbs, and the lowest performing schools are in the most impoverished areas of the cities. Though few educators will openly accept the argument, there is abroad in America the idea that some groups and categories of people are more academically inclined and able than are other groups. Such a view was set forth in the last decade in a book entitled *The Bell Curve.*[7] Although many, including myself, find the conclusions of this book hateful and repugnant and although the case has been made that the research and analysis that support such conclusions are critically flawed, many Americans accept this argument at least tacitly. (Fortunately, when confronted with what their tacit assumptions imply, many are appalled and remorseful.)

Another explanation of variance in student performance is that children in the suburbs do better in academic pursuits than do children in inner-city schools because resources are inequitably distributed.[8] Although resources certainly are very unevenly distributed, there is no clear and compelling evidence that there is a *direct* link between resources provided (variance in inputs) and benefits received (variance in outputs).

This lack of a direct link has led some policymakers and political pundits to the conclusion that having more or less money makes no difference to schools, unlike businesses, churches, and families, and every other organization. This conclusion is sheer nonsense and of more utility to politicians seeking votes from tax-averse constituents than to civic leaders endeavoring to improve the quality of America's schools. The conclusion that money does not matter is logical only when one assumes there should be a direct linkage between inputs and outputs. It is for this reason that understanding the processes that provide the link between inputs and outputs is so critical to school reform. It is variance in processes that leads to variance in outputs. Some processes may cost more than others do—but they may produce more as well.

HOLDING TEACHERS ACCOUNTABLE

Implicit in the idea that schools and teachers should be held accountable for the performance of students is the assumption that teachers can do something about that performance and that teachers know what to do. On the one hand this makes sense. If teachers and schools cannot affect student performance, why have schools? If teachers do not know what to do to affect that performance, why have teachers? On the other hand, many things in addition to schools and teachers affect student performance. Students who are truly mentally retarded will not learn as quickly or as much as students with greater intellectual capacity. Students who come to school with good work habits and who are prone to comply with adult directives and demands are likely to do better on tests than are students who have less well-developed habits of work and personal deportment. Indeed, as discussed earlier, it is the known power of such factors that leads many teachers to feel powerless and threatened in the face of demands for greater accountability.

To hold teachers accountable for the overall achievement of students in their classes, especially when the instrument of accountability is a standardized test, is somewhat akin to holding middle-level managers accountable for the profits or losses of the corporation for which they work. There can be little doubt that teachers contribute to the overall quality of student performance, just as middle-level managers contribute to overall corporate performance, but to try to sort exactly who is responsible for exactly what is an impossible task and probably harmful as well.[9]

People should not be held accountable for results that are outside their control. Does this mean then that teachers are in no way accountable for student learning? Absolutely not. What it does mean is that teachers should be directly, personally, and immediately accountable for ensuring that the work they provide students is increasingly effective at producing those conditions needed to increase the likelihood that learning will occur.

Accountability for improvements in student learning should be long term and should reflect the principle of collective accountability rather than individual responsibility. More specifically, individual teachers can and should be held accountable for ensuring that what is taught is aligned with what it is intended the students learn. Individual teachers also should be accountable for ensuring that the work they provide students improves continuously in terms of producing measurable student engagement, persistence, and satisfaction. Finally, school faculty as a group should be held accountable for the performance of students who have been in a school a sufficient amount of time for differences between that school and other schools to make a difference.

CONCLUSION

When schools align curriculum with what it is intended that they teach and when they produce the student engagement, persistence, and satisfaction that lead to learning they are engaging in their true job. These activities are measurable and schools can be held accountable for them. One way to gain a deeper understanding of these and other issues is to consider educational practices in the light of business practices. That is the focus of the next chapter.

CHAPTER FOUR

Getting Down to Business

Differences in the intellectual ability of individual students and in students' family backgrounds are frequently used by educators to explain why some schools are better than others. However, those persons who take seriously the idea that all students can learn difficult content at relatively high levels find such explanations denied to them. Indeed, these differences are no longer explanations; they are empirical descriptions of conditions to which the schools must respond and respond appropriately. Furthermore, it is assumed that there is an appropriate way to respond, a way that will produce the level and type of learning desired.

When the right to explain away variance in student performance on the basis of personal attributes or background is denied, some other explanation must be sought. The next logical explanation, of course, is input variables like class size, teacher preparation, and the number of computers in the classroom. Though I believe that such variables do make some difference in student learning, the evidence for this difference is not at all clear. What is more important is that most of these differences, like differences in measured ability and family background, are beyond the direct control of teachers, principals, superintendents, and school board members. Without the possibility of control, accountability cannot be assigned and improvement cannot be expected.

What then do educators control that might explain some—perhaps most—of the variance in school outputs? For what might teachers be held accountable? They control qualities and characteristics of the tasks that they provide to students and that they encourage students to undertake. They control the processes involved in the design and delivery of these tasks. They control the processes and means by which they endeavor to get students to do the tasks they want them to do and to do these tasks with commitment and enthusiasm.

Such processes are not *mere* processes. Rather they are *the* processes through which schools and teachers can make a difference. Indeed, differences in these processes are the only differences over which teachers and other educational leaders have some prospect of exercising control.

DIFFERENCES THAT MAKE A DIFFERENCE

It is not necessary to accept the innate ability argument (whether applied to individuals or to groups and categories) to accept that different people respond to the same processes differently and that part of the way they respond is shaped by the cultures of which they are a part and the experiences they have had. As James Coleman pointed out forty years ago, schools where the adolescent subculture places high value on academic achievement have more high-performing students (regardless of students' measured ability) than do schools in which the subculture values athletics or social life most highly.[1] The question for educational leaders is, How can a supportive student culture be created, especially among students who come predominantly from homes where academic values are not embraced or where there is outright anti-intellectualism? This is a process question.

Rather than simply asking for more money or smaller class size, educators need to acknowledge that money and resources alone will not improve student performance. When more money is provided but the system continues to employ the same processes as before, one should not expect improvement. However, if schools are to employ new processes, those who teach the more disadvantaged will probably need more money to put those processes into practice. First, however, educators will need to learn to use the money they now have differently. These are questions of process.

RELATIONSHIPS AMONG MEASUREMENT, CONTROL, AND QUALITY

Systematic improvement in the quality of any outcome is dependent on the ability to control those processes that affect that quality. To control in this context means to act on a process in ways that produce predicable results, or outcomes. One cannot know that a process is under control until one is in a position to measure the process. It is only through measurement that variance in processes can be detected. And it is variance in processes that results in variance in outcomes.[2] When processes are out of control, sometimes the desired results are produced and sometimes they are not, and no one will know what makes the difference. To measure a process, one must first understand it. The process must be broken down into its component parts so that each part can be analyzed to determine the extent to which it is contributing to the variance in outcomes.

Much of our current understanding of measurement, control, and quality and also of processes comes from management theorists. Business offers some other concepts that can help us understand improvement in education.

SOME LESSONS FROM BUSINESSES

Business leaders who are wise understand that to stay in business they must produce products and services that customers will buy at a price that results in a profit and that customers will be satisfied with. Wise business leaders also understand that to get and keep customers it is essential to understand those customers and their needs and values and to make those needs and values the business's central concern.

Teachers who are wise understand that if students are to learn what it is intended they learn, the work students are assigned or encouraged to undertake must be engaging, it must be sufficiently compelling that students persist when they experience difficulties, and when they complete the work, students must experience a sense of satisfaction and significant accomplishment. Furthermore, students must be willing to pay enough for the experience, in the form of time and energy invested, to ensure that the desired learning occurs.

Business leaders know they have done their job when the products and services the business offers get customers, keep customers, and satisfy customers, and make a decent return on stakeholders' investment. Teachers and other educators know, or should know, they have done their job when

- Students are engaged; they do the work assigned with a high degree of diligence and enthusiasm.
- Students persist with the tasks assigned, even when they experience difficulties and when they find the work tedious and demanding.
- Students take satisfaction in the results of their work and experience a sense of accomplishment and pride.
- Students learn what it is intended that they learn.

Of course it is possible to have students highly engaged and sufficiently committed to persist with the work and even have them take pride in their work without their learning what needs to be learned. When this happens, it is likely that students have been given the wrong work to do. Teachers sometimes conclude that such failure to learn means that students lack the ability or will to do the work assigned. Most often, I suspect, students have the ability to do the work assigned; they just do not see any good reason to expend significant effort to do that work. The fact is that schoolwork is not always designed to provide reasons for doing the work in terms that students find understandable and convincing. *Great teachers understand this, and they constantly work to ensure that the work they assign to students has those qualities that students find engaging.* Teachers who are less attentive to the qualities of the work they assign quite often find themselves "working" on the students.

As I have been describing, properly conceived, the work of teachers is to be found in inventing work—specifically knowledge work—that has attributes that appeal to the motives of students. Great teachers do not seek to motivate students. Rather great teachers understand that students are motivated, and they design schoolwork in a way that appeals to those motives.

Teachers do not cause learning; they do not make learning happen. Rather, they design activities for students that they believe students will find engaging and from which students will learn. When teachers design the work right and when they provide the right work (work that contains the right content), students do learn. The primary source of variance in student learning is the quality of the work the teachers and the schools provide to students.

The Need for Multiple Measures

Educators have developed many measures of learning. Teachers are delighted when test scores go up and are concerned when they go down. Unfortunately, when test scores and other evidences of student learning do not move in the direction intended, present thinking in education does little to help teachers gain control of the processes they must control or even help teachers estimate which processes are out of control. The plethora of strategies and tools available for measuring student learning is matched only by the paucity of measures in most other areas important to understanding the processes associated with improving the performance of students. This encourages many teachers to feel out of control and, as I described earlier, to attribute lack of improvement in student performance to forces and sources beyond the control of teachers and other school leaders. When failure to learn is framed this way, there is little chance that educators will believe there is much they can do to dramatically and continuously improve the level of learning in the schools in which they teach.

For example, many teachers believe that the fundamental problem confronting the schools is that parents are not doing their job, and because they are not, their children misbehave in school. Some parent training might improve the performance of some parents. Clearer and consistently enforced behavioral rules in schools might reduce some of the discipline problems. The exclusion of those students who persistently misbehave might reduce these problems even more. But the impact of such measures on the overall performance of students is not likely to approach a magnitude that will satisfy critics and convince the public that the schools are doing their job. As I pointed out in Chapter One, long before the creation of the special education enterprise, long before grade inflation, and in a time when corporal punishment for bad behavior was the rule and expulsion from school for repeated infractions was often swift and certain, it was still the case that only a relatively few students attained high levels of academic performance. What is needed today are schools that do for the first time what America's schools have never done: provide a high-quality academic education for nearly every child.

Those who see the solution to this problem as finding ways to get more resources for the schools are, I believe, engaging in wishful thinking or excuse making. It is doubtful that schools will be provided much more money than they now receive, other than adjustments for inflation. First, the increasing criticisms of America's schools, though often unjustified and based on erroneous data and unsupportable assertions, are eroding public confidence in and support for public education. Second, and perhaps more important, the taxpayers of America are increasingly people who have no children in school and who perceive themselves as having little direct interest in schools. Furthermore, the senior citizens among these taxpayers have needs such as medical services that are in direct competition for the same dollars that support schools.

If there is no new money, which seems likely to be the case, then schools will not be in a position to do new things of any sort unless their leaders are prepared to abandon old ways of doing things and are willing as well to invent new ways of doing what they elect to continue to do. This presents an opportunity for dramatic change, but it is a dangerous opportunity, as a look at business again illustrates.

Dangerous Business

My thinking on educational matters has obviously been heavily influenced by ideas promulgated by authors concerned primarily with corporate America rather than life in schools. Educators sometimes find such influence distracting and off-putting. Some fear that viewing students as customers will dehumanize students and make education nothing more than a crass commercial concern. Many fear that to think of schools within frameworks with which business leaders are comfortable is to think of schools as factories, children as products, and the curriculum as an assembly line.

This is not so.[3] What is most important to understand in this regard is that business thinking is not factory thinking. For the most part, even business leaders have rejected the factory as the best model for work in the modern world. Moreover, as businesses are becoming less involved with the world of manual work and more involved with the world of knowledge work, the problems that confront business are becoming similar to the problems that confront schools. For example, Peter Senge and numerous other business authors have written about the *learning organization*.[4] Senge is not writing about schools in this instance, though he does that as well elsewhere: he is writing about life in healthy corporations in which the work is primarily knowledge work. Given the school-like properties of some corporations, it is not unreasonable to assume that educators might learn a good deal from studying the ways corporations have solved and also failed to solve their school-like problems.

Learning from business does not necessarily mean learning how business leaders do things and then copying what they do. Business leaders have done some very dumb things, and the consequences have sometimes been disasters. David Halberstam, for example, presents a detailed account of how American automobile industries failed to properly address the issues of quality and customer service and how this failure almost led to the collapse of some of these industrial giants.[5] There are clearly some lessons here if educators would attend to them. Eastern Airlines is also a source of valuable lessons, as are the U.S. Postal Service and AT&T.

As an example of learning through negative illustrations from business, consider the tendency of teachers to locate their problems in sources beyond the control of the schools. This thinking is reminiscent of the thinking of leaders in the American automobile business during the 1960s and 1970s. When the automobile business began to lose market share to foreign competition, business leaders looked first for explanations beyond their control. It was professors and hippies who bought all those Volkswagens, they said. The American automobile business made American cars for "real Americans." When it eventually became clear that American automakers' declining market share was at least in part due to quality problems, the reasons for the quality problems were externalized as well. Some automobile industry leaders resorted to union bashing, others to lamenting the fact that Germany and Japan, their chief competitors, were operating modern plants built since World War II, whereas many of America's plants and much of its machinery predated that war. Yet another explanation was that the Japanese culture was more unified and the workers less individualistic. *Indeed, the school reform efforts that started in the early 1980s came about in part because business leaders in a number of industries were seeking a scapegoat to blame for their own failures.*

By the early 1980s, however, it was also becoming clear to some leaders in business that they could not wait for the world to return to "normal" or for the American customer to regain his or her good senses and once again buy good American products. Too many good Americans were willing to buy products no matter where they were produced—so long as these products responded to their needs and addressed values they held. As a result, business leaders began to discover ideas that management gurus like W. Edwards Deming, Peter Drucker, and Philip Crosby had been promulgating for a long time. By the mid-1980s, these basic ideas were being popularized by a variety of consulting firms and authors.[6] This was the beginning of the quality movement in business.

The quality movement, like all movements, has had its fads and foibles, successes and failures. Sometimes it has been more rhetoric than substance, but it is clear that many in America's business community have learned (or relearned) some very important lessons, including these:

- Quality is defined by the customer (Alpo is not good if the dogs won't eat it).

- It is therefore important to know the customer well and to understand the needs of the customer even better than the customer understands those needs.

- If businesses are to survive, they must be customer focused. This does not mean that all business leaders need to do is discover what customers want and give it to them. Rather, the creative business anticipates wants by discovering needs. Through market development based on these discoveries, business leaders help customers recognize how new products are linked to customer needs, thus transforming needs into desires and wants.

- Quality control is essential to business success, but quality control cannot be achieved until process control is achieved. The quality of a product or service is directly linked to the processes employed in creating and delivering that product or service.

- Profit is the result of doing one's business well and being in the right business. Profit happens because of the way one does one's business.

- The three most important questions business leaders need to ask are: What is our business? Who are our customers? and, What is our product?

SUMMARIZING THE LESSONS

Learning is to schools as profit is to business. Businesses cannot survive unless profits are made; schools should not survive if students fail to learn.

The centrality of profit in business and learning in schools often conceals the fact that there is little that can be done to affect directly either profit or learning. Sometimes businesses become highly profitable in the short run simply because they are located in the right place or are created at the right time. Some Texas ranchers who drilled oil wells on their land during the 1920s turned unprofitable businesses into profitable ones. Similarly, sometimes schools produce large numbers of students who meet or exceed standards for no other reason than that the students and their parents bring special social and cultural resources to the enterprise. It is not surprising that children who attend suburban schools usually do better than children who attend inner-city schools. What is surprising is the assumption that the schools these high-performing youngsters attend must be high-performing schools. They may be, or they may be schools that have the good fortune of being located in the right place (something like the farmer who got smart by discovering oil on his farm).

If one assumes that the primary source of variance in school performance is to be found in the nature of the child, then it is clear that the nature of middle-class and upper-middle-class children is more congruent with the current work expectations of schools than is the nature of the children of the poor. Parents who teach their children to read save a school a lot of trouble. When parents do not teach their children to read, the student is often viewed as "the trouble." Such a view, though perhaps comforting to those who teach in low-performing schools, condemns half or more of America's children to an inferior academic education.

In the long run, effective businesses and effective schools are those that can produce products that have known and predictable qualities that meet the needs of customers. This means that to be effective those who work in a business or a school

- Must know their products well.
- Must understand how variance in the quality of the product can be produced.
- Must be able to measure variance in the processes that result in variance in the product and thus be in a position to control and improve the product provided.
- Must have a clear understanding of who their customers are and know those customers well.

STUDENTS AS PRODUCTS
AND AS CUSTOMERS

Nowadays it is commonplace to hear students referred to as the product of the schools. More than one business leader has been heard to say that the schools are producing too many "unsatisfactory products." More than one proud superintendent has been heard to brag about a national merit scholar as "a product of our school."

From the perspective of those outside the schools, at least, viewing the student as a product of the school makes some sense. Students are products businesses need to continue staffing their work processes, and businesses would like them to meet certain requirements, just like other products necessary to a business's work. Increasingly, an individual's demonstrated ability to work with knowledge and knowledge-related products is critical to his or her success in adult life. Students who cannot do such work "up to standard" are by definition "below standard." The primary complaint of many businesses is that the schools are not producing enough students who meet the standards that must be met to do the work employees are expected to do.

However, viewing students only as products can have some unfortunate consequences, for both the students and the cause of school improvement. For example, when students are viewed as products, educators, policymakers, and the public are likely to fasten their attention on student characteristics as sources of explanation for performance. If the student is the product, then the raw material must surely be the "stuff" that makes up the student—such stuff as innate ability and parents' socioeconomic status. Therefore whatever variability there is in student performance is to be explained primarily by variability in the raw material—or so the argument goes. When students are viewed as products, compliance and control, rather than direction and motivation, too often become dominant concerns. Viewing students as products encourages teachers to view their task as shaping and molding students to meet predetermined standards, as controlling student behavior so that these standards are met, and as encouraging compliance, even if that compliance results from ritualism rather than authentic engagement.

From the perspective of those working inside the school or setting policy for schools, then, it is better to view the students as customers[7] and the experiences provided to the students as products. Schools produce experiences (intellectual work) from which students learn what they need to learn to be considered well educated. Students are customers for schoolwork, and schoolwork is the primary product of the schools.

Once educators view students as customers, they address many of the problems associated with viewing students as products. The word product reeks of depersonalization and alienation. Students as products are things rather than people. They are things to be molded and controlled. In contrast, once they view students as customers, rather than seeking control teachers seek to provide direction for student action and to transform student needs into wants and desires. Rather than seeking compliance, they seek to link what it is expected that students will learn to activities that will result in commitment. And rather than seeking to explain student failure in terms of student characteristics, they seek to improve the experiences the school provides to students.

Ensuring that students learn what it is intended that they learn and ensuring that what students learn is seen by parents, the community, and the society at large as desirable and of significant value is the business of schools. It is essential to keep in mind, however, that what students learn has much to do with what they do in school, and what students do has much to do with the qualities and attributes of the tasks they are assigned. If students find the tasks responsive to their needs, they are more likely to complete them with the commitment and enthusiasm that excellence requires.

QUALITY WORK AND IMPROVED PERFORMANCE

Beating a dead horse does not make the horse run. Insisting that schools with low test scores get test scores up does not help much either. To be sure, to the extent that low test scores are attributable to laxity and lack of focus, some rather dramatic improvements can be brought about simply by insisting that students meet and be expected to meet relatively high standards. This is certainly the mantra of those who advocate *high-stakes testing*. When high expectations are accompanied by curriculum alignment to ensure that what is being taught is also what is being tested, the results can be even more dramatic. Some principals have produced remarkable results, for example, by transforming the school they lead from an organization prone to accepting and perhaps expecting low performance from students to an organization where high performance is expected of everyone.[8] Unfortunately, these remarkable results seem seldom replicable, even in the same school district. Furthermore, when the initiators of the improvements leave, many of these turned-around schools revert to their prior performance levels.

To advance the cause of school reform it is first necessary to acknowledge that for the reasons I discussed in Chapter Three, teachers are basically right when they assert that teachers as individuals should not be held accountable for test scores. Teachers resent, and rightly so, the assumption that they are providing students with an inadequate education on purpose or because they are slothful. Teachers resist merit pay at least in part because they assume that all teachers should be meritorious, just as all doctors and all lawyers should be meritorious. (I fly a great deal, but I would be hesitant to fly with a pilot who needs merit pay to make him or her fly the plane as best as he or she knows how to fly.)

Fear and defensiveness in the face of calls for higher achievement result primarily from the fact that many educators do not know what more they can do or how they might do what they do in dramatically different ways. At present too few teachers view themselves as inventors of work for children, and too many see themselves as implementers of programs. Too many administrators manage by programs and too few understand how to focus on results, and those who are results-focused often focus on the wrong results. The understanding that is needed is that in the end it is not what the teacher does that counts. What matters is what the teacher is able to get the students to do with enthusiasm, commitment, and persistence.

CONCLUSION

Looking at businesses can help us to an understanding that what educators have the potential to control are variances in the processes that result in student learning. Once the idea that the work that is offered to students is the product of schools and students are the customers of schools is embedded in the school systems, schools have a foundation on which they can become change adept and begin the process of continuous improvement. We can acquire a further understanding of producing quality work for students by examining the practices of schools' new competitors.

CHAPTER FIVE

Learning from Competitors

Explaining variance in student learning by referring to the qualities and characteristics of the students or the students' parents is akin to a business's blaming the lack of profit on the customers. When teachers explain poor student performance by saying that television and electronic games have shortened children's attention spans, they are engaging in the same behavior that the business leader is engaging in when he or she explains a decline in profits or lack of growth by saying that customers as less loyal than they once were.

It may be true that consumers are less loyal to businesses than they once were, and it may be equally true that television and electronic games have conditioned students to expect immediate gratification and short bursts of activity rather than long-term consequences and sustained effort. But consumers' lack of loyalty and students' short-term view do not explain why a corporation does not make a profit and a school has low test scores. Changes in the competitive environment have something to do with the matter as well.

Instead of asking questions like, How can we force Americans to buy our products? or, How can we get Congress to impose a tariff to protect our goods from unfair competition? business leaders should ask, What is the competition providing our customers that we are not and how might we build these qualities and attributes into our product? In a similar fashion, when educators are faced with unsatisfactory student performance on measures of academic learning, they should ask questions like, Who are our competitors for the time and attention of our students? What do they provide our students that we are not providing? How might we provide these things, and are we willing to do so? If we are not able or willing to provide these things, can we provide alternatives that are equally attractive?

THE NEW COMPETITORS

Next to their concerns about lack of parental support, school violence, discipline problems, and large class size, teachers seem to worry most about the fact that students appear to watch a great deal of television, play a great many video games, and generally spend a lot of time in frivolous pursuits when they could be more profitably employed doing the work that teachers would have them do. Furthermore, when confronted with the awesome prospect that to succeed with students they must learn to compete with these new electronic devices, many teachers become agitated and defensive. They do not believe they can compete or that they should be expected to compete. They say things like: "We are not in the entertainment business." "Education requires hard work." "Everything students do cannot be exciting and entertaining." "That is the problem we have nowadays; the attention span of students is being conditioned by sound bites, and those sound bites had better be entertaining." "Teachers cannot compete with television and computer games." "What we need are parents who know how to turn the television off and tell their children to do their homework."

There is no doubt that the introduction of the radio, television, computer, and other electronically based means for storing, retrieving, transmitting, and processing information has transformed and is transforming our social and cultural landscape. It is also the case that schools and teachers are at a disadvantage when they are expected to compete unassisted with such giants in the "edutainment" industry as Disney and Dreamworks, to say nothing of Nintendo and MTV. It is equally true that high-level academic attainment is hard work, not always entertaining, often calls for sustained effort rather than short bursts of activity, and is sometimes unavoidably tedious and repetitious.

In spite of these facts, educators can learn many lessons from studying how their competitors go about their business. This chapter illustrates some of these lessons.[1]

VISITING AN ALLENTOWN BAR

In January 1994, a colleague and I visited a hotel bar in Allentown, Pennsylvania. Television monitors were everywhere, and the bar patrons were gazing at them intently. "What," I wondered, "could be the attraction?" There was no sports action on the screens. All I saw there were multiple-choice questions, such as, "Which President was given the nickname 'Old Hickory?'" Many of the patrons had a keyboard through which they communicated with an electronic device that recorded answers to the questions. Some participants were single persons sitting alone; some were members of teams sitting together at a table. Some were obviously chemically impaired. The teams usually designated one member of their group to staff the keyboard (the designated "scorer"). All team members contributed answers—or tried to.

I also observed that consistent with the views advanced by cooperative learning advocates, such teams had become quite proficient at arriving at a consensus about the answer team members thought was right and that participants understood that some members of the group were strong in one area (such as history) and others in other areas (such as science, geography, popular culture, or music). Furthermore, in the barroom as in the classroom, when there was uncertainty, it appeared that those who were perceived as expert in an area were looked to for leadership and direction.

REFLECTING ON WHAT I SAW

Given what I saw in that Allentown bar, there are at least two sets of conclusions one could draw about engaging people in an activity. One could conclude that eliciting and conveying information in a trivialized, disjointed, and irrelevant way is the key to holding people's attention and that therefore this approach should be enshrined in the school curriculum. I did not reach this conclusion, although I did see that electronic technology would allow educators to trivialize the curriculum further than it is already and to do so without risking boring students to the point of rebellion. I fear, indeed, that some large companies that are marketing software to schools are even now exploiting this potential.

The alternate set of conclusions arises from asking this question: *How is it that chemically impaired people of probably at best average education and academic motivation can become actively engaged in the pursuit of fragmented, trivialized knowledge and isolated facts when they are in a barroom, but teachers cannot get the same engagement from students in a history class, science class, or English/language arts class?*

Here are the observations and conclusions that are the results of my reflections on this question. I am continuing to do "research" on the matter.

Observation. The barroom game was organized around trivialized content. Furthermore, much of the trivia was related to academic subjects (history, literature, science, and so forth), which many students seem to find uninteresting. Yet the participants, few if any of whom were likely to have been professional academics, were intensely engaged in the activity, so intensely engaged that many study relevant facts during the week so that they can better support their team on Friday night. This game is played in many other bars, and there are in fact now national competitions, with prizes for the winners including trips to exotic places. National Merit Scholarships are not on the line, but there are consequences of significance to those participants who compete for prizes, although one need not enter the competition to play the game.

Conclusion. The relevance of content and the organization of content are less important than are the organization of the task and the nature of the work students must do to learn the content and master the related skills. One of the reasons so many students fail to learn difficult content is that they find the activity associated with this learning lacks those qualities that encourage them to become engaged. And one of the reasons so many students fail to become engaged, give up when they experience difficulty, and find little satisfaction in the academic aspects of their school experience is that the work they are given to do is not focused on products, exhibitions, and performances on which they place value.

Observation. The barroom game involves a public performance (what Theodore Sizer refers to as an exhibition[2]) that has meaning and significance to the participants.

Conclusion. Teachers who organize the work they assign students so that the students see some linkage between what they are asked to do (and to learn) and some product, performance, or outcome they care about are more likely to engage students than are teachers who fail to make this link.

Observation. The barroom game communicates clear performance standards that are understandable to the participants. Furthermore, the participants perceive these standards to be fair, reasonable, and significant (that is, meeting these standards is perceived to be important). In the case of the barroom game, the standards have to do with speed and accuracy. Getting the right answer fast is the desired goal, but accuracy is more important than speed. Players who get the wrong answer are penalized in the scoring process.

Conclusion. Teachers who attend to communicating clear standards for student work and ensuring that students view these standards as fair, reasonable, and significant are more likely to gain commitment than are teachers who are less careful about such matters.

Observation. In the barroom game, participants are given honest, accurate, and useful information about the quality of their performance in relation both to the standards of the game and to the performance of others engaged in the same activity. By virtue of satellite uplinks, even international comparisons are possible. The winner in a bar in Winnipeg can be compared to the winner in Allentown (I was in Winnipeg when I saw this happen). Even the losers in the local bar seemed to take pride in the performance of the local winner when winning performances were compared among sites. He or she suddenly became "we."

Conclusion. Properly presented, honest feedback to students regarding how close they have come to meeting the intended standards and how their performance stacks up compared to the performance of others can be a source of inspiration to try harder rather than a devastating blow to low performers' self-concepts. The key seems to be to ensure that students find the standards worth pursuing and see a reasonable prospect that they can make a successful effort to meet these standards.

Observation. In the barroom game, participants have considerable control over the degree to which they will risk adverse consequences for failure to meet standards or to perform to expectations. Put differently, in the barroom game, although participants are given very clear feedback about how well they are doing compared to the standards and compared to others playing the game, failure to stack up well against the standards or against others has only minimal negative consequences—unless the participant chooses to put himself or herself at risk in order to gain higher rewards. For example, players may, if they choose, remain anonymous throughout the game. They may sit alone at a table or in a booth. Though their score on each item will be displayed for all to see, they may have that score recorded under any name they choose. Thus a solo player using an alias is able to judge the quality of his or her performance quite accurately without the threat of public humiliation.

Other ways of safeguarding participants from adverse consequences for failures are present as well. For example, when participating in a group, persons who are uninformed on a particular subject are not compelled to reveal their ignorance. All they need do is keep their mouths shut. The only time these silent partners will be asked a question is when other members of the team are equally uncertain of the answer—in which case one guess is nearly as good as another. There is little threat of loss of status or regard under such circumstances.

In addition, though the standards are absolute (one either knows the answer or one does not; one can recall the answer quickly or one cannot), there is some flexibility and some possibility of limited success even for the least informed. Indeed, as time passes, access to some measure of success is more dependent on one's ability to read and to reason than on the recall of specific information. The designers of this game provide clues that permit one to rule out wrong answers systematically, so that in the end only the literally illiterate and those with absolutely no power of reasoning (or the stupefied drunk) will fail to get a few points from each question.

Conclusion. Teachers who provide students with some protection from adverse consequences for failure to meet standards on initial tries and some opportunity to test their knowledge and skill without facing humiliation if they fall short are more likely to get students to pursue and achieve high standards than are teachers who fail to provide such protection.

Observation. Barrooms encourage conviviality. Usually those who come to bars are with companions or seeking companionship. In fact it was clear that the only reason some participants were engaged in the activity was that they wanted to be with their friends, doing what their friends were doing.

Conclusion. Teachers who design their activities in ways that encourage and permit students to affiliate with each other are likely to engage more students than are teachers who are less attentive to group activity as a source of positive motivation.

Observation. The barroom game is designed so that participants have some choice in the way they go about their work. For example, teams can be formed—and they often are—but an individual can also choose to play the game alone and remain anonymous if anonymity meets a need. Cooperative learning is valued, provided for, and even encouraged, but those whose learning and performing styles are more solitary can be accommodated as well. Similarly, as described earlier, participants can choose the level at which they want to compete. Those who are timid, uncertain, or just exploring can maintain anonymity. Those who find competition stimulating have the opportunity to compete to their heart's content. Whooping and hollering are permitted.

Conclusion. Teachers who provide students some choice and some sense of personal control over how they will conduct their work and when they will work with others are likely to engage more students in assigned tasks than are those teachers who are less flexible about working arrangements. Affiliation is a powerful source of motivation, but there are times one just wants to be left alone to cry in one's beer and to sort out one's confusions.

Observation. In the barroom game the content is organized in such a way that there is a wide range of opportunities for success. Participants have many opportunities to contribute to the group. Even individuals who are well along the way to being drunk sometimes suddenly come to life on a question that has to do with baseball trivia or popular culture.

Conclusion. Teachers who design tasks in such a way that all—or nearly all—students are held to common standards yet all will also experience some level of recognizable success are more likely to increase engagement than are teachers who are less attentive to students' needs for achievement.

THE BIG LESSON

Each of the little lessons I learned from my research in barrooms can be summarized into this one big lesson: With care and planning, schoolwork can be designed so that all students are engaged in precisely the same activity at the same time, yet the activity is customized to the point that each student has some degree of control over how he or she will approach the task. It is also clearly possible to design each piece of schoolwork so it appeals to a wide range of motives: for example, some students may do the work to demonstrate mastery, others to learn new material, others to experience the conviviality of a group, and still others for the intrinsic joy of learning.

AFTERTHOUGHTS

I have also had some more general ideas as a result of pondering the significance of different levels of engagement in different contexts. These ideas present further challenges for schools in this new era of competition for students' attention.

Learning from Game Design

For some time now I have been intrigued by the fact that many students neglect their schoolwork because they find electronic games more engaging. The easy explanation for this is that the games are entertaining, as they are intended to be, whereas schoolwork requires disciplined effort and from time to time tolerance of a degree of boredom. Phrases like "short attention spans," "the need for immediate gratification," and "lack of discipline and self-control" frequently come up when teachers are discussing why students find computer games more engaging than schoolwork.

The light, sometimes frivolous, action-oriented approach taken by many computer games and mass media presentations (MTV, for instance) does indeed give some advantages to the edutainment industry. There is no question that playing an electronic game is often less demanding and more entertaining than is even the most exciting academic exercise. There is, however, more here.

First, those consumer and media businesses that are trying to engage the minds and hearts of the young understand some things that too many educators overlook, look past, deny, or find repugnant. Chief among the things these competitors to the schools understand is that students are *volunteers*. They understand that they must *earn* youngsters' attention and commitment. More than that, they understand that students are more likely to engage in an activity, to pay attention and act with commitment, when it is somehow related to a product, performance, exhibition, or result about which they care and that is responsive to needs they have. Certainly, entertainment meets needs, but students want and need substantial activity as well. When substantial activity that meets needs is lacking, students become bored. Entertainment at least temporarily alleviates that boredom.

The schools' new competitors also seem to understand better than do many educators that students do not mind failure; what they dislike is the implicit punishment that so often accompanies failure in schools. On the one hand, protecting students from failure does no one any good, and it encourages poor student performance. On the other hand, punishing students for pursuing high standards and failing to meet them encourages students to pursue lower standards or to disengage entirely.

Educators tend to punish failure, or just as bad, they try to prevent failure by lowering standards. When one watches students play computer games and sees them fail to achieve the desired result yet come back for more, it becomes clear that there are ways to design activities that require students to meet high standards but that do not, implicitly or explicitly, rely on punishment and extrinsic rewards.

There are many other things educators could learn from the design of electronic games that would help in the design of engaging schoolwork. Furthermore, they need not go to bars to learn these things, but what they must do is accept the proposition that students are volunteers and that the work schools provide to students, rather than the students themselves, is the real product of the schools.

Teaching as a Social Transaction

In the field of sociology the concepts of *social exchange theory* proceed from the assumption that it is useful to study the social values that are satisfied by any human interaction. For example, youngsters who join a gang might be seen by a social exchange theorist as exchanging their support of the gang's activity for status, affiliation, and security. Like all social theories, this one has seen a great deal of debate regarding its validity. Rather than enter that debate here, I prefer to downgrade this theory to a category I am more comfortable with using—the metaphor.

I suggest, then, that our understanding of teaching and learning would be greatly enhanced if educators allowed themselves to play out in full the implications of a transactional metaphor that assumed that what is going on in classrooms is a series of social exchanges wherein the teacher is trying to get from students something the teacher must have to do his or her job (the students' attention and commitment) and the students are willing to provide what the teacher wants to the extent that the work and tasks the teacher offers appeal to their needs and values.

In this social transaction, the ideas of the student as the customer and of work as the product are pivotal. Furthermore, the quality of the work provided to students is at least as important as the quality of the work the students do. Rather than improving students, the business of the school becomes improving the educational experiences provided to students. The assumption is that it is only by improving these experiences that students will become more engaged. And it further assumes that students who are authentically engaged in schoolwork will learn more than will those whose level of engagement is lower. They will certainly learn more than the retreatists and the rebels, who are not engaged at all.

Overcoming the Illusion of Monopoly

Critics of schools often fasten on schools' monopoly status as an explanation for lack of enduring school change. Like all monopolies, the schools have no motive to change, they say. The way to encourage change is to introduce competition through vouchers, charter schools, and privatization—or so it is sometimes argued.

If one assumes that all that educators want and need from students is attendance and compliance, then the public schools do enjoy relative monopoly status. Adopting the transactional metaphor for teaching, however, gives us a different view of the matter. From the transactional viewpoint, what is going on in school is an exchange between students (as customers) and teachers (as inventors and providers of work for students). This transaction is a social and moral one. What teachers want from students is their attention and their commitment. What teachers too often get is attendance and compliance.

What students want from schools and from their teachers are not new gizmos and widgets, but activities that respond to their needs and satisfy their motives and values. What students too often get are tasks and assignments to which they attach little significance and meaning and toward which they feel little compulsion to act other than in the most ritualistic fashion.

What the new competitors of schools are showing is that when student are provided with activities that respond to their needs, students do become engaged, they do persist when things are difficult, and they do experience a sense of accomplishment and satisfaction. Students who are engaged and who persist will learn. Whether what students learn will be of value depends upon the ability of teachers and schools to create work that is engaging and that at the same time brings students into significant and profound interactions with the content they need to know and the skills they need to master to deserve to be called well educated in the context of modern society.

Given this transactional framework, it seems that even though schools—both public and private—*often behave as though they are monopolies, they are not.* Yet because they persist in the illusion of monopoly, they allow many of their potential customers and most of their real market go unserved or underserved. They often offer their customers that which they can conveniently produce and leave it up to the customer to buy or to refuse to buy.

The primary product of the schools today is academic work that if properly pursued results in academic learning. Those who find academic work attractive or at least tolerable are likely to find schoolwork engaging, whereas those whose values and needs cannot be satisfied by academic work will be less engaged. Indeed, one of the laments of public school educators is that private schools do not have to enroll everybody, and they can get rid of students who do not buy what the school has to sell. This is probably true enough. It is also generally true that students who are willing to do academic work in private schools also do well in suburban public schools that offer strong academic programs and emphasize academic work.

The problem is that some students in suburban schools, some in private schools, and many in urban schools and rural schools find little meaning in academic work as that work is done by academics. The consequence is that academically speaking these students learn too little. Furthermore, in the effort to accommodate (as opposed to serve or respond to) students who are not academically oriented, schools often resort to strategies that reduce the quality of the academic program as well. This is one of the reasons that families who place a high value on academic work opt for private schools, where students who do not value working in the manner that academics work are sometimes excluded.

The result is that public school educators have often settled for a few students who become authentically engaged in work that produces high levels of academic learning. For the rest it has been sufficient that they are in attendance and are compliant. But this no longer matches Americans' expectation that schools will ensure that all students are academically well prepared. It is no longer enough to provide only an opportunity.

To deal effectively with this new expectation, educators must come to understand and believe the fact that learning is the result of educators' doing their business and that the business of schools is to produce intellectually demanding tasks and rigorous and disciplined experiences that engage students, inspire students to persist when they have difficulties, and produce in students a sense of satisfaction and accomplishment. Measuring learning results in schools is important, just as measuring profit in business is important. But educators, like successful business leaders, must understand that to produce their desired results, they must get customers, keep customers, and satisfy customers. Their focus therefore must be on the customer (the student) and on the products (the work) that will meet the needs of the customer.

CONCLUSION

It has always been the case that many youngsters resisted learning what their elders felt they needed to learn, but the coercive power of traditional adult authority was sufficient to keep this resistance in bounds. The acceptance of an adolescent subculture, the wide availability of all kinds of information and entertainment, and the erosion of adult authority now threatens those boundaries.

To me, the exciting part of the lesson I learned in the Allentown bar is that when activities are properly designed, students will do many things they might not otherwise do and as a result will learn many things they might not otherwise care to learn. As one who believes that part of the function of education is to ensure that the accumulated wisdom of past generations is effectively transmitted to future generations, I find this encouraging.

If educators are to reestablish the boundaries needed to ensure that schools can teach what they must teach for our society to survive and thrive, teachers must replace the traditional authority they have assumed with the expert authority they need to design work that students will engage voluntarily and that will result in their learning what adults believe they need to know to carry on with the building of our democratic society. Understanding what the new school competitors are doing that schools are not doing should persuade us all that if teachers are to function successfully without the support of traditional authority, the only authority they have to rely on is that expert authority, which proceeds from a detailed understanding of students and what motivates them, along with a profound understanding of the nature of the engaging work that must be created for students. The next chapter offers a framework to assist teachers in this endeavor.

CHAPTER SIX

Assessing the Quality of Schoolwork

*Q*uality is best defined as "conformance with customer requirements."[1] Customer needs and values determine requirements. For operational purposes, these requirements are translated into standards. Standards specify how much of which qualities must be present to meet the requirements of the customer. It is critical therefore to know who the customers are and what needs and values they bring to the transaction.

Schools have many customers in addition to students. Parents are customers as are members of the business community, religious leaders, political leaders, and taxpayers in general. Each of these groups and constituencies has expectations of the schools; in other words, each has requirements that it wants to see met. Parents want their children to learn, and they also want them to be safe and happy. Conservative religious leaders want students to learn as well, but there are also things they would rather students did not learn. In addition, some of the things these religious leaders want students to learn cannot be taught without violating the Constitution of the United States as that document is interpreted by the Supreme Court. Business leaders want students to learn those things they need to know to become members of a world-class workforce. Politicians and taxpayers generally want to ensure that students are learning enough to justify the expense of educating them.

With the exception of parents, who are often as concerned with the safety and happiness of their children as they are with what their children learn in school, most of the schools' adult customers are primarily concerned with what is learned, how much is learned, and at what cost. It is for this reason that most of the debate over educational content and educational quality tends to focus on test scores, school finance, and the setting of achievement standards for students.

These matters are important and should be discussed and debated. However, the debate over standards for student performance and the impact of different levels and types of financing should not distract attention from the fact that on a day-to-day basis, the students are the primary customers of the school and of teachers. Schools do not produce test scores; students produce test scores. Once again, what schools are intended to produce is knowledge work that students find to be engaging and from which students learn those things that will satisfy the requirements of the adult community, as these requirements are expressed in test scores and other measures of quality, such as dropout rates and school safety, that the community takes into account.

It is through working on the tasks given to students and designing them in ways that increase the likelihood that students will become engaged in them that teachers have the possibility of improving student performance. It is only by attending to those qualities, or attributes, that make schoolwork so compelling to students that they will persist when they experience difficulty that teachers can hope to encourage students to invest the level of effort needed to learn at high levels. It is only by ensuring that the tasks are challenging and meaningful to students that teachers can help students to experience a sense of satisfaction and accomplishment upon completing the work and can realize the goal of transforming students into intentional, lifelong learners. It is only by creating schoolwork that has all of these qualities that teachers have any prospect of ensuring that students learn what it is intended that they learn. It is therefore by *Working on the Work* that teachers ensure that the tasks students carry out will produce the results that the adult customers of the schools must have for their needs and requirements to be met as well.

WORKING ON THE WORK

What then are the qualities, or attributes, that are likely to make schoolwork more engaging? The somewhat lighthearted discussion in the preceding chapter sketched the answer I give here with more precision. There are at least ten qualities on which teachers can work: qualities that can be made more or less present in the tasks students are assigned and encouraged to undertake. These ten qualities address

- Content and substance
- Organization of knowledge
- Product focus
- Clear and compelling product standards
- Protection from adverse consequences for initial failures
- Affirmation of the significance of performance
- Affiliation
- Novelty and variety
- Choice
- Authenticity

To create tasks, assignments, and activities that students find consistently and predictably engaging, teachers need to have a deep understanding of each of these qualities. They must consciously work to ensure that these qualities are present in the tasks and assignments they offer students, and they must understand their students well enough to know which of these qualities are likely to be important to students and under what conditions the importance an individual student attaches to one or more of these qualities is likely to change. This undertaking is what is meant by the term *Working on the Work* (WOW).

The WOW[2] framework is a mainstay of the Center for Leadership in School Reform (CLSR), a nonprofit organization of which I am the founder and CEO. This framework was designed as a tool that could be used to inform pedagogical decisions, support planning efforts, encourage disciplined dialogue among teachers, and serve as a means of assessing the "fit" of specific projects to the overall direction of the school. The WOW framework is not a lesson plan format, nor does it assume that all students respond to the same qualities in the same way. It does not assess the "goodness" of a lesson. It is intended to be used by teachers and school administrators when evaluating programs, classroom activities, and units of work intended to be assigned to students. It can also be useful in the design of schoolwork and in assessing schoolwork when many students fail to be engaged by the activities provided or when particular categories of students are disengaged.

The WOW framework is not a program. To view it as a program is to diminish its power as a tool for planning and analysis. It is better to think of it as analogous to the operating system in a computer.[3] A computer program must be designed to be consistent with the assumptions of the operating system on the computer on which the program is installed. The operating system enables the program to run. The operating system is, metaphorically speaking, the framework within which programs operate.

The Working on the Work framework functions in a similar fashion. Regardless of the program provided, the WOW framework causes educators to ask the question: "Is this program likely to enhance those qualities of schoolwork that students care about and that lead to increased engagement?" If the answer to this question is yes, then the program is compatible with the WOW framework. If the answer is no, then the operating system (the WOW framework) will not accept the program. Similar observations may be made to assess activities, assignments, and tasks created by teachers.

The WOW framework proceeds from the assumption that it is only by altering the quality of experiences students have in school that teachers can hope to improve the quality of student learning and student performance. To improve the quality of experiences that students have in school, it is essential that teachers work continuously to improve the quality of the work they assign to students and that they encourage students to undertake. It is also important that teachers learn to assess each of the ten qualities listed previously to determine whether the quality is at all present in the tasks they have designed and, if it is, the extent to which it is present. Chapter Seven discusses the uses of the WOW framework. The remainder of this chapter outlines the framework by translating each quality into a standard and then listing and discussing indicators of compliance with the standard, which in turn should assist teachers with the important undertaking of continuously improving the work given to students.

Process Standard 1: Content and Substance

Among themselves, teachers and administrators have a clear and consistent understanding of what students are expected to know and to be able to do, and there is community consensus regarding these matters.

INDICATORS OF HIGH COMPLIANCE WITH THE STANDARD

- Teachers and principals can articulate what students under their tutelage are expected to know and to be able to do.

- Parents and other relevant adult customers of the schools are aware of performance expectations and the standards by which performances will be assessed, and they agree that these standards are important.

- Students are provided regular opportunities to assess their own performance in terms of the standards established.

- The ideas, propositions, and facts that are presented or made available reflect the best understandings of experts in the field being studied and are consistent with the views and lines of argument presented by scholars in the relevant disciplines.

- Standardized tests (local or state sponsored or both) have been carefully reviewed to determine the content students are expected to master, and these expectations have been taken into account in the selection of content.[4]

- Curriculum materials are available that will support students' working on and with the content and skills it is agreed should be emphasized; that is, curriculum alignment is practiced.

- Teachers provide students with a wide range of activities that call on them to work with content and processes that have been identified as "worth knowing and worth mastering."

- Teachers know which students find the content uninteresting and attempt to compensate by building other qualities into the work associated with learning this content to make the work attractive to these students.

INDICATORS OF LOW COMPLIANCE WITH THE STANDARD

- Great uncertainty or confusion exists about the substantive intentions of instruction.

- Teachers are not clear about what they are expected to convey to students, or they resist the notion that anyone other than the individual teacher should determine curriculum priorities.

- Classroom activities seldom call upon students to engage the content and processes that will be covered in official assessments such as end-of-course tests and state-sponsored tests, or if they do, the instruction is pedantic and relies heavily on rote memorization and quick recall.

- Student boredom or lack of interest in the subject is accepted as normal and is expected.

- Considerable variability is found from classroom to classroom and school to school in the content that is emphasized, the skills that are practiced, and the concepts and processes that are developed.[5]

DISCUSSION. The richness and profundity of the knowledge on which students are asked to work should be of major concern when educators are considering the content to be included in the curriculum. Rich and profound knowledge requires students to expend considerable energy and to gain control over complex and difficult processes if they are to employ this knowledge with positive effect. Theodore and Nancy Sizer call this process *grappling,* by which they mean a process that causes the student to feel empowered to come to personal terms with a story, problem, or project and to perhaps add to it and make it his or her own.[6]

Learning to write complete sentences and to decode words is not the same thing as learning to write persuasively and to read critically, thoughtfully, and with substantial understanding. To function in the world of educated men and women, one must write persuasively; to gain access to the ideas contained in great literature, one must be able (and willing) to read well, not just passably. It is imperative that students learn these things, whether or not they find them inherently interesting. Yet too many students today, as in the past, fail to acquire the skills and understanding they need to write well and read well. Unlike the case in the past, however, those who cannot read well, think well, and present their views persuasively and those who are incapable of mathematical reasoning and the ability to compute will find themselves increasingly excluded from the opportunity structure in America's economy. Furthermore, large numbers of such people can be dangerous to the survival of democracy, for in this information-based society, they may be manipulated by those who lack a moral rudder yet do possess such skills.

It is important that teachers know students' interest level in the content and that they endeavor to make the content as interesting as they can. However, some content is dull and boring to most students, and mastering some skills calls for almost mindless repetition. Such work requires discipline—self-discipline. What teachers must do is to attach such tedious work to results that are important to the students so that the students will see that the activity is important even if it is boring and tedious.

Unfortunately, it is often assumed that the acquisition of these skills and abilities has to do with the interest students have in the content. There are those who say that students who are not interested in the subject should not be in the class. (This is why some high school teachers like to teach elective advanced placement courses.) Some argue that some students just cannot learn difficult subjects and leave the matter there. However, leaving the matter there is no place to leave it—especially in a democracy where the ability to access, control, and use information is becoming the currency of the realm.

If it is indeed the case that mastery of profound knowledge and rich content is necessarily limited to the children of the rich and of the educated and to children born with special intellectual gifts, then the dream of democracy cannot be realized. Our democracy is based on the assumption that through hard work nearly every person is capable of benefiting from an elite education. It is this dream that guides the Working on the Work framework.

Given this dream, it is time for educators who share it to commit themselves to inventing work that is engaging to all students, not just to those born with a predisposition to doing the kinds of work schools now require them to do or with the home support that encourages them to persist. It is also the obligation of educators to ensure that the content with which students are to work reflects that which is most highly valued and viewed as most essential in the larger society, even when some of that content is boring to some students.

Process Standard 2: Organization of Knowledge

The content presented is organized in ways that are most likely to appeal to the personal interests of the largest possible number of students.

INDICATORS OF HIGH COMPLIANCE WITH THE STANDARD

- The presentation format is designed to take into account the level of student interest in the topic. If the interest is low, then the teacher emphasizes other attributes of the work that seem most likely to promote engagement and persistence. (As the lessons from Allentown described in the previous chapter illustrate, students can be provided things to do that they find interesting even though the content has no inherent value or meaning for them.)

- Teachers use a variety of media and formats in order to appeal to the widest possible range of students.

- The content presented is rich: meaning that as much as is possible and practical, students are called on to conduct real experiments and to read books and articles that convey powerful ideas in a powerful way.

- Serious efforts are made to cause students to use what they are learning to analyze problems, issues, and matters of concern to them.

- Serious efforts are made to encourage students to develop an *interdisciplinary perspective*—for example, to see how what they are learning in a history class might have relevance for what they are learning in mathematics and language arts.

INDICATORS OF LOW COMPLIANCE WITH THE STANDARD

- Teachers give little attention to the inherent interest and value to the students of the content with which they are asked to work.

- When the content presented is of little interest or relevance to some students, teachers give little attention to ensuring that the work is designed to increase the engagement of these students in the tasks.

- The format of instruction fails to encourage in-depth discussion and analysis.

- The format of instruction calls on students only to memorize rather than to use what they memorize and to remember what they use.

DISCUSSION. Sometimes content is presented in ways that are fragmented and disjointed; sometimes it is unified and focused. Sometimes the information is easily accessible; sometimes it is difficult for the student to access, organize, or manage. Such things make a difference to the likelihood that students will find the work associated with mastering specific content to be engaging work. Knowledge and information that are arranged so that student work products and problems of concern to the student are the point of focus are more likely to be engaging than are knowledge and information that are presented in fragments and unrelated pieces.

Students who find the content interesting are not difficult to engage. Thus it is tempting to argue that the best way to ensure engaged students is to ensure that the content is inherently interesting or relevant to the lives of the students. Sometimes, however, the effort to make content interesting leads to trivialization and distortion, in which case the cure is as bad as the pathology it is intended to address.

There are in fact many things students learn in school that are neither interesting nor relevant to all students yet are likely to be very important to them as adults and as citizens. Furthermore, it is important to understand that sometimes there is no way to make the content interesting to some students. What can be done, however, is to organize the content in ways that make access relatively easy and the use of the content relatively clear and then to create work that has enough other attractive qualities that students will engage the tasks assigned.

Process Standard 3: Product Focus

The tasks students are assigned and the activities students are encouraged to undertake are clearly linked in the minds of the teacher and the students to problems, issues, products, performances, and exhibitions about which the students care and upon which students place value.

INDICATORS OF HIGH COMPLIANCE WITH THE STANDARD

- Teachers systematically assesses students' interests to determine the kinds of products (the term I will use from now on to include problems, issues, products, performances, and exhibitions) that will be of interest to the students.[7]
- In so far as possible, the work assigned is linked to a product that is valued by the students.
- The teacher endeavors to customize products so that individual students can engage in a common experience yet do so for reasons that may differ from student to student. For example, some students may engage in a history project because they love the

subject. Others may engage in the same project because they like working with their peers, and the project is designed in a way that fosters peer interaction.

- Students demonstrate an understanding about the connection between what they are doing and what they are expected to produce.

INDICATORS OF LOW COMPLIANCE WITH THE STANDARD
- Teachers have given little if any thought to the kinds of products students might be called on to produce.
- The products students are called on to produce are not valued by students.
- The products students are called on to produce do not require students to learn particular skills and to develop specific insights, nor is the activity associated with the creation of each product systematically linked to what is to be learned.
- The work does not require students to demonstrate what they have learned.
- Teachers have little understanding of or appreciation for the kinds of products students find compelling.

DISCUSSION. One of the more certain ways to increase student engagement and persistence with academic work is to link this work with some problem, issue, product, performance, or exhibition that students find compelling. Having a product focus is not, however, the same thing as being committed to the project method or to interdisciplinary themes as a preferred mode of instruction. Projects can be just as dissociated from the motivations of students as the most fragmented rote memorization exercises. Complex, long-term projects are likely to call on students to master knowledge from a variety of disciplines. However, it should be remembered that the disciplines themselves are nothing more—or less—than the sum of the projects scholars have undertaken over a long period of time. Thus projects need to call upon students to participate in interdisciplinary inquiry. *What is important is that the outcomes of the tasks assigned are perceived by the students as things that are worthwhile and significant to them.*

One final point needs to be made. Increasing the degree to which tasks are focused on valued products is a powerful means of increasing engagement, but all tasks are not easily linked to specific products. Indeed, sometimes the effort to link products to tasks so trivializes or distorts knowledge that what is learned is meaningless or in error. (This is one of the more telling criticisms of the project method.) It is useful for teachers to ask the question: Is there some problem, issue, product, performance, or exhibition about which students would care that I can link to what I want them to learn? It is not, however, useful to insist that all work be product focused. Some work cannot be focused in this way, and a product focus can be absolutely harmful when it leads to trivialization and distortion.

Process Standard 4: Clear and Compelling Product Standards

When problems, issues, products, performances, or exhibitions are a part of the instructional design, students understand the standards by which the results of their work will be evaluated. Furthermore, they are committed to these standards, see them as fair, and see a real prospect of meeting these standards if they work diligently at the tasks assigned or encouraged.

INDICATORS OF HIGH COMPLIANCE WITH THE STANDARD

• When the tasks assigned to students include the creation of products, students understand and can articulate the standards by which these results of their efforts will be assessed.

• The range of products students are encouraged to produce is such that the products appeal to a variety of student interests; in effect, products are customized.

• Students are encouraged to assess their own work in terms of the standards set and to participate in group-assessment processes.

• It is commonplace for each student to have personal evaluation conferences with the teacher to assess the quality of one or more of the student's products and help the student become increasingly clear on the nature of standards and how they should be applied.

• Student success in solving problems or creating a product that meets the specified standard is the primary goal. Assessments are conducted with this view in mind.

INDICATORS OF LOW COMPLIANCE WITH THE STANDARD
- Students are unclear about the standards that apply to their products and are usually dependent on the teacher to tell them whether or not what they have done meets the standard. Neither do they know when the conditions set by a problem have been met or when an issue has been adequately explored.

- Teachers pay little attention to the kinds of products students find of interest, and when they do use a product to motivate, it is usually a product chosen because the teacher finds it interesting or specialists in the disciplines find it interesting rather than because students find it interesting or relevant.

- When students perceive a product to be uninteresting, the teacher does little to enhance values such as affirmation of performance or opportunities for affiliation to offset this barrier to learning.

DISCUSSION. Students are more likely to engage and persist with work when the standards for the products are clear and compelling. Children and young adults (like all of us) prefer to operate in a world where they know what is expected and where what is expected is something they care about or can be brought to care about.

Recent efforts to develop and communicate to students clear examples and models (sometimes called *rubrics*) of the products expected indicate that the need students have for clear expectations is coming to be better understood. What is less well understood is that until students learn to care about the products illustrated by a rubric, no amount of clarity and precision will substitute for that caring. Standards have relevance only when those to whom they apply care about them. Teachers, like other leaders, must become as skilled in getting students to see the desired performance standards as important as they are skilled in providing experiences that make the meeting of the standard possible.

It is also important to understand that at times students will have to be brought to produce products, such as essays, that some may find uninteresting. When this condition arises, it is once again the job of the teacher to shape the activity associated with the task so that other motivations are actualized and other values are brought to the fore.

Process Standard 5: Protection from Adverse Consequences for Initial Failures

Students are provided many opportunities to try to complete a task without being penalized for failures associated with lack of knowledge and skills. Instead, when failure occurs, the reasons for the failure are diagnosed by the student and the teacher, and new efforts are encouraged.

INDICATORS OF HIGH COMPLIANCE WITH THE STANDARD

- Teachers accept failure to meet standards on initial tries as a normal part of the learning process and do not apply sanctions (positive or negative) to these initial efforts.

- Students have a clear understanding of the expectations they are to meet in the end, and they use these standards to evaluate their present performance.

- Efforts are made to ensure that students have access to the resources needed (people, time, and technologies in particular) to provide optimum opportunities for success.

- When failure occurs, the teacher or another adult works directly with the student to diagnose the cause of the failure and to correct the situation. For example, if a science teacher discovers that a ninth grader cannot succeed in science because he or she cannot read the required materials, rather than continuing to assign tasks at which the student is certain to fail, the teacher ensures that the student is taught to read. In the meantime, any science taught to this student will have to be taught through media that do not call for reading. (Of course, if there were high standards throughout the system, this situation would not occur in the first place.)

- Peer evaluations and public discussions of products are commonplace in the classroom and in the school.

INDICATORS OF LOW COMPLIANCE WITH THE STANDARD

- Each time a student product is evaluated by the teacher, that evaluation becomes a part of the record the teacher uses to "justify" a grade.

- Nearly all evaluations and assessments are conducted by the teacher alone and are communicated only to the students and to the students' parents.

- Time is treated as a given. Typically, the time allocated to a task or project is the amount of time the teacher judges necessary for the average student to do an average job. Thus the "above average" student is bored, and the "below average" student fails to achieve.

- When students fail to learn after numerous tries what it is intended they learn, little thought is given to designing new tasks that may result in increased engagement and increased learning. In effect, failure is accepted as normal.

DISCUSSION. The level of engagement of students—especially students who work more slowly than the majority—is clearly affected by the extent to which students have opportunities to engage in tasks at which they are not proficient without fear of embarrassment, punishment, or an implication of personal inadequacy. Students, like most adults, either avoid situations that bring pain or discomfort or redefine the situations so that they can accommodate to them. For example, the student who regularly fails to comprehend mathematical operations defines himself or herself as "not mathematically inclined" or as a "C student in math." Enhancing the opportunities students have to test themselves against the standard and ensuring that when they fail to meet the standard they receive additional punishment-free opportunities to succeed seems a likely antidote to student defeatism and perhaps a spur to greater effort. Whereas "learners who come to believe that failure is inevitable develop a sense of futility and hopelessness—a belief that success is beyond their reach. Slowly, over time, they stop trying. How likely are these students to meet our new high achievement standards?"[8]

The unfortunate fact is that the way schools are currently organized makes punishment-free opportunities difficult to achieve. Consider grading practices. Each time a grade is given, it is perceived as either a reward or a punishment. Any person who receives less than the highest grade is implicitly receiving either a slight or heavy rebuke—A's are excellent, B's are pretty good, but F's are failing. The demands that teachers have enough evidence in their grade books to justify each final grade given make it difficult for, say, a teacher with 150 students in five sections of English composition to provide feedback to each student without making the feedback count in the grade book. When the propensity to grade is combined with the rigid time frame in which schools typically function—in spite of the fact that it is known that students vary considerably in the speed at which they learn—the linkage between failure and punishment is almost inescapable.

Students, and sometimes their parents too, do escape, however. The student simply begins to accept the fact that he or she is incapable of other than mediocre work, and parents come to believe that their child's performance has to do with "ability" more than with effort.

The Working on the Work framework assumes that effort accounts for most variance in academic achievement, and certainly for more than innate ability does. Those who achieve effortlessly could achieve much more if they invested some effort, and those who do not achieve could achieve enough to meet reasonably high standards if teachers appealed to their motives and provided appropriate support. Put another way, given time, support, leadership, and motive, there are few things schools expect students to learn that cannot be learned by all students.

Process Standard 6: Affirmation of the Significance of Performance

Persons who are significant in the lives of students, including parents, siblings, peers, public audiences, and younger students, are positioned to observe, participate in, and benefit from student performances and to affirm the significance and importance of the activity being undertaken.

INDICATORS OF HIGH COMPLIANCE WITH THE STANDARD

- Students, individually and in groups, frequently have opportunities to display for others what they are doing in class and in school. For example, sixth-grade students might be encouraged to write stories for second graders.

- Parents and guardians are invited into the standard-setting process for students and function as full partners in the evaluation of their child's performance in school and in the classroom.

- Adults other than parents, teachers, and guardians have opportunities to view performances and products and to comment on what they see (with attention given to protecting the student from public humiliation and harm).

• Work is designed in a way that clearly communicates that the effort the student expends is important not only to the student personally and to his or her learning but also to the functioning of the group and the needs of others who are significant to the student.

INDICATORS OF LOW COMPLIANCE WITH THE STANDARD

• Few adults other than the teacher are in a position to observe student performances or to evaluate student products. Similarly, there are few opportunities for peers and other students to view these performances and products.

• Parents and students receive evaluations conducted by teachers and other school personnel but are otherwise excluded from the evaluation process.

• The primary relationship that drives activity in the classroom and in the school is the relationship between the individual teacher and the individual student. Little attention is given to designing tasks that encourage broader relationships and that make successful learning by each student a matter of concern to others such as parents and peers who are a significant part of the student's social network.

DISCUSSION. Designing schoolwork in ways that encourage those persons sociologists call *significant others,* those such as parents, peers, and younger or older students, to communicate that they too consider the work students are being asked to do and the products associated with that work to be important often increases student engagement. This is what is meant by *affirmation.*

Affirming is of course not the same as *praising.* To affirm is to "say positively, declare firmly, assert to be true, confirm, ratify."[9] To affirm is not to approve or disapprove; to affirm is to declare that what happened matters and is important. Affirmation does not imply approval. Affirmation suggests significance. Affirmation attaches importance to an event or an action, thereby fastening attention on that event or activity. Products that count matter to people who count in the lives of the student. If the products expected in school are of little concern to those who count in the life of the students, then the likelihood is that the product will not count to the student.

It is unfortunate that the myth has grown up that teachers are always significant influences in the lives of students. Sometimes they are; sometimes they are not. Teachers seem to be much more powerful sources of affirmation for little children on the average than for older youngsters.[10] Why? In part it is because as children grow older, their social networks expand, and those who are significant referents for them change. Teachers simply have more competition for the attention and loyalty of adolescents than they have for the attention and loyalty of a child of six years. Rather than fighting this competition, teachers should do all they can do to exploit the power of these other individuals and groups and turn them into partners.

Currently, few adults other than teachers are typically in a position to affirm the work of students because in most cases it is concealed from everyone except teachers and perhaps a few peers. This is one of the reasons that portfolio assessment has—or should have—such great appeal. Portfolio assessment makes student products available for scrutiny by a variety of potential sources of affirmation, whereas conventional systems of grading and reporting make only the teacher's evaluation available to others and not the work on which the evaluation was based.

A critical point here is that one way teachers may be able to get students engaged in work that involves content that is uninteresting to the students is to get the products of the work affirmed by people who count in the lives of the students. They make these products visible to others and cause these others to show that they take these products into account. (In years gone by, the spelling bees and ciphering matches that were public events in many rural schools probably also had such affirming effects.)

Process Standard 7: Affiliation

Students are provided opportunities to work with others (peers, parents, other adults, teachers, students from other schools and classrooms) on problems, issues, products, performances, and exhibitions that are judged by them and others to be of significance.

INDICATORS OF HIGH COMPLIANCE WITH THE STANDARD

- Schoolwork, both inside the classroom and outside, frequently involves two or more students working together on a common product, and the work is designed to encourage interdependence.

- Students frequently work with parents and other adult members of the community (including senior citizens) in completing tasks and assignments.

- Students are frequently called on to develop products that are useful or of interest to others such as other students or community leaders.
- Teachers ensure that all students know enough about group processes to analyze and evaluate the operation of groups of which they are a part.
- Electronic technology, including the Internet, is used to build cooperative networks among students as well as among students and adult groups.

INDICATORS OF LOW COMPLIANCE WITH THE STANDARD
- When group work is provided, its design makes it possible for one or two students to do the work even though four, five, six, or more students are assigned to the group.
- Students are seldom provided opportunities to interact in significant ways with people outside the classroom, and few people outside the classroom really know what students are doing.
- Most student products are individual projects that can be completed without attention to the needs of anyone other than the teacher.
- Teachers give little attention to helping students develop group process skills and seldom provide instruction in group problem solving and group work.
- Electronic technology is used primarily as a tool for conveying information to students, not as a tool to assist students in the creation of products.
- Little attention is given to building student networks beyond the classroom or to using personnel outside the school and the classroom as resources to facilitate student work.

DISCUSSION. Work that is designed to permit, encourage, and support opportunities for students to affiliate with others is likely to encourage some students to engage the work that otherwise they might not find engaging. It is generally understood that most students enjoy and are motivated by being members of vital and well-organized groups. (Many students even enjoy poorly organized groups. Indeed, some students participate in actions that look a great deal like mob activity.) Groups and the affiliations that groups provide are powerful forces (for both good and ill) in the motivational structures of schools and classrooms. Teachers and school faculties that seem to produce the highest levels of engagement seem as well to understand the power of groups and how to use groups for positive ends. They also seem to know how to offset the negative impacts groups may have from time to time. For example, the social dynamics of student groups sometimes lead to a certain amount of unfocused activity or activity focused more on the affiliation needs of children than on the task at hand. Effective teachers understand these things and monitor group work to ensure that the ends for which the group is established are the ends that are being served.

Skillful teachers design work so that affiliation is one of the rewards students get from that work. Sometimes this reward comes in the process of doing the work (when it is group work), and sometimes it comes as a result of doing the work (for example, lonely practice at home gets one into the high school band). Skillful teachers also understand that group work is not simply work that students do together (like the parallel play very young children engage in before they have learned the skills of cooperative action). Group work requires interdependence as well as independence.

Those who advocate cooperative learning as a pedagogical strategy understand this very well. When teachers and administrators do not understand this strategy, they may easily end up with group work that is actually five or more students working together yet independently on a task. Such poorly designed group work is a reason why such work sometimes develops a bad reputation, especially among the parents of students who are quick, aggressive, and intellectually gifted. On the one hand parents see such work as holding their child back because he or she is working with students who learn more slowly; on the other hand they see their child doing all the work and others getting credit for it. However, the affiliation and affirmation provided by properly constructed groups are critical elements in the proper design of quality work for students. The skeptical reader should recall that many of the most highly engaging activities in schools (band, choral music, team sports, drama) involve students of various ages and talents and are organized around groups and cooperative ideals, yet individual attainment is not stifled, and stars are born and recognized.

Process Standard 8: Novelty and Variety

The range of problems, issues, products, performances, and exhibitions is large and varied, and the technologies students are encouraged to employ are varied as well, moving from the most simple and well understood (a pen and a piece of paper, for instance) to the most complex (sophisticated computer applications, for example).

INDICATORS OF HIGH COMPLIANCE WITH THE STANDARD
- Varied formats and varied modes of presentation are commonplace.
- Students are expected to play various roles in group work: sometimes a particular student is a follower; sometimes he or she is a leader.
- When content is judged to be inherently without interest to students, teachers are especially attentive to creating activities that are of high interest to students.

INDICATORS OF LOW COMPLIANCE WITH THE STANDARD
- The mode of presentation and the instructional format are generally lacking in variety.
- Students are seldom called on to play roles or perform functions other than those they show a "natural" tendency to perform. Thus those who seem to be born leaders are expected to lead; those who seem not so inclined are expected to follow.
- Rigor is confused with rigor mortis. It is assumed that uninteresting subjects cannot be presented in ways that stimulate interest or that any effort to create interest is likely to trivialize the content.

DISCUSSION. *Novelty* and *frivolity* are not synonyms. Novelty adds freshness and new life to the tired and the repetitious; novelty improves performance because it insists that one continue to learn to master the new situation. Frivolity is activity without substance. Novelty can be and should be substantial.

Giving students novel things to do and novel ways of doing things is simply one more way of increasing the likelihood that they will engage the work provided. For example, the introduction of computers into writing classes sometimes motivates students who would otherwise not write. But what is sometimes forgotten is that novelty has a way of wearing off. What is new today is taken for granted tomorrow. The motivational power of computers and other forms of electronic technology will only be realized when these tools are used to provide students with new forms of work to do and new products to produce as well as new ways to do old work and new ways to produce old products. Access to a computer is novel only to those children who do not have a computer at home or regular access to computers in school.

Process Standard 9: Choice

What students are to learn is usually not subject to negotiation, but students do have considerable choice of what they will do in order to learn what it is intended that they learn.

INDICATORS OF HIGH COMPLIANCE WITH THE STANDARD
- Students are provided with numerous opportunities to select modes of presentation.
- When being tested or being challenged to perform before others, students are given many opportunities to participate in decisions regarding the processes to be employed in the test or performance and the standards by which such work will be evaluated.
- A wide range of technologies is available for student use (from pencils to sophisticated computer programs, presentation technologies, and laptop publishing), and students are encouraged to use all of them at some point in time.
- Within sensible limits, students have a great deal of control over when and how they will participate, and teachers make every effort to make activities invitational and voluntary as opposed to compulsory and coerced.

INDICATORS OF LOW COMPLIANCE WITH THE STANDARD
- Teachers rely heavily on a limited range of presentation styles—predominantly lecture, predominantly group work, or predominantly independent library research, for example.
- The range of technologies available for student use is limited; textbooks supplemented by workbooks are the norm. Modern electronic technologies are not available, or if available, they are seldom used.

DISCUSSION. Choice implies some degree of control over events. Individuals who have choice are empowered. Empowerment increases the likelihood of commitment. Today, however, the idea of choice, like the idea of group work, has become tainted in schools.

In the not-too-distant past it was relatively common for radical reformers to assert that students needed choice in what they learned. Some even went so far as to argue that the interests of the students should dictate the curriculum. There are still those who would advance such an argument, although I am not one of them. Schools exist because the adults in society believe that there are things the young need to learn in order to ensure cultural and social continuity. About these things students should have little choice. Children need to learn to read, for example, whether or not they come to school wanting to read and whether or not their parents insist on and support them in this endeavor. Children are not simply family members; they are also future citizens, and as such they will have duties and obligations that they cannot fulfill adequately unless they can read. There are other understandings that are basic as well. For example, all citizens in our democracy need to be conversant with the history of America and the world; they also need a general grasp of basic geographical facts, skill in the use of maps, and so on. Indeed, I find much that is attractive about Aristotle's idea that to be truly educated, one must have an *educational acquaintance* with the basic disciplines. It is also important to understand that for Aristotle, an educational acquaintance is not a simple or shallow introduction to the disciplines. Rather, it is enough understanding of the basic assumptions of the disciplines and their methods to be able to distinguish sense from nonsense. In an age when nonsense has so many convenient outlets, this is not a trivial goal.

For now, however, I am willing to leave to others debates about what it is essential for students to know and to be able to do. I am not as interested in schools' providing *learning* choices as I am in their providing *doing* choices. I am also interested in making educators more conscious of the fact that whether adults like it or not, students have choices about what they will and will not do. Anyone who does not believe this has not been in schools, churches, synagogues, or other places in which adults sometimes try to get the young to do things they do not see some sense in doing. Certainly, rebellion can be stopped and minimal compliance ensured through coercion. But commitment, which is essential if substantial learning is to occur, must be earned. Certainly, the young can be compelled to attend school, but their attention at school must be earned.

It is critical therefore, as we create the schools of the future, that we understand that students, like other customers, are volunteers and they do have choices about what they do. By providing choices that are attractive to students and that cause students to work with the knowledge and information they need to work with in order to be culturally literate, personally competent, and possessed of civic virtues, the schools may indeed be able to satisfy those critics who currently believe that the schools are not doing the job they must do.

To provide such choices to students, it must first be acknowledged that what students do determines what students learn and that there are many things students can do to learn particular content. Variety in doing is the only way I know of ensuring constancy in learning.

Process Standard 10: Authenticity

The tasks students are assigned and the work students are encouraged to undertake have meaning and significance in the present lives of students and are related to consequences to which students attach importance.

INDICATORS OF HIGH COMPLIANCE WITH THE STANDARD

- The quality of solutions to problems, analysis of issues, products, performances, and exhibitions have consequences for the student about which the student cares.
- The tasks students are assigned are perceived by the students to be within reach if effort is expended.
- Tasks are designed in ways that increase student *ownership* of the quality of the results and that foster both individual and collective success.
- Most products are made public and most evaluations of products are public as well: for example, students evaluate each other, or the teacher evaluates student products in a public way.
- The consequences of meeting standards and of failing to meet standards are known to the students and understood by them to be important to their current circumstances as well as to their future prospects.

INDICATORS OF LOW COMPLIANCE WITH THE STANDARD

- Students consider the consequences associated with failure to meet standards to be inconsequential or beyond their control, sometimes requiring products students judge to be unattainable.

- Students are alienated from their work. They do not see the work and consequent learning as having anything to do with what they care about. Consequently, they carry out their tasks with minimum enthusiasm.

- Many of the questions students ask are designed to elicit approval for meeting minimum standards rather than to obtain assistance to excel.

DISCUSSION. The word *authenticity* is bandied about quite freely among educators, so freely that the power of the concept is sometimes lost. What it refers to here is a sense of realness about experiences. When experiences have this sense of realness about them—for example, if they carry real consequences, as winning or losing a football game does—then individuals' engagement with them is likely to increase.

Authenticity in schools is enhanced when teachers attend to building affirmation into the work given to students. What teacher has failed to note how much more attentive most students are when they are preparing for a performance their parents are likely to attend? The presence of a parent not only affirms the performance, it gives it authenticity as well. Authenticity is also enhanced by associating the work with real-life products from which students gain feelings of pride and satisfaction. For example, the production of a documentary videotape on the Civil War is likely to possess more authenticity for students than a series of lectures on the same topic will possess when the only benefit of these lectures is that students will be able to pass a test that indicates they were listening to what the teacher said and were smart enough to figure out what was likely to be on the test.

It is also critical to understand that an authentic experience for a student is not necessarily a real-world experience from an adult's viewpoint. That which is authentic to the student is that which the world of the student defines as real. Puppy love may be only infatuation to an adult, but it is real and thus authentic to an adolescent. The status system of the playground may seem of little real-world importance as one gains an adult perspective, but it is quite real to students. Similarly, the routine of adult work life that is real to an adult may seem unreal and not too compelling to the child.

CONCLUSION

The framework laid out in this chapter requires educators to think about their business in a very different way than they have historically considered it. The most important shift required is a shift in the way teachers view themselves and their profession. Rather than seeing themselves as performers, teachers must begin to view themselves as leaders. Students are volunteers. The task of the teacher is to design work that encourages students to volunteer their energy to the accomplishment of tasks that will result in their (the students) learning what it is intended that they learn. Many of the things that students need to do they would not do if they were not somehow led to do so. Providing this leadership is a vital part of the role of the teacher. Effective leaders are persons who understand the needs of those whom they set out to lead and respond to those needs in ways that are productive both for the individuals being led and the common goals of the group. Working on the work is one way for teachers to emerge as the leaders they need to be. Chapter Seven looks more closely at ways to use the WOW framework and at the significance of thinking about teachers as leaders.

CHAPTER SEVEN

Using the WOW Framework

T he Working on the Work (WOW) framework, like any other framework, is useless unless it is applied in a systematic and disciplined way. Both the standards and the indicators need to become the center of consideration when teachers are planning units of work, when they are trying to understand why some tasks appeal to some students but not to others, and when they are trying to evaluate new instructional programs to determine the likelihood that these programs will enhance student engagement. These standards and indicators can also provide a language for fruitful discussions among teachers and administrators and as a framework for team planning and team analysis of instructional issues. Finally, the WOW framework has utility for a disciplined approach to the design and delivery of professional development experiences for teachers and administrators. Staff development will be much improved when the activities provided by staff developers for teachers are as attentive to the standards suggested by the WOW framework as activities provided by teachers for students should be.

PLANNING WORK FOR STUDENTS

The first and primary use of the WOW framework is *to help teachers think through the lessons they present and the tasks they assign to students.* Teachers should ask themselves questions like, Which of the ten WOW qualities are most important to the students with whom I am working? Am I attending to these qualities as I design work for these students? How might I include more of these qualities in the work students are encouraged to undertake? What are my colleagues doing to incorporate these qualities, and what might I learn from their efforts? If over time I look for indicators that the work I provide contains the qualities suggested by the WOW standards, are there any that are missing or deemphasized? If so, is this a conscious choice based on my understanding of the students and their needs, or is it simply an oversight?

One of the strengths of the WOW framework is that it provides a discipline for planning units of work, from daily lessons to yearlong programs, that exploit the power of a wide range of approaches and pedagogical models and also avoid excursions that lead away from the primary business of the school. For example, the literature of education contains considerable discussion of the concept of *developmentally appropriate strategies.* The WOW framework encourages teachers to make informed judgments regarding the pedagogical strategies likely to be most effective with children at different developmental stages. It is clear, for example, that middle school students care much about values associated with affiliation. Most middle school students are likely to respond positively to an activity when that activity provides them with opportunities to work with peers or on occasion with adults. Kindergarten and first-grade students, in contrast, often need to be taught how to perform in groups and are typically not particularly motivated by such activity. High schools students often have mixed reactions to group work. On the one hand, like their middle school counterparts, they place great value on peer interaction and peer approval. On the other hand many find group work in schools an unwanted impediment to their own achievement goals. Regardless of the developmental stage, then, an understanding of the quality of affiliation is important, and the primary school teacher who tries to use opportunities for affiliation as a source of motivation is as likely to be disappointed as the middle school teacher who fails to take the need for affiliation into account.

Similarly, wise primary school teachers know that their students are usually highly motivated when they know that adults, especially their parents, see the students' performance in school as important. Teachers can take advantage of this fact by inventing varieties of ways for parents and other adults significant in the lives of students to affirm the importance of the students' work. Wise high school teachers understand that affirmation by peers is important to most high school students, and they take advantage of this fact by designing work so that students' contributions to that work are accorded importance not only by the teacher but also by peers. Such group work must have well-differentiated yet interdependent roles for group members and the teachers must ensure that these roles are well understood. Otherwise, what should be group work will turn out to be work that one individual could do given the time and commitment. For example, writing a group report does not necessarily require group work, but one way of ensuring that it requires group work is to ask each student in a group to be responsible for a different section of the report—which the student gives to the teacher—and one student to serve as overall report coordinator and to edit the report to ensure an even flow of content and style.

In using the WOW framework effectively as a planning tool, it is necessary to assess the interest value of the content being taught. Some students find certain subjects or topics interesting that others do not. If it is assumed that all students need to learn some things in common, which I do assume, then it is likely that many students at various times will be called on to learn things that are not particularly interesting or appealing to them.

There are at least four ways to handle lack of student interest in the content. First, educators can treat uninteresting content, like bad-tasting medicine, as a necessary evil. Students who want to be educated, in this view, must tolerate a great deal that they do not find interesting to be certified as educated. Second, educators can seek ways to spice up the content and make it more "relevant" to the lives of students. Third, educators can forego teaching this content. Fourth, educators can accept the level of interest in the content as a given and then ask the question, What other qualities in addition to content and substance might be built into this work that would result in students' coming to grips with the content even though they do not find it particularly interesting?

In the first case it is unlikely that any except students who are highly motivated by academic pursuits and academic attainment, such as entry into a highly selective college, will seriously engage the material and then only ritually. Many others will engage in passive compliance, and some may even rebel. The result will be that few students will learn what it is intended they learn because they did not do what it was intended they do at a level of effort commensurate with the requirements of the task.

In the second case, the strategy of making the content more interesting often leads to trivialization of the content—something akin to a Classic Comics approach to the study of the writings of Sir Walter Scott. Entertainment values rather than educational values become the guiding principles on which plans are made and materials are developed.

The third strategy simply bypasses the responsibility adults have for ensuring that all youngsters, as a part of becoming members of the adult community, know the things they need to know to function well in the society and the culture. If what is being taught is not important to social and cultural continuity as well as to individual success in that culture, then it ought not to be taught at all. There is too much else to do. If, however, what is being taught is worth teaching, then it is the obligation of the school and teachers to design work that is interesting to the students, even if the content they must learn to do that work is not of interest to them.

However, using the fourth strategy, and systemically and routinely employing the WOW framework, it is possible for teachers to continuously improve the quality of the work they provide for students and thus the level of learning that students will eventually exhibit. By asking questions like, "Is there some problem, issue, product, performance, or exhibition that is of interest to students the successful completion of which would require the students to know what I want them to know or be able to do what I want them to be able to do?" teachers can begin to gain an understanding of what is meant by Working on the Work. If the answer to this question is, "I can't think of such a product," then the next question might be, "Is there is some way I could use the students' needs for affiliation or affirmation as a means to increase engagement?" It is through posing such questions, reflecting on their own experience as well as the research of other scholars and the reports of other teachers, that individual teachers can set themselves on the road to continuous improvement.

Diagnosing and Assessing

Most teachers have developed units of work that seemed to them to be somewhat routine, only to find that the tasks stirred up a surprising amount of interest among students. Similarly, most teachers have invented work that seemed to them to be almost certain to spark students' interests, yet all that happened was some ritual engagement, some passive compliance, a great deal of retreatism, and some rebellion. Faced with such results, teachers are often at a loss for an explanation. I have even heard some explain such events as caused by a "full moon."

The WOW framework offers teachers a set of tools useful in diagnosing such situations. First, by fastening their attention on student engagement, persistence, and satisfaction, teachers have the potential of fastening on things that are immediately observable and that can, if there is the will, be measured. Teachers can determine what proportion of students are engaged and at what level from authentic engagement through rebellion. It is also possible for teachers to gain insight into why what they observe is happening. It may be, for example, that the teacher has been very attentive to affiliation needs when many of the students do not value affiliation as highly as the teacher thinks they do, and at the same time, the teacher has paid little attention to affirmation needs that many students do value. Instruments and procedures for measuring the WOW attributes of schoolwork are presently very primitive, but this should not stop teachers from trying to measure these things. Some measurement is better than no measurement at all. Indeed, without measurement there can be no control, and as I have said before, without control there can be no systematic and purposeful improvement.

In conducting such an analysis, teachers should remember that all ten of the work qualities described by the WOW standards will not be operative at once. WOW, once again, is not a lesson plan format or a checklist. Rather, it is a framework to help teachers to answer the questions, What is going on here? and, Why is this so? Sometimes all that is going on is that most students find the subject uninteresting, and the work has not been designed to appeal to any motive other than interest in the content. At other times the teacher may have worked diligently to increase the presence of attributes that few of the students in the classroom care about and have worked hardly at all to incorporate attributes of real concern to these students.

Without engagement, persistence, and satisfaction, it is not likely that students will learn what it is intended that they learn. Therefore engagement, persistence, and satisfaction should be the key results sought by teachers. Those who see *performance standards* as the sine qua non may question this assertion. However, as I have emphasized before, substantial learning is not easily assessed on a daily or even weekly basis, whereas curriculum alignment, engagement, persistence, and evidence of satisfaction can be measured at some meaningful level nearly every day.

Of course it is possible—indeed it is commonplace—to assess whether students are learning what it is intended they learn without assessing levels of commitment, persistence, and satisfaction. The problem with such truncated assessments is that when the test scores show that students are not learning what it is intended that they learn, it is hard to determine why this is the case. The result is that teachers gain very little new insight from a review of such scores, unless the problems are simply failures of curriculum alignment.

Given a lack of clear data to the contrary, the most commonly held explanation for failure to learn holds that students do not learn what they need to learn because they do not possess the aptitudes required to learn those things. A second explanation is that students fail to learn what it is intended they learn because they are not compliant with the demands of the teacher—"If you do what I tell you to do, you will learn what I want you to learn." A third, though less widely used, explanation is that the students have the aptitude to learn what it is expected to learn and they invest enough energy in doing what the teacher wants them to do, but the things the teacher wants them to do have little prospect of producing the intended learning results. (How many of us invested great energy in learning how to diagram sentences only to find that diagramming sentences did not teach us how to write?)

American education, democratic though its inclinations are, gives much more credence to the aptitude argument than schools in many other cultures do. Yet as Resnick and Hall make so clear, this mode of explanation has unhealthy effects on the organization of schools and on the willingness of students to engage demanding course work, because "students who are held to low expectations do not try to break through that barrier; they, like their teachers and parents, accept the judgment that inborn aptitude is what matters most, and they have not inherited enough of that capacity."[1] Such a view makes teaching and teachers relatively impotent. About all a teacher can do is present the material and find out who can master it. Some teachers do this presenting in ways that are more interesting and engaging than others can muster, but for the most part in this view, variance in learning outcomes is attributed to factors well beyond the control of teachers and even parents.

The effort paradigm is not without its problems as well. Some performances are beyond the physical or intellectual capacity of some individuals no matter how long or how hard they try. Many little boys and little girls may aspire to be like Tiger Woods or Michael Jordan, but only a handful of children will grow up to perform even on one occasion as these two great athletes perform. It is equally true, however, that these athletes would not perform as well as they do unless they were willing to invest effort, and those who aspire to be like them will be better than they might have been had they not had such exemplars of standards to encourage them to make a greater effort.

In the world of academics not all students will turn out to be great writers, great orators, or exceptional men and women of science. Yet it seems reasonable to assume that if students can be brought to invest enough effort in work that brings them into meaningful contact with matters academic, they will learn enough of what they need to learn to be thoughtful and productive citizens who have command of the full range of cultural and intellectual life that is available for them to experience and enjoy.[2] The problem, of course, is discovering what, in the students' view, makes the work assigned to them worth the energy they are being asked to invest.

Teachers sometimes overestimate the level of student engagement in their classes and confuse passive compliance with authentic engagement. Careful attention to soliciting data from students that permit teachers to assess students' level of involvement will clarify and discipline these judgments. Then, when students who were assumed to be engaged are upon more careful assessment judged to be less engaged than assumed, WOW provides the teacher with a set of standards and indicators that may help her or him to understand why this is the case and what might be done about it. For example, students who fear that they do not presently have the skills to perform up to standard may engage in passive compliance or retreatist behavior simply out of self-protection. The teacher who understands this is in a better position than the teacher who does not to create strategies for protecting such students against adverse consequences for failing to meet standards until these students have had the time and experiences needed to develop the skills and understandings the performance requirements call for.

The WOW framework suggests other possibilities for eliciting effort, or persistence, as well. Students who are rightly afraid of failure because they lack skills and are also unwilling to practice in front of more accomplished peers where their deficiencies might be publicly noted might well be assigned a position of some responsibility with younger children that calls upon them to read to these children from the kinds of books these younger children would normally read. Thus the older student is encouraged to develop reading skills as a result of receiving the affirmation that is too often lacking for low-performing students.[3]

Increasing numbers of teachers and school administrators seem to be willing to embrace the third explanation for failure to learn, the possibility that the school or the teachers are giving students the wrong things to do. Indeed, this is one of the reasons that those who argue for curriculum alignment are gaining so much prominence nowadays. They are making profound and meaningful the commonsense observation that students are more likely to learn what one wants them to learn when the students are somehow brought into contact with that content and afforded opportunities to practice the related skills. For example, many teachers want students to read, yet they give students few tasks that call on them to read and little time to read, to listen to others read, or to be heard reading out loud. Surely, if we learned nothing else from the time-on-task research of the 1970s,[4] we learned that if students are to learn things, they must spend time doing the things it is intended they learn.

There is, however, more to this matter than curriculum alignment. As Resnick and Hall point out, there is a vast body of research that shows that even the skills and understandings needed to show marked improvement on measures of intelligence can be taught.[5] The problem is that once the context in which the learning occurred is changed, students cease to use, or to see the applicability of, the cognitive skills and understandings they have been taught. It is not enough therefore to ensure that students are exposed to the appropriate content and provided opportunities to practice the appropriate skills. Students must also be provided the opportunity to engage this content and practice these skills in a context where the expenditure of effort makes sense to them: a context where it is assumed that success is possible.

Too often, even those who believe that effort counts provide tasks for students that assume that success is in limited supply. Rather than pursuing learning goals, which are accompanied by the assumption that greater effort produces enhanced ability, students are encouraged to pursue performance goals, which are accompanied by the assumption that effort and ability are negatively related and that the need to expend greater effort is evidence of lack of ability. The result is that in the typical school, "we expect teachers to grade on the curve in the belief that, if everyone gets an A or B, standards must be too low. We seldom assume that uniformly high grades mean that everyone worked hard and succeeded in learning what was taught."[6]

Learning goals have to do with what it is intended that students understand, know, comprehend, and feel. Learning goals have to do with what Sizer has called *habits of mind*.[7] Performance goals have to do with what it is intended that students do to demonstrate this understanding. Performance goals can be stated more or less behaviorally or in the form of demonstrations. Learning goals are stated in cognitive terms, and their accomplishment must be inferred from observation of a variety of performances in a variety of settings. Furthermore, as indicated earlier, it is possible to achieve performance goals without achieving the desired learning goal.

To understand whether students are expending enough effort on a task, it is important to understand both the learning goals and the performance goals associated with the task and to assess as well the extent to which the learning goals are being supported by or suppressed by the performance goals, which are the center of so many of today's efforts at assessment of student learning.

The WOW framework can make a major contribution to resolving the aptitude-effort question by helping teachers discover the extent to which students are engaged in the activity the teacher wants them to be engaged in, whether the students are persisting with the activity long enough to learn what they are intended to learn, and whether they find personal meaning and satisfaction in what they have accomplished in the process. If on the one hand they have done all these things and still have not learned what the designers of the performance tests would have them learn, then it just may be that the teachers are having the students do the wrong things or that the performances being tested should not be tested at all.

If on the other hand it turns out that the students are not engaged in the work, teachers can use the WOW framework to figure out why this is so and what might be done to remedy the situation.

Evaluating Curriculum Materials

Two key questions should dominate the selection of curriculum materials, whether these materials come in the form of textbooks, computer programs, videotapes, or distance learning opportunities:

- Are these materials aligned with what we intend our students to learn?
- Are these materials organized in ways and accompanied by strategies that make it likely that our students will become engaged in the activities suggested, persist when they have difficulty, and experience a sense of accomplishment when they have completed the activities?

The answer to the first question indicates whether curriculum alignment exists. Educators should also ask this related question, Is the level of difficulty within the reach of the students with whom the materials will be used?

The second key question has to do with the qualities of the work suggested by the WOW standards. One obvious and more specific question to ask is this: Is the content presented in a way that will be of optimum interest to the students with whom it will be used? Other specific questions are these: Are the activities recommended in the materials likely to increase affirmation of students' work by parents and other adults significant in our students' lives? Does design of these materials and activities encourage students to work together as well as independently? In a similar fashion, questions based on each of the ten qualities might be used to evaluate materials for use with a particular group of students.

Those who are making decisions about the adoption of new programs and materials almost always have implicit or explicit criteria against which these materials are evaluated. For example, textbook adoption committees frequently worry about scope, sequence, coverage, reading level, interest level, use of graphics and pictures, and so on. Such criteria bear on concerns that the WOW framework raises as well. For example, the scope and sequence issue is related to the way knowledge is organized. Reading level has to do with organizing material in a way that is accessible to students. Coverage is in fact a question about content and substance as is interest level.

What the WOW framework might contribute to such deliberations also goes beyond such obvious concerns, and where it goes might reveal much that needs to be known prior to selecting a program or that needs to be understood as a condition of selecting a program or set of materials.

For example, some persons see computerized programs as the answer to nearly every problem that confronts schools. Computer salespeople are quick to show videotapes that feature many students busy at the computer terminal playing the game or doing the activity that these product representatives are trying to sell. They are also prone to produce data, sometimes of dubious merit, that demonstrate great gains in test scores.

The WOW framework encourages those who are considering the adoption of materials and programs to ask additional questions: questions like, If this material is as good as the providers claim that it is, why is this so, and what can we learn from it? It may be that computer-based programs seem highly engaging to some students because working on a computer is a novel experience for them. If this is so, given the increasing numbers of computers in homes and the increasing access students have to them, the novelty of working on a computer may soon wear off, and engagement in computer-based work may diminish. Under these circumstances, the purchase of a computer program on the assumption that it is the program itself that is engaging may be a disappointing purchase.

Similarly informative questions that might be asked about materials or programs are these: What products, performances, or exhibitions do these materials support, encourage, or require, and what reason is there to believe that the students for whom they are intended will find these products compelling? What, if anything, have the designers done to ensure that the standards they suggest for evaluating products will have meaning for the students? Are the suggested standards stated in ways that students will find compelling or that they can be brought to embrace?

These questions are just a sampling. Imaginative teachers and administrators, using the WOW framework as a systematic guide and investigating each quality, can come up with equally important questions of their own that are relevant to their particular situation. I would insist, however, that to fail to use the WOW framework in a systematic fashion, quality by quality, is to run the risk of missing much that might otherwise be revealed.

USING THE FRAMEWORK TO GUIDE DISCUSSION

The WOW framework can help teachers shape a productive dialogue among themselves and with school principals.

Disciplining Discussion

Nowadays there is a great deal of interest in the concept of dialogue and the utility of getting teachers and school administrators (especially building principals) engaged in serious and sustained conversations about teaching and learning in their schools and classrooms. Conversation and dialogue are indeed central to the creation and maintenance of what Senge[8] and others refer to as learning organizations.

Unfortunately, the adversarial mind-set that dominates so much public debate often detracts attention from the fact that two people talking in sequence does not constitute a dialogue. A dialogue assumes that all of the parties to a conversation are open to the possibility that what others are saying may be more reasonable and more in keeping with the facts than are their own views. This is not to say that dialogue does not have room for argument, debate, and even short-term inflexibility. However, dialogue does not seek compromise. Those who are engaged in serious dialogue are, or should be, seeking consensus. To engage in a dialogue the participants must be honestly seeking the explanation or proposed course of action that is the best, the most reasonable, and the most consistent with the facts.

The WOW framework provides a basis for disciplining conversations about teaching and about the classroom in order to transform confrontations into conversations and debates into dialogues. For such transformation to happen, the teachers involved must understand the basic concepts underlying the WOW framework. These teachers must also share the belief that students are volunteers and the belief that the teacher's primary task is to invent engaging work for students and then to provide students the support and leadership they need to do that work.

Given these understandings and beliefs, two or more teachers might profitably engage in a mutual examination of a unit of work, a task, or a set of tasks to discover what attributes of quality work are present and to explore what additional attributes might be introduced or how those that are already present might be enriched. The experience the science teacher has had in developing products that are interesting to students may have something to contribute to the thinking of the math teacher who is having trouble getting students engaged in work that will result in their learning basic algebra. The experience the elementary teacher has had in organizing students into work groups and study groups may be useful to the planning of the high school teacher who knows that his or her students want to work together but that when they do, it almost always turns out that one or two students take over the completion of the task.

In such conversations an observer is more likely to hear "what if" questions than "yes, but" statements. There will be honest consideration of questions like: What is going on in the classroom? What would lead students to want to do this work in the first place? What qualities are built into the work and are these the qualities that the students in this class are likely to care about?

Presently, few teachers are very experienced with such nonevaluative conversations. Evaluation and defensiveness, rather than analysis and expansiveness, are characteristic of all too many conversations among teachers about teaching. Furthermore, it has been my observation that the closer a conversation comes to dealing with the realities of a particular classroom and a given teacher, the more evaluative and defensive the conversation becomes. For example, on numerous occasions when my colleagues and I have been demonstrating how the WOW framework might be used to analyze classrooms, we have taken as illustrations classes that are exemplary of the best of today's practice. For example, we often use videotapes of Kay Toliver, who is by nearly everyone's reckoning an outstanding teacher. In the process of the analysis, it usually becomes clear that although the work provided to her students has many of the attributes of quality work, there are possibilities for improvement. When these are pointed out, there is a tendency for teachers to say things like, "I don't care what you say, that is still a good lesson," or, "That is not fair; look at all the good things the teacher has done." The prevailing focus on the ideas of contest and performance standards, as opposed to dialogue and learning standards, causes at least as much difficulty for teachers as it causes for students.

Dialogue proceeds from mutually determined rules and from mutually determined frameworks. Dialogue assumes that all parties to the conversation are at risk of learning things they do not know. One of the advantages of the WOW framework is that it fastens attention on what students are doing and what students are expected to do rather than on what the teacher is doing and what the teacher is expected to do. This takes the teacher and the performance of the teacher off center stage and places the work provided to students at the center of the conversation. This does much to reduce teachers' defensiveness and increase their engagement in the conversation.

It is an unfortunate fact that the role expectations of teachers in the typical school encourage teachers to be judgmental and impatient with analytical conversations. Teachers typically find it difficult to be involved very long in a conversation about a class before words like *good, bad, exciting,* and *dull* begin to be uttered. When asked to explain the bases of such evaluative statements, teachers will often point to the effects of the teaching; they will note that students seemed to be engaged, or attentive. When asked what it was that led the students to be attentive, teachers will often respond that "the teacher made the classroom interesting." When asked how that was accomplished, some begin to drop out of the conversation. After all, everyone knows the answer to that question. But do they? If teachers (or any others) do have pat answers to this question, why is it that we have so many students who are less than authentically engaged in the work they are provided?

Providing a Frame for Principal Leadership

Evaluation is one of the most potent instruments available to any leader in any organization. Because it is so potent, evaluation has great potential for harm as well as for good. Conducted in an adversarial environment, evaluation creates defensiveness and resistance. Conducted in an environment where the attitude of dialogue is absent, evaluation implies that the person doing the evaluating has superior knowledge, superior skill, or at least superior authority compared to the person being evaluated. Such evaluations also encourage defensiveness and animosity. Conducted in an environment of trust and in an atmosphere that supports dialogue, evaluation can be productive and useful.

In most schools, principals are expected to evaluate teachers, and this fact sometimes clouds the relationship between teachers and principals. The relationship becomes even more troubled when principals are required to use *behavioral checklists* in evaluating teachers' performances. One reason for these difficulties is that teaching today is based on a mastery model rather than a continuous improvement model. It is assumed that teaching is a craft that can be mastered, just as cabinetmaking is a craft that can be mastered and surgery is a set of techniques and skills that can be mastered. The result of this view is that experienced teachers become defensive over any negative feedback about their performance, for to accept such feedback as legitimate would be to acknowledge that mastery is not present.

Principals too are affected by the present relationship they have with teachers. Often principals are charged with not being sufficiently "hard-nosed" in their evaluations, a charge that is probably more true than most principals would care to admit. If it is so, it is also understandable. As one principal put the matter, "If you aren't ready to fire [experienced teachers], then you had better leave them alone. The central office might not like it, but I have to live with these people next year." This principal went on to say that union contracts and the timidity of school boards also made firing difficult and perhaps not worth the effort.

The result is that evaluative conversations between experienced teachers (the case of inexperienced teachers is somewhat different) and principals are typically either shallow and filled with pious platitudes or acrimonious and accusatory. It is rare for principals to work out ways to both go beyond platitudes and avoid acrimonious interactions. Thus the evaluation system that exists in schools almost foreordains that most efforts to evaluate teachers result in little improvement in either teacher or student performance.

The WOW framework, in the hands of a knowledgeable and skilled principal, can do much to alleviate this situation. Rather than observing the classroom to see how the teacher is performing, the principal observes the classroom (and perhaps interviews students and reviews assignments as well) to determine the extent to which students are engaged, persist, and experience a sense of accomplishment and satisfaction as a result of what they are asked to do.

The conversation with the teacher is then one in which the effort is to verify whether what the principal perceives about student engagement, persistence, and satisfaction squares with what the teacher perceives. If it does not, both teacher and principal need to invest time in a dialogue to determine how a more accurate and verifiable view might be developed.

The power of the WOW framework is that it assumes that even though not all teachers can be great performers, all teachers can design work that will engage students in activities that will result in students' learning from the work they do. The WOW framework also assumes that Working on the Work is a collegial endeavor as well as an individual responsibility. Continuous improvement begins at the top. If the principal is to help teachers improve what they do, the principal must continuously be learning to improve what he or she is doing. In schools, where providing quality work for students is "Job 1," the job of the principal is to learn and to help others learn how that job can be done.

The quality of the work provided in every classroom is the responsibility of the principal as well as of the teacher, and each should have an investment in ensuring that each day each student receives quality work to do. Principals who know what quality work is and how to design it and do not help teachers with this task are not doing what principals need to do. Principals who do not know what quality work is and how to design it do not know enough to be principals.

USING THE FRAMEWORK TO GUIDE STAFF DEVELOPMENT

There are at least two ways the WOW framework might be used to guide staff development in schools. First, the framework can serve as a content guide, indicating what might be taught and giving hints as to how this teaching should occur and by whom it should be done. Second, it can serve as a framework for designing staff development activities, just as it can serve as a framework for designing work for students.

A larger question the use of the WOW framework raises concerns the role that the teacher should be trained to fill in the first place.

Defining Content and Designing Development Activities

As a *content guide,* the WOW framework suggests much that teachers need to know and be able to do if they are to carry out their tasks. It is clear, for instance, that to identify and present content that is rich and well textured, teachers themselves must have a deep understanding of the content they are endeavoring to teach. This does not mean that teachers necessarily need to take more courses in history to teach history or have a Ph.D. degree in that field. It does mean, however, that teachers need to be provided opportunities to read books in their fields and opportunities to discuss what they have read with others who are similarly situated.

Similarly, the WOW framework makes it clear that teachers need to learn much about the attributes of engaging work. They might study affiliation, for example, by reviewing materials developed under the general heading of *cooperative learning* and through reviewing the research on this topic. They can also learn much about providing engaging tasks to students by observing colleagues who are especially adept at providing needed qualities to students (by protecting students from the adverse consequences of initial failures, for instance). Both teachers and principals need to be provided such opportunities to learn.

One scenario for such learning is that each month each teacher is invited to be prepared to share with colleagues at a staff meeting an example from his or her own class of the way one or more of the attributes of quality work has been built into the tasks assigned to students. This would serve both to affirm the importance of what the teachers are doing and to establish a way to share ideas.

As a guide for designing staff development, the WOW framework can also be useful. For example, one of the habits that needs to be encouraged in schools is the habit of reading. Generally, teachers and school administrators simply do not read enough, and what they do read tends to be written at a less-than-demanding level. In part, teachers and administrators do not have—or do not feel they have—the time to read. Schools need to be organized so teachers do have—or feel they have—the time to read.

It is also the case, however, that there is a certain mindlessness in the school culture and sometimes an implicit anti-intellectualism as well.[9] It has been my experience that those who read comparatively more are sometimes a source of derision among colleagues as well as a source of faculty pride. Too few teachers style themselves serious students, and those who do are most likely to be found in high school liberal arts studies like science, history, or English than they are to be found in kindergartens or special education classes. If this is typical, it is too bad, because some of the most profound material on teaching and learning is to be found in the area of elementary education.

However, a need to read is not likely to be encouraged by lamenting the mindlessness of schools and the implicit anti-intellectualism of some teachers. What is needed is a staff development program designed so that reading becomes a means of gaining things that teachers otherwise value, such as affirmation of performance and opportunities to affiliate with others, including superordinates. For example, a number of superintendents whom I know have developed "book of the month clubs" in which they read and discuss books relevant to education. The superintendents always participate in the discussions, thus signifying the importance each one attaches to the activity. Principals have developed similar groups, both with members of the faculty in their school and with other principals across their district or from other districts. Educators have a need for affiliation just as students do, and staff developers can use this fact to create engaging activities for both teachers and administrators.

One of the greatest challenges confronting those who design staff development activities is to make these tasks sufficiently compelling to teachers that they will engage in the sometimes tedious business of working through issues for which there are no readily apparent answers and for which all available answers have limitations. Some staff developers respond to this problem by becoming physical activity oriented—making sure the participants move around a great deal. Others adopt the pretense that teachers who complain about too much theorizing and not enough practical application or too much "sit and get" are probably not worth the effort in the first place.

To say that staff developers should practice with adults what they preach should be applied to children is only half right. As adults, teachers should also have learned what Working on the Work is intended to teach students: sometimes one must do a great number of things one finds uninteresting and tedious in order to gain access to things one cares about.

Defining the Role of Teachers: Three Views of Teaching

The view teachers take of their role has implications not only for what teachers do in classrooms but also for the way they plan what they do. More than that, the way teachers views their role goes far to determine whether or not they will see the WOW framework as useful to them in their daily work. At present, three views of teaching are dominant:

- The teacher as clinician
- The teacher as presenter of information
- The teacher as performer

The view of the teacher as clinician is widespread among educators, especially at the elementary level. The view of teaching as a clinical act, with heavy emphasis on diagnosis and prescription, is most common among special educators. Teaching in this view is often oriented toward behavioral objectives rather than learning goals. Indeed, assessing student behavior becomes the primary means by which learning is to be assessed.

Though the clinical view of teaching is most clearly present in the field of special education, others embrace this view as well. Madeline Hunter, who has influenced the thinking of literally tens of thousands of teachers and principals in America, has placed on the cover of many of her books and training materials the well-known symbol for a prescription, ℞.

Teachers who view themselves as clinicians tend to give a great deal of attention to the needs of individual children and endeavor to develop plans for instruction that are tailored to the unique learning styles and developmental needs of each student in the classroom. A clinical view of teaching proceeds from the assumption that the best kind of instruction is *individualized* instruction. In the language of special education, each child should have his or her *individualized educational program* or *plan* (IEP).

The view of the teacher as presenter of information assumes that the teacher is the primary source of knowledge in the classroom and perhaps in the life of the student. It is therefore the job of the teacher to transmit to the student that which the teacher knows and that which it is assumed the student needs to know. It is also important that this be done in the most efficient manner possible: quite frequently by lectures and activities that encourage memorization and quick recall.

Viewing the teacher as a transmitter of information leads naturally to the idea of the teacher as performer. This concept of teaching is deeply embedded in the thought ways of the American high school and to a lesser extent the middle schools and elementary schools as well. Teachers who have a flair for the dramatic, who are entertaining as well as informative, are highly prized both by students and by colleagues and parents.

Teachers who see themselves as presenters of information are likely to give emphasis to such matters as scope, sequence, and coverage. Given the learning objectives for which they are responsible, these teachers feel an obligation to ensure that the students *cover* each of these objectives, or at least follow along as the teacher covers these objectives. Such teachers often spend considerable time preparing demonstrations and planning to have students provide demonstrations. Demonstrations, after all, are the primary means by which skills are transmitted, and it is through student demonstration that the teacher is assured that the student has learned what is intended.

Teachers who view themselves as performers assume that if they give the right performance, the students will respond appropriately, so they spend much less time than does the clinician in figuring out what they want the students to do. What the performing teacher plans for and concentrates on is what he or she is going to do.

Defining the Role of Teachers: Teachers as Leaders and Inventors

Each of the views just presented has some merit. Teachers clearly need to understand students and their needs, and in so far as possible, they need to plan their classes so that they respond to these needs. Teachers are not the only source of information available to students, but they are a source of information. More than that, they should be mature and experienced guides to students who are just learning how to access and use information. There are as well some things that are better taught directly than caught indirectly—or so I believe. Finally, anyone who has spent much time around schools understands that the personality of the teacher and the way he or she performs make a considerable difference in what happens with students.

These prevailing views of teaching do not, however, concentrate the attention of teachers on what teachers need to attend to if they are to do well at the business of schools, which is to invent work for students and lead them to do that work. The clinical perspective transforms the school into something between a hospital and a mental institution. Analyzing behavior and seeking behavioral control become, implicitly if not explicitly, the agenda of the schools. Parents in many communities are uneasy with such a view, and some are down-right antagonistic to it.[10]

The presenter of knowledge perspective assumes that teachers have a relative monopoly over the knowledge students are to learn. If this was ever the case, it is no longer so.

The idea of the teacher as performer is also being challenged by modern circumstances. One need not be around the American high school long before one hears the complaint that teachers cannot compete with paid performers who have tremendous resources behind them and the time to exploit these resources fully. In addition, movies, videotapes, radio and television programs, computers, and other means by which information and performances can be communicated make the performances of master performers readily available to everyone. Teachers cannot compete in this arena not only because most lack the skills to do so but also because the support systems of professional performers are well beyond the capacity of schools and school districts to reproduce.

Teachers must understand that what they do—how they perform—is important to the extent that it gets students to perform as well. To get others to perform, teachers must develop professional expertise, but it is not the expertise of the actor or the entertainer. Rather it is the expertise of the *leader* who understands how context can affect his or her performance and performance requirements. It is the expertise of the sociologist and social psychologist who try to understand how groups and organizations shape and mold human behavior and how humans learn.

As part of this shift in their view of themselves, teachers will also need to come to view themselves as inventors of work for students rather than as clinicians who diagnose the psychological states of students and develop *intervention* strategies intended to somehow modify these states. Rather than motivating students, teachers need to be expert in identifying existing student motives and in creating or adapting activities that require students to engage intellectually important content as a condition of having their social and their psychological needs addressed.

Such a shift in the self-perception of teachers requires a shift in other areas of school life as well. For example, those who prepare teachers and those who design continuing education opportunities for teachers will need to be much more attentive to the literature on leadership than is now typically the case, and sociology and social psychology will play a much more dominant role in the preparation of teachers than they do now.

Learning theory and curriculum theory, which now dominate the attention of teacher educators, will retain an important place in teacher education. Learning theory is useful for helping teachers understand what students need to do to learn what they want them to learn. However, learning theory is not particularly useful in figuring out how to get students to do those things. To understand how a person gets others to do what they might not otherwise do, teachers need the social insight of the leader as well as the psychological understanding of the clinician. As Waller put the matter many years ago:

> Teachers . . . learn to teach by teaching. The teacher gets something from experience which is not included in his "professional" courses, an elusive something which is difficult to put between the covers of a book or work up into a lecture. That elusive something is social insight. What the teacher gets from experience is an understanding of the social situation of the classroom and an adaptation of his personality to the needs of that milieu. That is why experienced teachers are wiser than novices. That is what we must try to include in the regimen of those who aspire to be teachers.[11]

In a similar way, curriculum theory, when it is not learning theory dressed up in different clothing, has more to do with the ends of education than the business of schools. Curriculum theory is concerned primarily with what is worth knowing and when it can and should be known. Certainly curriculum theory is useful to those who are Working on the Work, especially with regard to Standards 1 and 2 (see Chapter Six). However, curriculum theory does not provide sufficiently powerful insights into how teachers get students to do the things they must do to learn what the curriculum intends.

Fortunately, since World War II and especially in the past twenty years, a vast literature has developed in the area of leadership. Most of this literature derives from the study of leaders in nonschool settings such as business and the military, but increasing attention is being given to conceptions of leadership in education. Unfortunately, with a few notable exceptions,[12] most of the effort to apply what is known about leadership to schools has centered on the role of principals and superintendents rather than the role of teachers. In the context of teacher preparation programs, teachers are still viewed as performers and clinicians rather than as leaders and inventors.

In the typical teacher education program, teachers learn much more about what they are to do and how they should go about doing those things than they learn about how they should go about designing engaging work for students and figuring out why the work they do design is sometimes not so engaging. Careful attention to the literature on leadership, especially leadership in learning organizations, has considerable potential for addressing this issue.

Viewing the teacher as a leader and an inventor, rather than as a clinician, a presenter, or a performer, seems likely to advance the cause of school improvement greatly. Like the clinical view, the idea of the teacher as leader requires that the teacher know and understand the needs of the students he or she is endeavoring to lead. Indeed, leaders who do not understand their followers and take their needs into account are likely to look back and find that no one has come along.

Like the presenter, the leader is sometimes the mature guide to information and sometimes the most efficient and effective source of needed information. Leaders do model and they do provide demonstrations. Indeed, much of leading is modeling and demonstrating along with some modicum of telling and directing.

Like the performer, the leader must establish rapport with the audience and must inspire affective responses as well as more cognitive ones. Leaders must inspire others to go places they think they cannot go and do things they think they cannot do. Leaders, like great performers, sometimes inspire flights of fancy and acts of imagination that could not occur without their presence.

As a leader, the teacher concentrates his or her attention on what he or she wants those who follow to do rather than on what he or she is going to do. In the context of teaching, it is understood that what the students do is much more important than is what the teacher does. The question that confronts the teacher is, How do I design the tasks, assignments, and activities I give to students or encourage students to undertake so that they will do what they need to do to learn what I want them to learn?

In addition, teachers who view themselves as leaders understand that for the most part, leadership and followership are best understood as group phenomena. Certainly the psychological makeup of individuals in groups makes a difference in the group, but just as certainly the makeup of the group shapes how individual differences will manifest themselves in the world of the classroom. For example, the class clown is more likely to be a disruptive influence in a classroom where the other students are not sufficiently engaged in their work to care if they are distracted or where they may even be seeking distraction from the work. The primary task of the teacher as leader and inventor, therefore, is to invent work for students that students will find engaging and then to lead them in the conduct of the work that has been created.

THE WOW EXPERIENCE SO FAR

As my colleagues and I at the Center for Leadership in School Reform provide technical assistance, training, and support to school districts, we find that when the WOW framework is consistent with other streams of action in the school, it is likely to be embraced and used (this is consistent with the view of systemic reform discussed in Chapter Two). For example, the assumptions underlying the WOW framework and those underlying Sizer's Coalition of Essential Schools are very compatible, and many persons who are involved with Sizer's work are using the WOW framework to discipline the *critical friends*[13] conversations used so much in coalition activities. When there is no existing system that accords with the framework, teachers and others tend to view the WOW framework in isolation from the ongoing business of the school and of teaching. They see it as just "one more project to implement" and "one more thing to be done." As a result, teachers may resist adopting the WOW framework as a guide to action, because they perceive that they already have more on their plate than they can digest.

Moreover, in the quest for accountability and standards, many states are developing policies that tend to distract teachers' attention from carefully considering what they are designing for children to do and that concentrate attention instead on what the students do on standardized tests. This leads to viewing the students, rather than the tasks prepared for them, as the product of the schools. This view of students as products creates considerable tension and confusion in the implementation of the WOW framework, because the framework views students as customers.

Another problem that confronts successful implementation of the WOW framework is the insistence by legislators and the academic researchers who advise them that innovations are to be embraced only once they have been "proved" to be effective. As Kanter observes, however, "Sometimes an idea stems from significant scientific and technical research, but just as often the need for R&D follows the idea (as in the development of technology that made colored paint stick to metal car bodies). What is always essential, however, is the idea itself: a concept resulting from new thinking."[14]

Given the conventional nature of most research-based educational programs (one is even labeled The Modern Little Red School House), it is unlikely that installing one of them will require significant changes in the structure or culture of the school. Indeed, part of the appeal of many research-based programs is they can be installed in existing systems with minimum support and only minor disruptions. Those that do require deep changes are likely to fail in school districts that are less than adept at supporting change.

The WOW framework clearly requires new thinking. It requires teachers to think of themselves as leaders and inventors rather than as performers and clinicians. It requires teachers to view students as volunteers and customers rather than as neophytes to be inducted into the tribe by powerful adult authorities. It requires teachers to renounce the notion that most of what affects the performance of children is beyond the control of teachers and schools and to embrace the idea that most failures in learning arise because the schools have yet to invent work that will motivate the student to expend the energy to do what needs to be done to learn what needs to be learned. Indeed, the WOW framework requires teachers, parents, and others to renounce the idea that individual ability is the chief source of variance in performance and to embrace the notion that effort and persistence are the primary source of variance.

Such dramatic changes in perceptions do not come easily. They require strong, persistent, and highly visible leadership. They require, as well, a great deal of coaching and new uses of time. Indeed, without coaching and time, the perceptual changes needed will not occur, and the cultural changes needed will not arise to challenge old habits of mind.

There is some research that tangentially supports the assertion that teachers who invent engaging work for students get better results than do those who simply perform for students or who are overly clinical and behaviorist in their approach. For example, some of the time on task research so prevalent a decade ago gives empirical support to the commonsense notion that if students do what the teacher wants them to do, they are likely to learn more. (What this research never did was to help teachers figure out how to get students to do what the teachers wanted them to do.) Similarly, that long stream of research that demonstrates the inferiority of the so-called lecture method for conveying new information to others and developing new insights in them supports the notion that in-depth understanding is not easily facilitated unless students are encouraged to actively engage the content to which they are being exposed.

But the kind of changes suggested by the WOW framework cannot be brought about on the basis of supportive research. The WOW framework is dependent on developing a cadre of *converts to the cause* whose personal credibility and willingness to take risks are sufficient to carry the day, and to change structures and cultures. Truly new programs call for truly new and different systems of support. Change-inept systems cannot provide such support. It requires support to make change-inept systems change-adept.

CONCLUSION

The WOW framework is not a program, and it is not a format for evaluating daily lessons. Rather, it is a set of ideas that can, if used carefully, help teachers make sense out of what is going on around them, and sometimes make sense out of what is not going on. It can also help teachers understand why things are as they are and thus provide increased control over learning situations.

The WOW framework can also discipline conversations among teachers and among teachers and administrators and can also guide the evaluation of programs and projects being considered for inclusion in the activities of the school. Finally, the WOW framework can be used as a guide for the development of staff development and leadership development programs.

It has been my experience, however, that the utility of the framework cannot be realized until teachers and administrators understand the importance of shifting the way they think about teaching, coming to see the teacher as a leader and inventor rather than a performer, presenter, or clinician. Such a shift challenges many of the tacit assumptions on which much of teacher education is based. It also challenges the basic beliefs that many teachers have about who they are as professionals and what it is that they do. This, indeed, requires a paradigm shift. Such shifts are not easy, and they are always accompanied by some pain and sense of loss. The leadership that is required to help people overcome this pain and loss in order to improve what they do is the subject of the next section.

Transformational Leadership

As Peter Drucker has observed, leadership is always important, but its absence is felt even more in situations of uncertainty and tumult.[1] There is perhaps no time in history when the changes in society have had such a powerful impact on schools as they are having in the present. Such change introduces uncertainty. Learning how to deal with uncertainty and learning to "thrive on chaos"[2] is the major challenge faced by most school leaders.

In this section my goal is to sum up what I have learned over the past forty years about leaders and leadership. The kind of leadership required to lead fundamental reform movements (transformational leadership) is very different from the kind of leadership required to make the trains run on time (transactional leadership), and it is the absence of transformational leaders, more than any other factor, that accounts for the slow pace of school reform. The chapters in this section are intended to offer current and potential leaders a better understanding of the leadership today's schools require.

CHAPTER EIGHT

Leading Structural and Cultural Change

Until the last half of the twentieth century, leaders in America were more concerned with building new organizations and creating new systems than with renewing and revitalizing old systems. Most industrialists, like Andrew Carnegie and John D. Rockefeller, were much more interested in creating systems that efficiently exploited natural and human resources than they were in developing and renewing these resources. Those who did give some attention to issues of resource development, as Henry Ford did, for example, were aiming mainly to ensure that the human and material resources they developed fit efficiently into the predetermined system of production they had created and intended to expand.

What was true of American business was also true of American schools. Beginning in the 1830s with the common school movement and continuing through the early 1900s and the high school movement and through the three decades following World War II, one of the dominant problems confronting educational leaders was managing expansion. The need for more money (capital) to support more schools and more schooling for more and more Americans undergirded nearly every aspect of the educational enterprise. And, as R. W.

Callahan has made so clear, those who designed America's schools and who conceived the systems that would come to dominate them were greatly influenced by those who originated America's industrial system.[1] The metaphor of the school as a factory was and is commonplace in the literature of education.

To be sure, there were critics who argued for reform in both systems. Sometimes these critics gained sufficient power to effect some alteration in the systems they criticized. For the most part, however, the structure and the culture of the American school system that were established between 1840 and 1920 continue to provide the framework of education in America today, just as the factory assembly-line model that emerged in America between the 1840s and the 1920s continues to undergird our present system of production. Like today's businesses, today's schools that are able to break the bonds these historical organizational forms impose will survive and thrive. Those that fail to do so are almost certain to perish.

PROCEDURAL CHANGE AND TECHNOLOGICAL CHANGE

Because the problems confronting past leaders were primarily problems of growth and efficiency rather than problems of quality and renewal, until recently few leaders in business or in education had much experience in leading systemic change. Even fewer were concerned with making the systems they led more adept at change. The kinds of changes with which organizational leaders have had the most experience in the past are procedural change and technological change, changes inherent in the new programs and projects installed in their organizations over the years.

Procedural change has to do with altering the way the job is done—usually the sequence in which events occur or the speed with which they occur. Sometimes procedural change involves nothing more than substituting one form of material for another. Changing a curriculum sequence so that state history is taught before U.S. history (or the converse) is an illustration of procedural change. Compacting an academic-year course into a five-week summer school course is another illustration. So is the revision of a reporting form or planning process.

Substantively speaking, most procedural change requires only minor adjustments in the system. When it requires more than that, it is likely to be rejected by the system. For example, when the summer school program is in fact the beginning of year-round schooling in the school district, considerable change in the rules, roles, and relationships that guide actions in schools and between schools and families will be needed. Unless there are systems in place to support such change, it is unlikely that it will even be attempted. If attempted, it is unlikely to last.

From the perspective of leaders, guiding procedural change is largely a matter of effective communication, monitoring, evaluation, and enforcement. The new procedure must be described and communicated to those who are to use it, through writing, workshops, and one-on-one conversations. To be sure, this communication must be persuasive, because old habits are typically valued no matter how inefficient they may be. It is also the case that in even the simplest forms of procedural change, those who must act on the change need to have some ownership of the change. Nevertheless, the complexity of this leadership task is relatively low.

After the procedural change has been communicated, some means must be established to ensure that the new procedure is properly implemented and that old patterns are not reestablished. Sometimes this involves nothing more than cursory inspection; sometimes it requires intensive feedback and support sessions. Much depends on how deeply ingrained the old procedure is, how much value employees place on that procedure, and how convinced those who must use the new procedure are that it will in the long run make their lives somehow better.

Successful leaders of procedural change also institute means of determining whether the change in procedure does produce the intended results and does not produce unintended and undesirable results. This step is often overlooked in educational settings. Even when evaluations are conducted, they are often conducted with an eye toward intended results and they ignore the unintended effects.[2]

One of the greatest dangers confronting leaders who are bent on procedural change is goal displacement, the inadvertent substitution of one goal for another. Leaders need to be clear on the goals they intend the change to serve. For example, airlines in their quest to be on time sometimes leave passengers standing at the gate who were late only because a connecting airplane from the same airline was late. Some airlines recognize the potential for conflict between goals and give gate agents considerable latitude in how the rules are applied. Other airlines become so obsessed with being on time that they leave customers standing at the gate even though the reason the customer was late was a late connection on the same airline. Procedural change that is not evaluated to ensure that it supports organizational values can over the long term distort those values.

Technological change has to do with changing the means by which a job is done: for example, switching from typewriters to word processors as a means of preparing a manuscript or switching from mercury thermometers to electronic thermometers as a means of checking patients for fever. In both examples the job that is being done remains the same; the means by which the job is done is all that is changed.

Technological change, like procedural change, requires leaders' attention to communication, monitoring, and evaluation. However, it also requires considerably more attention to training and support than procedural change does. People are likely to need new skills if technological change is to be implemented effectively. People cannot do what they do not know how to do. It is therefore the obligation of leaders to ensure that those they lead know how to do what is expected of them. Much of the best thinking about staff development in education has been associated with the implementation of technological change.[3] The research suggests that supporting technological change requires much more than awareness workshops; it requires as well opportunities for people to practice and to observe and opportunities to be coached and to coach others. When the effort to install technological change fails, one possible cause is that leaders have failed to appreciate and provide the quality of training and support that is required.

Another possible cause is that the technological change requires structural change too, and this requirement is overlooked or looked past.

STRUCTURAL AND CULTURAL CHANGE

In schools, procedural and technological changes are most likely to be introduced as projects and as programs. This does not present a problem so long as the requirements of the program or project are not too far outside the existing traditions of the system. For example, adopting a new textbook is a type of technological change. Because of the schools' long tradition of using textbooks, such adoptions usually do not cause major disruptions in the system. In cases such as textbook adoption or even the implementation of a new discipline code, the role of school leaders is that of implementers rather than inventors.

The task is to adapt or adopt programs and procedures within the system that exists rather than to change the system itself.

When the changes called for by a program or project are too far outside the traditions of the system, especially if they introduce a radically different means of doing the job or require a fundamental reorientation to the environment or to customers and clients, they have moved from the arena of procedural and technical changes to the arena of structural and cultural change: an arena with which educators, and leaders generally, have had less experience and about which there is less guidance from the research community.

When structural and cultural change is needed to support the new program or project, leaders must be attentive to this change and ensure that it is brought about. They must attend to the properties of the systems of the organizations they lead (including systems of recruitment, power and authority, and evaluation) at the same time they are attending to the technical properties of the new procedures and technologies they are attempting to install. Most of all, structural and cultural change requires that leaders communicate clearly and effectively a *picture* of what the new system will look like and the reasons why the organization needs to create such a system.

Not for Light or Transient Reasons

Thomas Jefferson recognized that structural and cultural change is a very serious business when he wrote in the Declaration of Independence: "Prudence, indeed, will dictate that governments long established should not be changed for light and transient causes; and accordingly all experience hath shown, that mankind are more disposed to suffer, while evils are sufferable, than to right themselves by abolishing the forms to which they are accustomed."

The fact is that people prefer habitual ways of doing things to new ways, and the deepest habits of people are embodied in the structure and the culture of the organizations where they live out their lives. When change begins to touch on these deeply held habit patterns and tacit assumptions, there is much more at stake than organizational efficiency and effectiveness. Careers are at stake, and feelings of personal worth are at stake, as is individuals' sense of social integration and belonging.

Structural and cultural change should not be undertaken lightly or often. Such change will have profound effects on life in the organization and relationships between the organization and its larger environment. Unless the organization is change adept, such change can be catastrophic as well.

The Cutting Edge of Ignorance

Because structural and cultural change is a rare occurrence in the life of organizations compared to procedural change and technological change, structural and cultural change is not as accessible to study and analysis as these other forms of change are. Therefore much less is known about leading structural cultural change in schools or in businesses than is known about leading procedural change and technological change. Leaders and followers alike are operating more on the cutting edge of ignorance than on the cutting edge of knowledge.

What we do know is that changes in structure and culture involve discontinuities and breaks with the past. Such changes are likely to be cataclysmic and profound in their impact. Structural and cultural changes define epochs in the lives of organizations and societies, whereas the less dramatic technological or procedural changes occur within epochs and are defined and given meaning by the structures and the culture that gave rise to them in the first place.

LEADING SYSTEMIC CHANGE

Structural and cultural change—that is to say, systemic change—usually involves procedural and technological changes as well. The introduction of structural and cultural change calls upon leaders to do all the things they must do to lead procedural and technological change and more. To lead structural and cultural change, leaders must be prepared to lead movements and to mount campaigns. It is not enough to manage people, products, and procedures; they must become masters at managing symbols as well.

The leadership required is transformational rather than transactional.[4] Transformational leadership requires the leader to embrace and cause others to embrace new and revolutionary assumptions. Transactional leadership requires the leader only to improve operational effectiveness based on well-established and commonly accepted assumptions.

Leading structural and cultural change calls on leaders to think systemically, to conceptualize connections between and among events, and to help others see these connections. At a more personal level, leaders must assure others that the abandoning of valued habits and the embracing of new approaches that reorganize and reorient work are not things to fear. At the same time, leaders must cajole, coach, and inspire hope. Most of all, leading systemic change calls on leaders to be wise and sometimes demanding but always to be supportive of and reassuring to those they lead. Such leadership is not simply a technical task; it is a moral task as well.[5]

Ensuring the Support of Others

The ability to recruit followers and to enlist their active support in the pursuit of group and organizational goals is the defining attribute of the leader. Those who have this ability should be among the most valued members of any group for they are the people who make things happen. Only persons who have this ability can hope to lead change that requires systemic change.

Such leadership ability is not to be confused with authority. People who occupy positions of authority in organizations have more opportunities to lead than do others, but being in a position of authority does not automatically make one a leader, and especially not a leader of systemic change. Through the exercise of power, those in authority can coerce men and women into compliance. Compliance is not, however, commitment. In the difficult task of bringing about systemic change, it is commitment rather than compliance that is required. Commitment is volunteered and must be earned. Commitment cannot be commanded or demanded. Generating commitment is the task of the change leader. Such leaders understand that leading an army of volunteers requires skills different from those needed for leading draftees.

Effective change leaders understand better than most that change, especially structural and cultural change, is a messy business involving considerable risk, the necessity for sacrifice, and the likelihood of setbacks. They also accept that it is normal and understandable for most of us to avoid risks, to shun sacrifice (though we admire the sacrifices of others), and to be discouraged by setbacks, sometimes to the point of abandoning the effort. It is for this reason that effective change leaders are so important to the process of change, for they inspire others to do that which they are unlikely to without leadership.

Among the key tasks of leaders are to ensure that in spite of fear and uncertainty, followers maintain a clear focus on the future and are persistent and constant in their pursuit of goals. Most of all, change leaders seek to ensure that the actions they take are strategic actions: that is, actions designed to produce a desired future state as contrasted with actions intended simply to relieve short-term pressures.

To accomplish these tasks, change leaders must be prepared to

- Develop among followers a clear understanding of the need for the change being advocated; a clear image, or vision, of what the change means for each of them; and a sense of urgency about moving the change agenda forward. *It is through the pursuit of this goal that a focus on the future is established and maintained.*

- Develop among followers a clear understanding of the anticipated results of the intended change, the means by which these results can and will be assessed, and the processes by which decisions on specific actions will be made. *It is through the pursuit of this goal that direction is maintained and that constancy of purpose is ensured for lasting change.*

- Ensure that the resources and technology needed to support the change are in place, the internal and external coalitions needed to sustain the change are established and supported, and the training and support needed by followers (and by the leader himself or herself) are available and accessible. Most of all, the change leader must ensure that the organizational structures and operating systems required by the new program or project are in place. *It is in this way that the capacity to act strategically is ensured.*

Clearly the pursuit of goals as grand and complex as these requires more than one leader. Structural and cultural change requires a coalition of leaders acting in concert over a substantial period of time. It requires what Margaret Wheatley has referred to as *leaderful* organizations: organizations that possess a leadership system rather than a system dominated by a single, powerful leader.[6]

Inspiring Belief and Using Beliefs to Inspire

People express their values as beliefs about what is good, desirable, and worthwhile. Such beliefs serve as standards for assessing the merit and worth of any effort to bring about or inspire change. Participants in the life of an organization feel inspired to change primarily when it becomes clear to them that their values can be more fully realized if a particular change occurs or that some important value or set of values is threatened unless change occurs.

Change begins with beliefs: beliefs about what the present circumstance of the system is, beliefs about what it should be, and beliefs about discrepancies between the way things are and the way they should be. It is important for leaders to understand these facts. It is even more important for leaders to understand that in leading change, beliefs and the symbols by which beliefs are expressed are among the most basic tools of the leader's trade and that they must learn to express beliefs in clear and compelling ways as well as to hear and understand others' expressions of beliefs.

Quite often, aspiring leaders who are trying to recruit others to follow them in some change venture fail because they do not take into account that others may not share the leaders' beliefs regarding the way the world should be. Even more frequently, aspiring leaders fail because they do not understand that even though many of their intended followers share the leaders' vision of the future, these followers do not share the leaders' sense of urgency about realizing this vision. Potential followers are often indifferent about what aspiring leaders see as a crisis. For example, at a time when critics are calling for radical change in the structure of schools and "break-the-mold schools," fully 75 percent of the teachers in America believe that "given the circumstances," the schools are doing about as well as can be expected.[7] Teachers believe there is a crisis all right, but as described in the previous chapters, they also believe the crisis has little to do with factors under their control.

Many of those who would lead school reform are equally out of touch with the beliefs of the lay citizenry regarding what is wrong and what is needed. Although most knowledgeable reformers understand that schools are being asked to do things they have never done, under circumstances that are unprecedented, much of the citizenry including many parents believes that the problem is that America's schools have lost their way. Change is needed all right, but it is, in their view, change that takes our schools back to the "good old days" when all students learned to read, all parents were supportive, and teachers and adult authority were respected without question.

Leaders who would move educational reform forward and put it on the path of continuous improvement must find ways to debunk this myth of an educational Camelot without being, or appearing to be, defensive. It is not enough to say that the schools are not as bad as ill-informed critics say they are or even that schools are better today than they have ever been (two sentiments to which I personally subcribe). Leaders must also acknowledge that schools are much further from meeting expectations today than they have ever been and are therefore in need of radical change if they are to survive.[8]

However, effective leaders must recognize as well that debunking myths is a dangerous enterprise. If old beliefs are eroded and new and more compelling beliefs are not offered to replace them, the result will be despair, apathy, and resignation to what is perceived to be an inevitable doom. It is critical therefore that change leaders be well grounded in the history of the systems they are trying to change and have a clear-eyed view of the facts. They must be prepared, as outstanding teachers themselves, to use what they know to create cognitive dissonance among potential followers. They must create doubt and uncertainty where ill-founded beliefs encourage indifference and self-congratulating or self-serving interpretations of events. Simultaneously, again like outstanding teachers, they must use the uncertainty they create to inspire others to reorganize their view of the world so that both leaders and followers can develop control over emerging events and not give in to hopelessness and despair.

To tear down the myth structure of schools without replacing it with equally compelling myths is irresponsible. Myths contain hopes and aspirations as well as descriptions of realities. Though they can be used to maintain the status quo, they can also serve to inspire action. Lincoln's Gettysburg Address, for example, stands as a monument to positive mythmaking. Standing in the midst of a battlefield of a civil war that even as he spoke was still tearing the nation asunder, Lincoln developed an idealized (mythical) vision of an America "conceived in liberty" (the slaves would not have said so) and "dedicated to the proposition that all men are created equal" (many women nowadays would object to this phraseology). Certainly, a case can be made that the ideas of liberty and equality on which our nation was founded did not, and do not, square with the facts, with our practice. Yet the fact is that because we believe we ought to believe in liberty and equality, women have received the right to vote, the Civil Rights Act of 1964 has been enacted, and the public schools are now integrated. Sometimes powerful myths are more likely to produce change than is an emphasis on reality.

Some of the great truths and principles by which our society aspires to live are conveyed in the myths we choose to perpetuate. One of the tasks of leaders is to ensure that myths are used not to conceal reality but to illuminate it.

In sum, great leaders must be great teachers. The basic materials with which they work are beliefs: their own beliefs and the beliefs of those they would lead. Among the first tasks of the leader is ensuring that followers are challenged to examine what they believe about schools, children, and the schooling enterprise. This examination should take place in the light of the evidence that supports these beliefs. It should lead to the reconstruction of beliefs as well as to the projection of the likely consequences of acting on them.[9] It is especially critical that teacher leaders and community leaders, as well as those who occupy positions of authority in the system, be confronted with this challenge.

Creating Concepts, Ideas, and Visions

Visions, in the language of leadership, involve pictures one carries around in one's head. Ideas and concepts can have properties similar to visions. It is not too much of a stretch, in fact, to think of a vision as a special category of concept. A vision is a mental image intended to organize or categorize experiences. Both visions and concepts function to give meaning to present experience and permit those who hold them to better control future experiences. Leading systemic change requires nothing more, or less, than that leaders develop and deliver an elaborate concept development lesson, the intent of which is to engage intended followers (in effect a leader's students) in activities and experiences that cause them to reorganize experience and make new, expanded, and improved meaning out of what is presently going on and what might be anticipated to occur. Once developed and shared, visions transform otherwise mundane activities into inspiring experiences. For example, in a vision-driven school, improving test scores may be transformed into the goal of creating a school in which each child succeeds at important academic tasks each and every day.

Effective leaders understand that realistic goals and measurable goals need not be uninspiring goals. Extending the previous illustration, effective leaders understand that not many teachers will fight hard simply to improve test scores. However, many teachers will sacrifice much to ensure that most students are successful and all students are more successful than they were. In a school staffed by such impassioned teachers, test scores are certain to improve.

In schools where many students are not learning much and most students are learning less than they could learn, the belief that every child can learn more than he or she is now learning, combined with the belief that it is the obligation of the school and the community to ensure that this occurs, produces a vision (a concept of school) that is obviously at odds with present reality. Such a discrepancy can inspire corrective action, or it can lead to conflict and denial. Whether improvement or denial occurs depends upon people's depth of commitment to the basic beliefs upon which the vision is based.

If leaders and followers sincerely believe that all children can learn more than they are now learning and if they sincerely believe that it is the obligation of the school and the community to ensure that students do learn more, radical change is likely to be the result. If, however, the belief is not strong and the commitment is not great, then the result will be a revision of the vision, making it all right to believe that many students are learning about all they can learn, even though what they learn is not very much or very worthwhile. When this happens, the honest leader should declare that leaders and followers have replaced the belief that "our school is a place where teachers believe that every child can learn more than he or she is now learning," with the belief that "our school is a place where teachers believe that some children learn something, sometimes, depending on factors that are largely out of the control of teachers and schools."

Finally, as this discussion has implied, a vision must be shared by all involved in the change. Without a shared vision, distrust among participants is likely, and factions and factionalism are certain to grow. In change initiatives where persons rather than ideas are the driving force, the fickleness of personal loyalties and the uncertainties of individual choices (leaders do move, die—or just get tired) make long-term commitment problematic and the quest for short-term advantage almost mandatory.

Common visions, like a common culture, create shared meaning and inspire shared commitments over time. Past leaders can continue to inspire action in the present. Why? Because they were a part of the vision-building process, and part of the vision is also part of their legacy. United Parcel Service, for example, uses leadership legacy as a means of ensuring continuity in a highly fluid and constantly changing organization. Among other things, company executives receive a copy of a book containing statements by the founder of UPS. The Walt Disney Company does the same sort of thing. No doubt General Electric will find some way to incorporate Jack Welch's views into its corporate vision, just as Alfred Sloan Jr.'s vision has shaped the views of thousands of General Motors executives.

Real change requires profound shifts in ideas and in sentiments. Charismatic men and women charging about on white horses can raise havoc, produce temporary order, and even bring about some change, but in the long run, this change will be suppressed. In spite of the democratic rhetoric of the Revolution, a continuing monarchist vision eventually gave to France first Robespierre and then Napoleon. For lasting change to occur people must change the way they see the world and the way they feel about it. It is the obligation of the serious leader of change to ensure that it is the new ideas, the visions, that are the focus of loyalty rather than the men and women who give voice to these ideas. Effective change leaders are intellectual leaders as well as leaders of sentiment and affect.

Articulating Mission, Goals, Assessment Needs, and Intended Results

Systemic change interrupts habitual ways of doing things. When habits are interrupted, confusion and uncertainty are the result. In times of uncertainty, people tend to revert to habitual ways of doing things and to seek out leaders who value these ways above the ways of the new order. This is the reason so many revolutions produce counterrevolutions of a most reactionary sort. Effective change leaders understand this tendency and do all they can to counteract it. They are extremely careful to articulate the organization's mission in clear terms, and they cause others to be clear about intentions and expectations. They translate the mission into goals, and they are fastidious about designing assessments to measure progress toward goals. They are clear about the results they hope the change will achieve, and they insist that others be clear as well.

They do all of this not only because they are concerned about results but also so that followers will have clear benchmarks to help them know they are doing things right while they are still becoming comfortable with the new definitions of the right things to do. Effective change leaders seem to understand intuitively that in the midst of change, definite information is limited, and they use whatever guideposts they can create to give themselves and others a clear sense of where the organization is as well as how it is doing in getting where it is going.

It sometimes escapes those who speak admiringly of visionary leaders that road maps are useless if all one knows is where one is going. It is important as well to know where one is presently located. The destinations described by visionaries are inaccessible if they and their followers do not have a clear idea of where they are presently located. Therefore, careful assessment of present circumstances and realistic appraisals of the prospects of advancement toward the objectives suggested by the vision are critical to effective leadership in the midst of change. It is such assessments that provide points of stability and calm in what can otherwise appear to be nothing more or less than pandemonium and chaos.[10] Without some sense of calm and stability, panic will certainly set in, and with panic often comes the counterrevolution and the emergence of an authoritarian leader.

Supplying Incentives for Change

Structural and cultural change requires unusual exertions of effort, unusual commitments of time, and sometimes considerable personal sacrifice. It is small wonder that those who try to lead serious change efforts frequently confront a great amount of resistance. Overcoming resistance to change is such a common problem, in fact, that it frequently appears as a topic on the agendas of seminars and training sessions for change leaders. However, overcoming resistance is only part of what leaders must do. At the same time, they must create commitment to change.

Encouraging others to initiate and sustain a change effort over a sufficient period of time to ensure that new habits are formed and new ways of doing business become institutionalized requires commitment building as well as barrier removal. Change leaders who attend to providing positive incentives for change are much more effective at creating such commitment, and along the way, they overcome change resistance as well.

The intent of incentives, of course, is to induce others to do things they might not otherwise be inclined to do. To serve such a function, incentives must promise to satisfy needs that are not presently being satisfied and to support or enhance values that are important to the person or persons toward whom the incentives are directed. The specific incentives leaders provide will depend on the context in which the leaders are operating, but several categories of incentives are available to the discerning leader.

Incentives that bring positive recognition and honor to the recipient are especially powerful. For example, persons who enlist early in support of a change effort might be afforded opportunities to report on their work at conferences or before community groups. Properly framed, such opportunities can be perceived as a perquisite available to those who are supportive of the change. Attentive leaders will find many similar opportunities to provide recognition. For example, they might ensure that visitors who come to the school are introduced to the teachers who are doing the most to advance the change initiative and that these teachers are also available as seminar leaders for peers and perhaps even superordinates.[11]

Given the scarcity of positive recognition in school environments, however, leaders must take care not to create unhealthy competition and jealousy. Positive recognition is a powerful symbolic incentive, but the reason it is powerful is the same reason it is dangerous in un-skilled hands: Positive recognition is a scarce resource in schools, and limited rewards lead to big fights over little things. Unfortunately, in their effort to enrich the schools' inherently impoverished reward structure, leaders sometimes get so carried away with the idea of positive recognition that a potentially powerful symbolic reward is distributed, somewhat as Pavlov distributed rewards to his dogs and Skinner to his pigeons. This is not only degrading but ineffective in the long run.

Followers know when the leaders are behaving in ways that suggest they find the followers callow, shallow, and somewhat stupid. Leaders who have integrity will seldom fall into this trap, and if they do, they will acknowledge the error of their ways to those who count most: those they want to follow them. Indeed, one of the most powerful forms of recognition leaders can provide to followers is to trust them even when the leader feels vulnerable, stupid, and alone.

A second category of incentives frequently used with effect in the school setting comprises incentives that enhance the followers' sense of personal efficacy, their importance to the enterprise, and the significance of the enterprise to others, including its significance to those who are perceived to be leaders. One of the reasons that management consultants like Tom Peters have so much positive to say about management by walking around is that the resulting face-to-face interactions not only provide the leader with a more accurate view of the world he or she is leading but also enhance followers' feelings of self-importance and the importance they attach to what they themselves say and do. The personal attention of leaders is a resource that is in scarce supply. Used strategically, this attention is a powerful source of motivation, but again, in the hands of the ham-fisted or the egomaniacal, such a resource can be dangerous indeed.

The critical point here is that the more skilled a leader becomes at providing direction to others and encouraging and supporting others in pursuing that direction, the more likely the leader is to generate the sense of involvement needed to inspire commitment to a change effort. Furthermore, an effective leader knows that the genius needed to move a change effort forward is more likely to be locked up in potential followers than in his or her own head. The effective leader knows that it is his or her obligation to liberate this resource in ways that are beneficial to followers as well as to the change effort.

A third set of incentives has to do with collegiality and what sociologists refer to as the *shared ordeal*.[12] Sociologists have long recognized the power of group affiliation as a mechanism for inspiring people to behave in heroic and self-sacrificing ways and to see adversity in positive and motivating terms.[13] Facing difficult situations with others can serve to strengthen commitment, whereas lack of collegial support can weaken commitment. Medical schools, some business schools, fraternities, and sororities understand the positive power of the shared ordeal, just as those who want to "brainwash" prisoners of war understand the power of isolation as a means of weakening commitment.

Effective change leaders do all that they can do to inspire a sense of collegiality. They miss few opportunities to symbolize that "we are all in this together," and behind the symbols there is substance. Change leaders take personal risks; they absorb the blame for failures of the group rather than scapegoating individual group members. They encourage followers to work together and do not tolerate "I said, she said, he said" conversations. And when such finger-pointing conversations begin, effective change leaders are prone to get all the actors together to tell each other what they have tried individually to tell the leader. The effective change leader does not play one follower against another, nor are such leaders easily co-opted by others.

One of the most effective techniques I have observed in promoting collegiality is reported by Margaret Wheatley.[14] The technique, which could well be an adaptation of the medical school morbidity and mortality conference, gathers all participants in a significant event together in a postevent session in which three questions are asked and answered: (1) What happened? (2) Why did it happen? (3) What can we learn from what we experienced? In the hands of a leader skilled in group facilitation, much can be learned through such a process. Equally important, such conversations reinforce the collegiality that leaders and leadership groups must share with followers if these leaders are to serve as effective sources of direction for significant change initiatives. Without trust and the interdependence that trust creates, bringing about real change while maintaining such values as respect for the dignity and worth of every person is nearly impossible. With trust and collegiality, and with strong and responsive rather than authoritarian leaders, the quest for excellence has an enduring foundation.

CONCLUSION

To make the changes that will ensure that schools can meet public expectations and become places where most students are successful and all students are more successful than they were, leaders must attend to structural and cultural change. To guide schools to become places that focus on producing work that engages students and that build community, leaders must envision new systems resting on new beliefs that can support these goals. The major skills and competencies that will assist leaders in this challenge are described in the following chapter.

CHAPTER NINE

Empowered Leaders: Questions of Style and Substance

It has been observed that major changes seldom occur in organizations unless somewhere, in the foreground or the background, there resides a monomaniac with a mission. There is more than a bit of truth to this observation. Just as too much can be made of the idea of great leaders, too little can be made as well. In the following pages, I look at the importance of both top-level leaders and shared leadership to the change endeavor and at the character traits and competencies among leaders that support strong leadership.

There is no substitute for strong leaders who know where they are going and who are committed to getting there. For a change to be implemented effectively in schools, the superintendent (or in the case of school building–level change, the principal) must either assume a clear and proactive leadership role or publicly empower others to function in his or her stead. It is unlikely that substantial change in the life of a school or a school district will occur until and unless the principal or the superintendent recognizes the need for the change and officially endorses and supports actions to bring the change about. Furthermore, there are few, if any, cases of substantial change in any organization—including schools and school systems—where there has not been an identifiable person whom others perceive as the chief advocate or champion of the change and to whom others look for direction, encouragement, and support, especially when difficulties arise, as they always do; when enthusiasms falter, which is certain to occur; and when courage fails, as so often happens. Significant change requires that change leaders be clearly identifiable and that these leaders be strong.

It is therefore absolutely essential that the person who occupies the top-level position in the organization undergoing change be very clear about the need for change as well as about the direction the envisioned change will take the organization. The top-level leader may also be the primary source of direction for the change effort, but if unable to take on this role, he or she must have the ego strength and confidence to encourage and permit another person to be the official change leader and to speak about the change effort and to lead it on his or her behalf.

THE SHAPE OF LEADERSHIP

Even when the changes called for are relatively minor in scope, the change process usually requires more leadership than any one person can provide, no matter how talented that person might be. Thus one of the fundamental tasks of those in authority is to understand the concepts of shared leadership and participatory management and to empower others to lead.

Delegation Versus Shared Leadership

Rational systems (sometimes called bureaucracies) assume that jobs can be rationally defined and that authority appropriate to the job's tasks and duties can be delegated to the people who occupy those jobs. Rational systems also tend to be centralized systems and hierarchical systems. In a bureaucracy one of the more frequently asked questions is, To whom do you report? Recognizing that no one person can carry out all the tasks that must be completed in a complex organization, organizations develop elaborate job descriptions. The idea behind such descriptions is to delegate responsibility for carrying out specific tasks and functions on behalf of the organization.

In the Weberian ideal bureaucracy, responsibility and authority are matched through a process of delegation: delegation of authority is supposed to accompany delegation of responsibility. Yet one of the complaints often heard in bureaucratic systems is that although responsibilities have been assigned, those "in charge" have not granted those who have the responsibilities sufficient decision-making authority to function effectively. Terms like *micromanagement* have been coined to describe the tendency of superordinates to interfere needlessly (and harmfully) in the work of those below them, supervising the way the work is done rather than monitoring the results of that work.

Another problem associated with bureaucratic models is that when authority *is* effectively delegated, the various bureaus, departments, programs, and operating units have a tendency to take on a life of their own within the organizational system, forming separate *silos* that cut vertically through the system. Often competition among these organizational units rather than cooperation then becomes the norm. Shared leadership is an effort to counteract such adverse effects of delegation in a bureaucracy without giving up the theoretical advantages the model intends to produce (coordinated action, relative autonomy among subunits, the creation and rational use of expertise, and so forth).

Shared leadership as I am using it here does not refer to equality or parity among leaders such as co-principals. It means that those who occupy positions of authority share with subordinates the responsibility for decisions that are made within the subordinates' unit and that subordinates can in effect borrow the authority of their superordinates in carrying out these decisions. The superordinates are responsible for the actions of the subordinates and also responsible for ensuring that the subordinates have what they need to carry out the task. Similarly, subordinates are responsible for the actions of the superordinate. Leadership and followership are viewed as a piece.[1]

Shared leadership recognizes the concepts of shared fate and shared accountability. Shared leadership requires a great deal of trust and confidence among the leaders and those they lead. It requires that leaders know each other and that all members of the leader-follower team have a reasonable assessment of the strengths, weaknesses, and tendencies of each of their peers. Most of all it requires fluidity and flexibility in determining who shall lead at any given time. As a group, the shared decision-making team is less like an orchestra, where the conductor is always in charge, and more like a jazz band, where leadership is passed around among the players depending on what the music demands at the moment and who feels most moved by the spirit to express that music.

Employing this pattern of leadership requires careful attention to the development of shared commitments, beliefs, and values. As discussed in Chapter Eight, systemic change begins with a careful analysis of beliefs and values. It is only after top leaders deeply understand the values and beliefs that will guide them that they are in a position to judge what kind of changes are needed and why they are needed. Those in authority, whether they are leading or following, consistently must seek to operate, and expect others to operate, in ways that are consistent with these commitments, beliefs, and values.

The Guiding Coalition

One of the first steps in bringing about change is the creation of a coalition of persons to support and sustain the change: what Kotter refers to as a guiding coalition.[2] The guiding coalition, as I described in Chapter Two, is not a random collection of persons. Neither is it a group representative of constituencies. Rather it is a group of individuals who among themselves have sufficient power, technical skill, credibility, and leadership skill to start and sustain action in the organization even in the face of adversity. More than that, this coalition is capable of acting as a team, and it is empowered to be in the forefront of the change process. One of the chief tasks of the change leader is the creation, development, and nurturance of this coalition.

Building the Coalition as a Team

Having identified persons who will serve as a guiding coalition for the change initiative, the official change leader's next task is to help this group learn to function as a team. There are many books on team building, and the number of consultants prepared to help build teams is legion. Indeed, there is probably not a public school system in America that does not have one or more staff members who have received specific training in team building and who are likely to be useful in a change endeavor. Therefore, this discussion focuses not on the details of team training but on some more general guidelines about the formation of groups.

First, it seems obvious that leading systemic change requires a sustained team effort. What is sometimes not so obvious is that team leadership and the leadership of teams are two different things. Teams that practice leadership need leaders as well: leaders of leaders. Without such leaders, teams will seldom even be formed, and if they are formed, they will not be sustained. Without strong individual leaders, few of the resources members bring to the team are likely to be deployed and used in ways that have maximum benefit to the cause being pursued. Rather than a team, what will exist is a group of individuals working in parallel; a collection of people acting independently side by side. Building teams, therefore, is an essential leadership act.

Second, teams do not form until the persons who are to be members of the team have a task to confront that causes them to function as a team. That is why team training without real problems for the team to confront so often fails. One of the mistakes sometimes made by specialists in group dynamics is to assume that group skills can be taught outside the group context. Until people develop the will to be a group, there is no group. After the will exists, then help in group dynamics can be useful. Group work is hard work, and without a will to stick together groups will fall apart.

Third, when teams run into trouble, expert help should be available to them, whether in the form of an outside consultant or a local expert. Instruction in such specific areas as conflict resolution has much more impact when the group is confronting a real problem in a particular area. Furthermore, in the hands of a skilled group facilitator, the normal problems confronted by a group as it is forming can be transformed into powerful learning opportunities.

Fourth, most of work that needs to be done to create a well-operating team has to do with developing concepts rather than with developing skills. For example, if the guiding coalition is to function as a team, team members must proceed from a common set of beliefs and assumptions regarding where they are going and why they are going there. They must also have a sense of urgency about their cause. This means that the top leaders of the change initiative must be especially attentive to encouraging team members to examine the beliefs that guide the change initiative and to come to grips with the assumptions on which the initiative is proceeding. There is, for example, a vast difference between a change effort that is motivated by a passionate commitment to the proposition that nearly every child can and should learn to read serious literature by the time he or she is nine years old and a change effort motivated by a concern that fourth-grade test scores are too low and something must be done to get them up.[3]

Influence, Power, and Authority

The words *power, authority,* and *influence* are sometimes used as though they were synonyms. This is unfortunate, for such usage conceals much that needs to be revealed if one is to understand leadership and the role of leaders in a serious change effort.

Leaders work through others. Leaders are properly known by what they get others to do and accomplish. What the leader does has significance only to the extent that others follow.

Influence, power, and authority are the primary mechanisms available to those who would get others to do things. Influence has to do with the ability to get others to do things by virtue of personal relationships or affective commitments that exist between leader and follower. This does not mean that those who exercise influence are always personally known by those who follow them, nor does it mean that such leaders are always loved by those who follow them. What it does mean is that leaders who have influence are trusted, admired, and seen as persons who can be counted on to make decisions that are not only sound but also aimed at the common good. Influence is important to all leaders, but it is crucial to democratic leaders and those who would lead in a participatory environment.

Power, in contrast, is organizationally derived. Power derives from the position one occupies in a social system and has to do with the ability to induce others to follow directives, carry out orders, engage in tasks, and mobilize resources. A person's power is based on his or her control of organizational resources that others need and value. These resources may be symbolic, such as the right to determine status through bestowing promotions or awarding honors, or they may take the form of remunerative rewards, such as salaries and bonuses. Sometimes power derives because the position a person occupies grants him or her the "right" to inflict pain, deny access, or limit mobility. (Etzioni, upon whose insights the preceding paragraph is based, calls this latter type of power *coercive power*.[4]) Persons who employ power occupy positions in the organization that make it possible for them to do so. Sometimes they are officially and publicly entitled to the power they exercise by virtue of that position. In such cases, these persons have authority as well as power, for authority is nothing more or less than the organizationally acknowledged right to exercise power on behalf of the system.

Of course there are also persons who have power in organizations who do not have authority, and quite often these persons use their power to become petty tyrants and gatekeepers. Who has not come across a school secretary who uses his or her control of the superintendent's calendar as a means of ensuring that others in the organization give the secretary the deference to which he or she feels entitled? There are also persons who have authority, but little power; for example, the superintendent whose school board has let it be known that his or her contract will not be renewed.

The critical point here is that leaders need not have power to lead, and all who have power may not be effective leaders. Leaders must, however, be able to exercise influence, for it is through influence that the work of leaders is done. Indeed, when persons attempting to be leaders find themselves reverting again and again to the use of the power to gain compliance with directives, it is likely that they are failing as leaders.

Power is a tool of compliance, but power does not generate commitment. Commitment is generated by and supportive of influence, and it is commitment that leaders need if they are to move systems into new arenas and invent new worlds and new modes of action. Given commitment, the exercise of power becomes an enabling mechanism; absent commitment, the exercise of power often becomes increasingly coercive and bent on compliance.

THE CHARACTER OF THE LEADER

Many of the scandals that have come to dominate the attention of the American press seem to center on the personal foibles of both elected and appointed leaders, and it has become commonplace to discuss the role that character should play in the selection and election of leaders. Character is an amorphous concept, and discussions of character issues and character flaws often do little to enlighten conversations about leaders and leadership. Yet I am convinced that in leading change, where symbols are so important and where people's uncertainty and fear increase their need to have confidence and trust in a leader, inattention to issues related to character is a sure path to disaster.

When I refer to character, I am not referring primarily to issues commonly associated with conventional morality even though such issues are important. Many of us have probably seen serious efforts at change set back because top-level leaders were less careful than they should have been in documenting their travel accounts or because some member of the leadership group became more interested in what he or she was doing in the bedroom than in the boardroom. In this regard the advice I once received from an experienced superintendent remains sound. His observation was to the effect that "anyone who tries to lead a serious change effort needs to be extremely careful about petty cash, personal use of the telephone, travel vouchers, the use of school board cars and property, and real or perceived intimate relationships with employees. When your opponents cannot get you on the grounds of incompetence or bad leadership, they seek other excuses to get rid of you." In short, change leaders, like Caesar's wife, must not only be virtuous, they also must appear to be virtuous.

Acknowledging the importance of virtues such as honesty in dealing with public funds, when leaders fail in these virtues, it is probably a symptom of weakness in other virtues as well, ones that are of greater concern in the selection of change leaders and that go to the core of a person's being. Furthermore, I have never seen a person who possessed these virtues who was not honest, careful, and decent in his or her relationships with employees. I have, however, seen many honest and otherwise virtuous leaders fail precisely because they lack these qualities:

- Integrity
- Persistence and constancy of purpose
- Self-awareness and ego strength

Integrity

Persons who lead structural and cultural change must be persons of unquestioned integrity; their word must indeed be their bond. Machiavellian tactics may work for a short while, and I have seen change leaders who were successful for a time and who employed tactics that made them appear to be among Machiavelli's prime students. One was even given to quoting Machiavelli and kept a copy of *The Prince* prominently displayed in his bookcase. In the long run, however, most Machiavellian leaders fail, for unlike Machiavelli's prince, they cannot have their enemies decapitated. They may be able to oust them from a position temporarily, but these enemies may easily show up later as new members of the school board or as de facto leaders of disgruntled teacher groups, parent coalitions, or other identifiable groups disaffected with the change effort. And regardless of where they show up, persons who feel they have been unethically treated will show up, and they will be heard! Those who become losers because of strategies they and others feel to be duplicitous are especially dangerous and prone to sabotage.

It is therefore essential that change leaders establish and maintain a reputation for openness and honesty. Even then, change leaders of great integrity will be subject to charges of manipulation and dishonesty, but as Alton Crews, former superintendent in Gwinnett County, Georgia, sometimes said, "Them's the fleas that come with the dog." At the very least, leaders who have a clear and deserved reputation for integrity will have some assistance when they need to scratch, and some trusting and committed supporters may even provide some flea powder.

Persistence and Constancy of Purpose

Change produces uncertainty, fear, and sometimes even paranoia. Change, especially structural and cultural change, sometimes creates in the organization a temporary state of normlessness, or anomie, and as Émile Durkheim has shown, normlessness is a dangerous condition for individuals as well as the organization.[5] Scholars in psychology and philosophy suggest that it is at such times in the life of nations (and, I believe, in the life of schools and school systems) that people are likely to seek the security of an authoritarian leader, for authoritarian leaders promise at least some security and orderliness.[6]

Authoritarian leaders are generally more oriented to the past than to the future. Their goal, most often, is to go back to a time that was better. The chaos introduced by substantial change is an invitation to the rise of such leaders. If an effort on the part of some people involved with the organization to revert to the past and to install authoritarian leaders is to be avoided, it is critical that those leading the change be, and be perceived by others to be, constant in their purpose, clear in their intentions, and willing to stay the course—even at some personal sacrifice and personal risk. Who has not heard in the midst of a change initiative the question: "Is the leader going to stay?" or, "What will happen when the leader leaves?" Those who are uncertain about the direction of the change are even less likely to commit to it when they are also uncertain about the leader's persistence. More than that, those who are opposed to the change will exploit uncertainty about the likelihood of constant and persistent leadership to encourage others to withhold or withdraw support.

As I have observed elsewhere, school districts generally lack the capacity to ensure continuity of direction.[7] This is due not to character flaws in those who lead schools but to the governance structure of schools. Until this structure is changed to support continuity and persistence in leadership, it is unlikely that many leaders who possess the qualities described here will survive long enough to lead the changes they intend to lead. The way schools are now organized, those who are most likely to gain a reputation for being effective change leaders are too often those who lack persistence and constancy of purpose. They are the principals and superintendents who have become known as turnaround specialists, and who come into a school or school district with a mandate to improve test scores. Styling themselves as hard-nosed leaders who understand how to make hard decisions, they bully the system and the people in it to respond. For a short time the system and people in it respond and the numbers get better, but in three to five years a plateau is reached. Sensing that more improvement is unlikely, these leaders then seek new employment in a different system, jobs they get because of their past record of performance and producing results, where the pattern will be repeated.

If one returns to the system that was turned around by such tactics, however, one typically finds a shambles of demoralized faculty and declining test scores. And one of the consequences is that the successor to the Rambo-style leader is likely to be dismissed because he or she fails to continue the "great progress" of the predecessor.

Systems that do not honor and encourage leaders who have integrity and who are willing to persist when the going is toughest get what they deserve. It is, however, the children who suffer.

Self-Awareness and Ego Strength

I am not a psychiatrist, Freudian or otherwise. Therefore, I do not use the terms *self-awareness* and *ego strength* in any specialized way but in the senses that laypeople commonly use them. I use these terms to communicate the fact that change leaders, if they are to be effective, must understand who they are, not only within themselves but also to others. They must be fully aware of their own strengths and weaknesses, and they must also be aware of the strengths others expect them to demonstrate and the weaknesses others will not tolerate. Leaders are not simply who they think they are, they are also who others define them to be. Myth as well as reality define the leader; fiction as well as truth shape their lives.

The change leader who does not know the truth is likely to begin to believe the fiction. When the fiction is positive, he or she is delighted; when it is negative, he or she is devastated. What change-adept organizations need are leaders who have the capacity, through persistent action, to rewrite the fiction when it is negative and to resist taking too much personal credit for the fiction when it is positive. Change leaders who believe unquestioningly in their press clippings, good or bad, are not likely to be effective leaders in the long run.

Change leaders who lack self-awareness and who also have weak egos are especially likely to be ineffective in the long run, especially if the weak ego is also a big ego, for then it is in need of constant feeding. Those who need to have their own importance confirmed and their own contributions recognized and lauded should not take on the task of leading serious structural and cultural reform. In the short run, leaders of structural and cultural change are more likely to be criticized than they are to be praised; they are more likely to be cut down than elevated.

Leaders with weak egos are likely to spend too much of their time and staff time responding to critics, behaving defensively (for instance, expending vital resources to employ "spin doctors"), and doing all manner of things to ensure they receive the credit they feel they deserve. Monomaniacs may be needed in the leadership structure of a serious change effort, but these megalomaniacs are deadly. Yet the line between monomania and megalomania sometimes seems a fine one.

Effective change leaders understand the necessity of keeping their necessarily big egos behind their work rather than in front of it. Their egos are not only big, which they must be if leaders are willing to lead, they are also strong and relatively self-sustaining. The feedback these big but strong egos need is the feedback they receive when the data indicate that the organization is closer today to the vision the leader aspires to than it was yesterday.

Because they have strong egos, these leaders are also in a position to give away success and absorb failure; those with weaker egos are prone to absorb success and give away failure. Effective and strong change leaders understand that subordinates, especially those who are less secure and less committed, need as much credit as they can get for whatever success comes about in a project. Furthermore, because these subordinates do feel insecure (after all, what they are trying to do may be unprecedented in their lives), they need as well to be protected from the adverse consequences of short-term failures. Leaders who are not willing to absorb the failures experienced by others or at least to share these failures are not going to be effective change leaders. Scapegoating, either up or down, is not healthy at any time, but it is devastating in the turmoil that surrounds a major change. Fixing a system makes it essential that leaders forgo fixing blame as much as possible, and when blame must be fixed, the effective leaders point their fingers at themselves, not at their followers.

WHAT LEADERS NEED TO KNOW AND BE ABLE TO DO

Given leaders with the requisite character traits, the question remains, What is it that change leaders need to know and be able to do? It is my view that what change leaders need to know and be able to do is shaped largely by the requirement that their attention be focused on developing within the systems they lead the capacity of that system to support and sustain the kind of changes they are endeavoring to produce, in effect to make these systems change adept.

Currently, the Center for Leadership in School Reform is developing a curriculum for a leadership development program that will enhance leaders' (and especially superintendents') skills, concepts, and understandings so their leadership initiates and sustains change-adept schools and school districts that will achieve uncommon results for all or nearly all students. That curriculum informs the following discussion of competencies and skills that leaders must possess if they are to be effective in leading structural and cultural change in our schools. It addresses competencies and skills in three categories of system standards: focusing on the future, maintaining direction and focus, and acting strategically.

Focusing on the Future

Effective change leaders see the patterns and forces that call for changes in schools and in communities, and they develop persuasive arguments and presentations for school personnel and community audiences in order to generate common understandings and common commitments to a significantly improved future.

COMPETENCY 1: MARKETING THE NEED FOR CHANGE. School districts and their leaders have traditionally focused on public relations—how to get the word out about the good things happening in schools and with children. Today, simply getting the word out is not enough. Instead, effective leaders come to understand their customers and the interests and needs that motivate them. That is, they come to understand marketing. They understand, for example, that younger, inexperienced teachers are likely to view changes they are expected to support differently from the way older, more experienced teachers view them. They understand that high school principals generally have a worldview that is different from that of elementary principals. They know that what parents expect from school is likely to differ from what business leaders expect and that parents will be concerned about aspects of a change process that will be of no concern at all to senior citizens and vice versa.

In sum, effective change leaders understand the concept of market segments, and they employ these concepts when they are developing strategies for communicating with various groups and constituencies. Change leaders also understand such marketing concepts as positioning and image. They understand, for example, that some symbols carry negative connotations with some market segments and some carry positive ones. They strive to associate their changes with symbols that have positive connotations and distance their changes from those that are negative.

They also understand that those who oppose their changes are likely to have similar marketing skills and will use them. For example, one of the favorite tactics of persons who are opposed to public education generally is to position any change effort undertaken next to ideas that have become loaded with negative connotations: for example, they might label a reform activity as one more case of "outcomes-based education" or as a "government intrusion."

Finally, leaders must listen to hear, rather than listen to speak. In other words, they must learn the skills of great teachers and see themselves as teachers in the community as well as teachers in the school.

Skills

- Learning the difference between marketing and public relations.
- Learning to segment the market based on different elements: for example, demographics, values.
- Identifying customers and the different needs that motivate them.
- Learning how internal and external markets differ.
- Creating marketing plans for different customers that enable the

leader to communicate the need for change to these various customers.

COMPETENCY 2: REFRAMING PROBLEMS. Frequently, leaders tend to look at and solve problems in the way in which the problems come to them. Because most problems have a way of reappearing, the solutions too are often the same disappointing ones that merely get dusted off for the next rendition. Moving out of this mode and producing real and sustainable change requires leaders to reframe problems so that they are compelling to those whose support is needed to sustain the change and responsive to differences in the audience being addressed and so that creative and innovative solutions can be developed.

To perform this critical function, change leaders need solid analytical skills. They must be skilled at asking the kinds of questions that reveal hidden agendas and that uncover difficulties not commonly seen. More than that, a leader must be able to conceptualize solutions to the problems identified in ways that can be articulated in relatively simple and clear terms yet are sufficiently profound to encompass the complexities that must be addressed if the change is to be effective. For example, it is commonplace for teachers to argue that one of the major problems confronting schools is that class sizes are too large. An effective change leader will try to reframe this problem in more manageable terms. For example, it can be argued that the problem is not class size. Reducing class size is a proposed solution to a more basic organizational problem: teachers do not have enough time, and students do not get enough individual attention. That is the problem. If teachers were encouraged to consider new and different ways to use time, organize space, employ technology, and organize and deploy people (adults and children alike), they might well invent solutions to the time and attention problem that would be much more satisfying than reducing class size.

It is the role of the change leader to frame problems in this manner and to ask "what if?" questions and to discourage "yes, but" responses. The change leader learns to take the obvious question, such as, Why do so many Hispanic students drop out of school? and ask the opposite, Why do so many Hispanic students who appear to come from precisely the same circumstances as those who are prone to drop out stay in school and succeed academically? They learn to observe what is not said, as well as what is said; and what is not done, as well as what is done. In sum, effective change leaders develop the skills that academics sometimes associate with *action research*.

Skills

- Learning what data to collect, and using these data analytically to ask questions and reframe problems.
- Looking for "aha"s (innovative ideas) from other industries.
- Identifying trends—for example, in demographics—and rethinking what these trends might mean.
- Understanding the differences among procedural, technological, and structural and cultural change, and knowing which kind of change a problem solution requires.

COMPETENCY 3: CREATING A SENSE OF URGENCY. It is not enough to market the need for change; the leader must also create a sense of urgency that moves the organization from complacency to action. Reframing the problem is one way to do this. Once people have a sense of urgency, the need for change overcomes their resistance to change and their comfort with what is known.

Skills

- Learning what strategies to use to create a sense of urgency.
- Identifying and using these strategies without causing employees to "shut down" out of fear and uncertainty.

COMPETENCY 4: BUILDING A SENSE OF COMMUNITY. Another critical role that the change leader in schools plays is that of community builder. This means being proactive in building a sense of community among those inside and outside the school and helping others come to understand the role education plays in preserving our society and economy and to recognize the need for the community to provide support for children that encourages them to engage the schoolwork that their teachers provide and successfully pursue substantial, intellectually demanding tasks and activities. With increasing numbers of community members not tied to the school or district, leaders need to think carefully about the needs and values that should be tapped to gain these citizens' support of the success of all students.

Skills

- Learning strategies to engage the community in useful dialogue and inquiry rather than in debilitating debate and confrontation.

- Becoming viewed as the chief executive officer who is the convener of community groups on behalf of educational matters that are important to the community.
- Collaborating with leaders of other youth-serving organizations and developing common understandings about the current and emerging needs of students that must be addressed if schools are to ensure that students learn what schools, parents, and communities expect.

COMPETENCY 5: FORGING COMPELLING BELIEFS AND COMMUNICATING VISION. It seems that every book for leaders calls for those in positions of leadership to create a vision and communicate it every day and in every way. Too often the creation of a vision becomes hooked into some step-by-step process that results in a vision developed by a group and not having much to do with organizational life. Vision, as I discussed in Chapter Eight, emerges from a set of compelling beliefs and provides meaning for the beliefs. Beliefs indicate a direction for action. It is critical for leaders to be able to gain the commitment of all those whose support is needed to the beliefs and vision. Although this does not mean that all those involved in the change must come together to develop a set of beliefs and vision, it does mean that all the constituents need to know how their needs and views fit within and are taken into account in the beliefs and vision.

Within the context of school reform, the effective change leader will be prepared to answer such questions as these about beliefs:

- What is the primary purpose of schools? What ends should schooling serve, and whom must the schools satisfy? When there are conflicting needs and expectations, whose expectations will take priority and why?
- Do I really believe that all children can learn and that every child can learn more than he or she is now learning in school? If so, what is my obligation when children fail to learn or when the learning of children fails to improve on a continuous basis? If I do not believe that all children can learn more than they are now learning, why am I trying to change anything?
- What do I believe about the primary sources of variance in learning? Do I believe that most of these sources are under the control of the schools?
- Given the changes that have occurred in family life and community structures, what should be the role of schools in providing moral

and civic education? Is it the job of the school to reflect the social order or should educators, in cooperation with parents and other community members, purposefully try to shape the future as well? If the work of people in an information-based society requires employing ideas, concepts, symbols, and abstractions to solve problems, produce products, and deliver services, what are the implications for curriculum and instruction?

• What is the proper focus of school activity? Are public schools public simply because they are supported by tax dollars, or is their public nature derived from serving public purposes such as providing children with a civic education and developing their sense of the common culture? Is it possible and desirable to focus the attention of the school on students and the common good, or should the particular interests of other constituencies (business interests, religious groups, organizations representing racial and ethnic groups) be of equal importance and of equal concern?

• What do I believe about the relationship between schools and parents, schools and families, and schools and other community agencies? Do I really believe that parents are—or should be—partners, or are parents only partners when they do what I and those who support me want them to do? What do I believe about the relationship between the schools and those parents who want forms of education for their children that I believe are inappropriate or potentially harmful to the child and to the larger society? What kind of relationships should the school have with other child- and youth-serving agencies, and by what rules should these relationships be governed and what system—for example, a collaborative—should be created? What responsibility does the district or school have in serving as the chief advocate for children and their needs?

• What do I believe about the obligation of the district or school to its employees? Do I believe, for example, that the continuing nurturance, training, and development of employees are critical? If so, do I believe the district or school ought to provide resources to support this belief or is development and training largely a matter to be left up to the individual and accomplished at the expense of the individual?

A leader who has taken the time to think through his or her answers to questions such as these and has bothered to test these answers on others is much more likely to be steady and constant when the inevitable difficulties and crises that confront change efforts emerge. I have observed that change leaders who waffle under fire usually do so because they do not know what they believe about these important matters. It is also sometimes the case that the waffling leader does know what he or she believes in, and it is personal status and survival in a particular job that causes the waffling. Such leaders are not only ineffective, they are harmful as well.

When it comes to the vision, imagining what the world would look like if it were organized in ways that were consistent with one's beliefs, it is important for leaders to know that although they may be visionaries themselves, they need not be. What is important is that they can articulate visions and inspire others to act in terms of the vision, even though sometimes these will be the visions of others who are less articulate, less credible, or less powerful. To fulfill this important function, leaders must become skilled in managing symbols and symbolic expressions, especially expressions that convey inspiring images and pictures to others. Leaders must learn to speak to the heart as well as the head.

The most effective change leaders I have known, in education and elsewhere, made extensive use of allegories, metaphors, and word pictures. Many of them were very familiar with classical literature such as the works of Shakespeare and the Bible and with the writings of profound thinkers in the field of education such as John Dewey, Alfred North Whitehead, and Bertrand Russell, and the listener could hear the literary and scholarly refrains in the background and the deep structure of the arguments, just as one cannot miss the sounds and rhythms of the King James Bible in Lincoln's Gettysburg Address, and Dr. Martin Luther King's "I Have a Dream" speech. They sought both the common ground and the higher ground. Their language was understandable to the audiences they were addressing, but the thoughts expressed took audiences beyond where they were and helped them see how far they might go. The words they chose were chosen to communicate and to inspire rather than to impress and awe.

These are skills and understandings that can be learned. One of the things that helps, I believe, is a habit of reading and thinking about great literature, inspiring novels, and other rich cultural experiences, including multicultural experiences, that takes one out of one's comfort zone and into a world that must be understood on its own terms and in its own way.

To speak metaphorically, leaders must learn to think metaphorically. Metaphorical thinking begins with a "what if?" question: for example, What if we thought about the school as an airport? Where would the control tower be? The principal's office? If the principal's office is the control tower, what are the classrooms? Are they free-flying aircraft? Who are the teachers? Are they pilots or flight attendants? If the teachers are flight attendants, who is the pilot? Maybe there is no pilot, and that is why there are so many "crashes" in schools. Maybe the control tower has faulty radar. Such thinking, along with the discussion it invites, allows leaders to open up for themselves and for others possibilities that were unrecognized and to identify problems that might otherwise remain concealed.

Of course not all metaphors help, and sometimes they can be misleading. The discerning leader must never become enslaved by any of the symbols or metaphors used to express visions.

Skills

- Getting clear about the questions, What is our business? Who are our customers? and, What are our services and products?

- Developing strategies for forging a set of compelling, comprehensive, and clear beliefs from which the district can act and to which diverse constituencies can commit.

- Developing guiding coalitions to support the leader in focusing on the future.

- Developing an array of communication techniques that ensure the beliefs and vision are always articulated in all things the leader does and says.

Maintaining Direction and Focus

Restructuring a system requires repurposing and the development of new commitments throughout the organization. The challenge for school leaders is to develop at all levels in the organization a commitment to focus on customers, on quality products, and on quality work. To maintain direction and focus leaders must develop systems to ensure that the actions and decisions that take place every day—at board meetings, at school councils, at departmental sessions, at the central office—are congruent with the district's or school's beliefs and vision.

COMPETENCY 6: ORGANIZING ALL DISTRICT AND SCHOOL ACTIVITY AROUND THE WORK OF STUDENTS. Among the leader's foremost roles is to ensure that everyone knows and understands the core business of the organization. Without a clear focus on that business, even the well-intentioned are likely to be side-tracked into adopting or buying programs that do not serve the core business. The core business of schools involves organizing all activity around students and the work of students. It means that students are provided high-content, engaging work from which they will learn what schools, parents, and communities expect. This significant shift in the work of schools requires the leader to keep a deliberate focus on maintaining the new direction.

Skills

- Getting clear about the questions, What is our business? Who are our customers? and, What are our services and products?

- Putting in place systems from induction systems to performance systems to professional development systems that focus on the work of students.

- Telling stories—at board meetings, at leadership sessions, at professional activities, at building-level events, at PTA meetings—about student work.

- Eliminating district policies, programs, procedures, and practices that get in the way of organizing schools around the work of students.

- Abandoning programs that do not focus on improving the work of students.

- Creating or adopting and then using measures to assess customer satisfaction. Measures might answer such questions as these: Do students find the work that they are provided satisfying, challenging, and interesting? Are students engaged in the work that they are assigned? Do students stick with the work they are assigned even when it is tough? Do parents believe that their children are safe and happy in schools and learning what they need to know and be able to do? Does the community believe students are learning what they need to know and be able to do?

COMPETENCY 7: FRAMING NEW ROLES. Today, the school superintendent is often leading the largest business in the community or one of the largest; yet often the superintendent is neither thought of nor treated as a chief executive officer. Why not? As school districts and schools begin to make the changes envisioned through Working on the Work, roles of all in the schools must shift in significant and challenging ways. The shift must begin with the superintendent as he or she takes on the role of CEO.

Skills

- Posing questions, and making this activity more commonplace than solving problems.
- Reading beyond the typical educational journals, and making this reading part of a weekly routine.
- Developing an ever deeper understanding of the change process, and acting on that deeper understanding.
- Devoting time and resources to the support of people's developmental needs, and ensuring that the organization maintains direction and focus. Practicing these skills becomes a significant aspect of the superintendent's work week.
- Causing problems to be solved in ways that are congruent with the system's new beliefs and vision.

COMPETENCY 8: USING ASSESSMENT AND MANAGING BY RESULTS. Leaders must lead by focusing on results that satisfy a set of compelling beliefs and vision. To create a culture in which results are valued and beliefs provide direction, those who occupy official leadership positions in schools must learn to manage by results and to cause others to be results-oriented as well. Thus skill in assessment and the ability to define results in publicly verifiable and measurable terms are essential to ensuring that progress is made and direction is maintained. Even visionary leaders can be diverted from their larger goals by pressing day-to-day concerns, and even the best-conceived plans can go awry and lead in directions both unwanted and unintended. Leaders who are committed to assessment and who are skilled in thinking about measurable indicators of results that will get them where they want to go are less apt to go astray.

As I mentioned in Chapter Eight, assessment is especially important in determining where one is. The refrain, "You can't get there from here," is often heard in educational reform, precisely because leaders sometimes have a much clearer picture of where they are going than they do of where they are. Clearly assessing the organization's capacity to support and sustain change is critical to the change process.[8] Developing and implementing plans to overcome deficiencies in these capacities is critical to the change process, and leaders who do not understand this and attend to it are certain to fail.

Assessment and attention to results are critical in other ways as well. Without a clear conception of what results should be measured and of how these results might be measured, there is little chance that direction can be maintained. Lack of imagination in developing this conception is certainly one factor accounting for the failure of many efforts to change our schools. Furthermore, leaders must understand that the results the organization must have to survive (profit in business, student achievement in schools) are seldom the results to which people in the organization must attend day to day if they are to produce these bottom-line results. I have never seen bottom-line leaders who are very successful in the long run, for what happens at the bottom line (whether measured in student achievement or profit and growth) depends in large measure on how leaders lead above the line.

For example, the organization I lead, the Center for Leadership in School Reform, is envisioned in part as a dependable and responsive organization that responds to the training and support needs of educators who are leading school reform. This vision is based on the belief that those who are leading school reform need and ought to have access to outside sources of consultation, technical assistance, and other forms of support that are in short supply locally and needed only periodically. The achievement of such a grand vision is difficult to measure, though the bottom-line measure, does revenue match or exceed expenses, is clearly important; not-for-profit organizations cannot operate at a loss for very long. I cannot, however, lead this organization strictly by considering revenue; I must also lead it by attending to what our clients need, for that is how we generate revenue.

One of the things our clients need from us is responsiveness. This translates into some relatively clear and simple measurable results. When the phone rings in the office, it should be answered on or before the third ring, for example. Telephone messages should be responded to within twenty-four hours. Making sure these things are done and checking up on how well we are doing these things is part of the leader's role. Having real numbers (how many calls were not returned promptly, how many times the phone was not answered promptly) can give direction to our system.

Even leaders who focus on results above the bottom line must exercise care, however. People learn what is expected by what is inspected and what is respected. Fastening attention on answering the telephone promptly may be harmful if the intent becomes just to answer the phone rather than to be responsive to clients. A hurried "What do you want?" does no more to increase responsiveness than does failure to answer the telephone. In an intensely results-oriented system, such goal displacement is a constant threat. Similarly, on a larger scale, district leaders may institute programs aimed at achieving district goals, but the programs may take on lives of their own and those who run them may tend over time to manage by programs rather than by results and to modify or buttress the programs rather than assess whether the desired results are being achieved. Therefore results-focused leaders must be skilled in cross-checking, in conceiving and measuring varieties of indicators of the same results.

Skills

- Training and leading others to use a results-oriented framework.

- Creating structures—rules, roles, and relationships—that will cause an organization to become results-oriented.

- Designing assessments that measure not only the bottom line but above the bottom line, and using imagination in finding ways to measure such things as student engagement, persistence, and satisfaction.

COMPETENCY 9: ENSURING CONTINUITY. As the district or school forges beliefs and vision, understands the need for change, and focuses on its core business, it becomes increasingly important that the superintendent or principal works to put systems in place to ensure continuity of purpose. Achieving such continuity does not mean maintaining the status quo but rather giving innovations that hold promise to achieve desired results time to succeed and resisting pressure to abandon them before they are well tested. It also means that superintendents work with school boards to set a course so that any subsequent changing of the guard does not result in discontinuity of purpose (as discussed in Chapter Two).

Skills

- Developing knowledge about succession planning, and identifying how to apply this knowledge to critical leadership roles in the district or school.

- Developing and putting into place systems that ensure promising programs are not abandoned before they can prove themselves.

• Identifying private, public, or nonprofit sector exemplars of ways to gain the support of those necessary to effective succession planning and to keeping good innovations going.

Acting Strategically

Once the district or school has developed the capacity to focus on the future and maintain direction with special emphasis on the core business, then the official leaders must cause other leaders, including teachers, to act strategically on matters that will support organizing schools around the work of students. All the leadership competencies in this area require leaders to ask consistently and continually: How will this improve the work that we provide to students? and, How will this improve the conditions that enable teachers to invent high-content, engaging work for students?

COMPETENCY 10: INVESTING IN PROFESSIONAL DEVELOPMENT. "Leaders can't lead unless they read."[9] Although much of leaders' time and attention is focused on how to create opportunities for all employees to learn and develop, leaders' own development is often undervalued within the organization and by the community. Yet the pace of change and the turbulence of organizational life require every leader to continue his or her development in purposeful ways.

Skills

• Taking stock of one's own skills and knowledge about leadership, and ensuring time is devoted to learning and for reflecting.

• Identifying a few like-minded leaders with whom to communicate ideas, to share articles and books, and to grapple with tough issues, and becoming part of a collegial group that focuses on the future and the core business of schools.

• Talking regularly with persons who are in other sectors, to gain new ideas and tools for focusing on the future and maintaining direction.

• Reading regularly in fields other than education where changes are occurring rapidly that might affect the future of schooling.

• Asking others what they read and how they keep up-to-date.

COMPETENCY 11: ALLOCATING RESOURCES STRATEGICALLY. In most organizations, resources are interpreted as dollars. Leaders must broaden people's view of resources from dollars to people, time, space, information, and technology—all of these are resources. Additionally, resources are generally thought of as things internal to the organization. It is rare for those in the organization, including leaders, to think of the outside resources they might tap: for example, technology now provides access to information resources that not too long ago were prohibitively expensive or time consuming for schools to acquire.

How the leader and the organization decide to deploy resources is also critical to successful change. Resources and results must be linked. This means that resources continually need to be used in new and innovative ways, and leaders must be prepared to help the organization change old ways of doing business.

Skills

- Thinking anew about how resources are defined.

- Developing ways to access resources beyond the confines of the district or school: for example, collapsing traditional boundaries.

- Developing structures in the organization that encourage people to use resources flexibly to achieve results.

COMPETENCY 12: FOSTERING INNOVATION AND CONTINUOUS IMPROVEMENT. Leaders have a responsibility to create structures that support developmental activities. Most organizations, including districts and schools, can get so caught up in the daily grind that innovation is often fragmented, if not actually frowned on as inessential or wasteful or self-aggrandizing. Effective leaders create conditions in which all personnel develop the capacity to think anew in responsive and responsible ways.

Skills

- Developing means to ensure resources are allocated for innovation and continuous improvement efforts.

- Enlisting leaders from other sectors in the community to reinforce the importance of innovation and continuous improvement.

- Creating structures that enable individuals (trailblazers) to scout and try out things.

- Developing structures to support teacher leaders and other leaders throughout the system who undertake innovation.

- Developing ways that those in the organization can become boundary spanners—learning from other schools and other kinds of organizations.

- Creating a *kitchen cabinet* to consider how best to take advantage of technologies in order to improve the quality of the work provided to students.

COMPETENCY 13: EMPLOYING TECHNOLOGIES AS A TRANSFORMATIONAL TOOL. Effective change leaders know that emerging technologies are changing the way in which every organization does its work and produces products and services for its core business. The same is true in schooling, where technology can no longer be only an add-on to the everyday life of schools.

Skills

- Developing new understandings about the potential impact of private, commercial enterprises that are capturing students and delivering academic content in new and compelling ways.

- Demonstrating how new technologies help leaders do their work.

- Tapping into nontraditional sources to gain new perspectives on emerging technologies and potential applications, as well as on the ways young people are now using technology, in order to inform needed change in programs and the work provided to students.

COMPETENCY 14: FOSTERING COLLABORATION. District leaders have both the position of power and the responsibility to convene those whose support is needed if children are to succeed with their schoolwork. Such collaboration should be viewed as a district responsibility, a necessary action to call together those who can act on the issues that face children so that those issues can be better addressed and so that the schools can better do their core business. In particular, leaders are recognizing that creating partnerships and alliances with groups and agencies that have historically been viewed as adversaries (for example, alliances between school boards and the local teachers' union, between local businesses and schools, between public schools and private schools) is a growing need in education.

Frequently, however, when educators are invited to collaborate, their response now is an almost automatic yes, without exploring how the collaboration will help them achieve desired results. Scarcity of resources, for example, can result in alliances that are well intentioned but ineffective. Effective collaboration rests on well thought out relationships and understandings about what each organization is trying to achieve.

Too few educational leaders take seriously the need to study the realities of those groups and agencies with which they need to form alliances. Yet without an accurate perception of these realities, serious negotiation and collaboration is difficult, if not impossible. For example, too few educators seem to understand that not all—perhaps not even most—religious conservatives are committed to the agenda of the zealots who see public education as a handmaiden of the devil. Indeed, it may be the failure of educational leaders to recognize that religious conservatives have legitimate concerns about the effects of the secularization of American society (Alexis de Tocqueville had similar concerns) and about the role of schools in that secularization. Educational leaders, if they are to gain wide support of those in the community, need to stop trying to address the zealots and to start trying to address the audiences to whom these unsavory types are trying to appeal.

School prayer, for another example, is a symbolic as well as a legal issue. Leaders who treat such issues as simply legal quarrels miss the point and are almost certain be at a disadvantage in what some see as the coming "culture wars." Similarly, too few educators really understand the nature of American business and its diverse interests. Too few understand, for example, that the educational interests of the owner of the local dry cleaning establishment are very different from the interests of the CEO of a Fortune 500 company. Business interests are no more a monolith than are the interests of parents, senior citizens, or teachers. Learning to understand these varied interests and to identify points of creative tension among them as well as points where they have concerns in common with the agenda of educational reformers is critical in building the alliances that need to be built if the power of the community is to be turned to supporting schools and school reform. Thus effective change leaders need a detailed and intimate knowledge of the nature of the enterprises and groups with which they must deal in the larger world.

The skills school leaders need to foster collaboration and build alliances are the skills of the diplomat and the skills of the negotiator. Diplomats are especially skilled at identifying and articulating mutual interests and in seeking the common ground. Negotiators have skill in avoiding win-lose situations and seeking to create win-win solutions. In addition, school leaders must also recognize the need for partnerships among sometimes adversarial groups and agencies as well as between them and the schools. School change leaders who have skills as third-party negotiators can help establish these important partnerships.

Skills

- Learning from some of the many useful books on negotiating skills,[10] or from some of the readily available training programs in the art of negotiation.
- Understanding what it means to collaborate.
- Assessing existing and potential collaborative arrangements for their usefulness.
- Setting expectations for each collaboration from the outset.
- Taking part in networks that support the results that the district is trying to achieve.
- Conveying the needs of students to those in the community whose support is needed to address these needs.

SUPPORTIVE SKILLS

Finally, leaders at all levels require a few additional general skills that apply across all the more specialized competencies.

Team Building

Strong leaders in the modern organization know how to lead in a participatory environment where shared decision making and teams are the rule rather than the exception. Leaders must, therefore, be skilled in team building and in leading teams. In addition to a bit of common sense, skilled team leaders know something about group dynamics; they are astute observers of human behavior in groups; and they have a great ability to ask the right questions"—because team leaders move teams in desired directions more by the questions they ask than by the answers they give. Indeed, most of the great change leaders I have observed do most of their work by way of questions rather than by way of answers.[11] They know that followers are more likely to believe and act on answers the followers themselves provide than they are to act on answers that someone else, including the most powerful leader, hands to them. Even Moses had some difficulty in persuading his people to accept the Commandments he delivered, and he had exceptional authority.

Strategic Thinking

Effective change leaders are skilled in distinguishing between strategy and tactics. They see the grand design and do all they can to move the system they lead in the direction indicated by the design. They are constantly seeking leverage—trying to determine what they can move that will move other things as well. For example, the superintendent who is concerned about dropout rates at the high school may concentrate attention on preschool programs and reading in the primary school. Actions and projected consequences, direct and indirect, are the focus of the change leader. In short, ideas like those advanced by authors like Peter Senge in *The Fifth Discipline*, Peter Drucker in his many books (for example, *Management: Tasks, Practices, and Responsibilities*), and Andrew Grove (for example, *High Output Management*) are well understood by the effective change leader who is also a strategic thinker.[12]

Strategic thinking does not, however, mean strategic planning. Strategic thinkers are constantly asking the question, What must we do today, if we want to be at X point five years from today? Sometimes, the best thing to do today is to develop a strategic plan; sometimes, however, strategic planning is only a strategy for delaying action while pretending to move. If strategic plans are to work, leaders must think strategically as well.

And to think strategically one must be prepared to act strategically, which means that one must be prepared to stop doing old things as well as to embrace doing new things. Leaders who insist on strategic action are requiring those who follow them to behave in counterintuitive ways, ways that cause trouble as well as ways that move toward solutions. Strategic action does not always promise to solve immediate problems. Rather, it transforms problems in ways that promise better solutions in the future than are possible under existing circumstances. Thus strategic action requires leaders who have courage. It also requires leaders who are prepared to go into the unknown with confidence and who can inspire others while doing so.

Dealing with People

Effective change leaders tend to be relatively secure, self-sufficient persons, capable of getting by with amazingly little external reinforcement for what they do. Such independence is critical to survival in times of difficulty in the change process, but it is also a rare quality. Most persons need continuing reassurance from others that what they are about is on the right track, especially when the ground being covered is new to them.

Sometimes change leaders fail to understand this need in others and fail to respond in reassuring ways. Self-confidence is essential to effective leaders. Unfortunately, self-confident leaders sometimes forget that not all those around them share this trait. In the midst of change, one of the primary tasks of the leader is to assure others of their worth and significance. As Deming has observed, if change is to be embraced, leaders must learn how to "drive out fear" and assure followers that there will indeed be a tomorrow.[13]

This means that leaders must be skilled in spotting anxiety and capable of hearing what is intended as well as what is literally expressed. They must listen for underlying meaning as well as for the literal words. Often persons who are anxious because they fear they cannot do what will be required of them argue against doing what is required on the grounds that it should not be done. Leaders will be ineffective if they fail to recognize resistance created by anxiety and assume it is either resistance created by lack of incentive to change or resistance genuinely created by the belief that the change being advanced is ill advised or unnecessary. Rather than taking actions intended to relieve anxiety (such as providing needed training and support), leaders in such circumstances often try again and again to persuade the resister that the desired change is good and necessary—only to fail in their effort. In such cases it is not persuasion that is needed; it is support, encouragement, and empathetic understanding.

CONCLUSION

Much that I have presented in this chapter is based on my own experiences with leaders, leavened with my understanding of the perspectives of those who study life in organizations. One goal of this chapter is to provide the reader who is called on to provide leadership to a change effort with a template for self-assessment and a guide to skill areas in which he or she might need some additional development or support. One of the best pieces of advice I ever received as a leader was "hire to your weaknesses." To take this advice one must be strong enough to admit one's weaknesses and wise enough to identify them. I hope this chapter helps leaders be both stronger and wiser.

Another goal is to provide those who are in a position to select leaders (school board members, superintendents, principals, and elected union officials) with a framework for assessing the likelihood that a candidate will be successful. Some of the attributes I have identified here can be acquired through training and conscious efforts at self-improvement. I know one superintendent, for example, who found it very difficult to express her vision and her beliefs about schooling to others in public forums. Through a rigorous self-improvement effort—including practicing in front of a mirror and in front of her family—she has become one of the most articulate spokespersons about the nature of schools and the schooling enterprise that I know. Indeed, I am concerned that this skill has become so finely tuned that she may find the lure of the lecture circuit more attractive than the pressures of the job of being superintendent.

Though I believe character traits are acquired, I am not persuaded that by the time a person reaches the point in life when he or she is likely to be called on to lead a change effort, deficiencies in these traits can be remedied. The best advice I can give, and this is based on hard-won experience, is that when past performance raises serious doubts about the candidates' integrity, persistence, self-awareness, or ego strength, organizations should not employ these persons to lead a change effort—no matter how attractive their other skills and no matter how charismatic they may appear to be. A self-serving leader lacking integrity can single-handedly destroy otherwise solid efforts to bring about change in schools.

A final goal is to provide those who are in a position to create and implement systems for identifying and developing educational leaders with a framework for thinking through the issues they must confront in designing their programs.

I am convinced that it is through the identification and the development of leaders and through the creation of systems that encourage these leaders to lead that the schools of America may yet be revitalized. The final chapter in this section looks at various ways the different school leaders can get started in creating change-adept schools that focus on the business of providing engaging work to students.

CHAPTER TEN

Who's on First?

A Personal View

I have been writing about school reform for many years, and I have given more speeches and lectures on topics related to school reform than I care to recall. Often afterward I am told that the task I describe is so huge that it is unmanageable. And even those who are not afraid of the unmanageable want to know, "Where do we start?" and, "What can I do?"

My hope is that the preceding chapters, though revealing the complexity of the task ahead, also clarify and organize that complexity in ways that reveal how it can indeed be managed. That leaves the questions, Where do we start? and What can I do? This chapter offers some initial answers to those questions for all those who must become leaders if our schools are ever to meet today's expectations that all, or nearly all, children will succeed in school: state legislators, boards of education, superintendents, union leaders, central office staff, principals, teachers, parents, and nonparents.

TO STATE LEGISLATORS

- Stop trying to solve the problems that educators need to solve. Concentrate on causing educators to focus on the right problems. Do not legislate answers but provide incentives for teachers and administrators to address the right questions. The key question is, What can be done to ensure that the work and activities teachers provide to students are engaging and sufficiently attractive to the students that they stick with it when they have difficulty, and result in students' learning that which the community intends that they should learn?

- Create a policy context in which educational leaders are able to lead rather than simply respond and comply. Do what you can to ensure continuity of effort rather than start, after start, after start.

There is no question that too many schools do not take parents seriously enough and that this is a situation that needs to be corrected. Rather than mandating how this correction will occur (for example, each school will have a school site council), mandate a result (for example, each year the state department responsible for public instruction will survey a random sample of parents from each school district and school to determine the extent to which parents feel they are adequately involved in decisions regarding their children and the schools). The legislature could also mandate desired response levels and appropriate actions when specific levels fail to be obtained.

Similarly, it seems apparent to most educators that there is something seriously wrong with the way school boards are elected or selected. Most incentives for being a school board member, such as representing a special interest, are misguided and harmful.[1] In some locales (Chicago, for example), school board relationships with schools have deteriorated to the point that the boards are being bypassed and special appointed boards are being created.

The desperation that leads to such actions is understandable, but before we give up on locally elected school boards, legislators should think through ways school boards might be elected or selected that would maintain local community control over the governance of schools without making it impossible for leaders to lead.[2]

It is time for legislators to give serious consideration to such proposals and to encourage local communities to experiment with them. Neither superintendents nor principals can lead and attend to meeting the needs of their most important customers, students, when they must deal continuously with the demands of individual school board members who are pursuing special interests more than the common good.

TO LOCAL BOARDS OF EDUCATION

- Come to understand that you have not been elected because you know how to run the schools. You don't know how to run the schools. You have been elected to ensure that the schools are well run by those you employ to run the schools. Your job is to ensure that the schools are run in ways that will produce the results the community wants and will support. Stick to that job.

- Recognize that your most important role in the district is that of community leader rather than educational leader. Your job is to educate the community about education and ensure that what the community wants (and gets) is that which the wisest members of the community would provide if given the opportunity to do so.

Schools are complex social systems. Running them requires the full-time attention of top-level leaders. It requires detailed knowledge of events and systems that is generally not available to persons elected to serve part-time on local school boards. Most superintendents find it difficult to get all board members to attend a board retreat at the same time, let alone get them to undergo the kind of intensive effort it would take to learn how to lead a school or school system.

However, school board members, better than superintendents and even principals, should know the standards the community has for well-run schools and are therefore in a better position than superintendents and principals to determine when the job is being done. Creating the conditions in which leaders can lead, helping those who are employed as leaders to develop the capacity of the system to support change, and providing feedback on the way the community is appraising the job being done are, or should be, what school boards are about.

Unfortunately, too many school board members think their job is to respond to the community. It is not. Their job is to create systems that respond to the community and to provide the community with leaders who ensure this responsiveness through the actions they take. The job of the board is to engage the community in a dialogue to ensure that the standards the community endorses are those most likely to lead to excellence.

The true constituents of boards of education are the community's children and its future rather than voters and present interests. To be sure, the wants and desires of present constituents must be attended to or board members will not survive as board members. Nevertheless it is the role of the board member to educate the tastes and sentiments of her or his constituents so that the education they want and the policies they will support are those that hold the most promise for building the kind of communities we all want and need to move productively into the twenty-first century.

TO SUPERINTENDENTS

- Develop a few clear and simple messages about the beliefs that guide the school system and the core business of the schools. Frame these messages in terms that can be easily understood by the audiences you are addressing, and seize every opportunity to deliver these messages and then to deliver them again.

- Gather around you a collection of people who among them have credibility with those whose support is required to implement needed changes, the authority to allocate resources, technical skill, and leadership ability. Help this guiding coalition to embrace a common set of beliefs and a common vision, and then empower its members to act.

The job of the superintendent, like any chief executive's job, is certainly much more complex than these action steps suggest. However, it is my belief that if a superintendent could do only two things, these are the two that would be most important. Anything that interferes with doing these things effectively and well should be changed, and any barriers that cannot be changed should be abandoned.

Among the clear and simple messages they craft, superintendents should include a thirty-second statement about their beliefs and vision, a three-minute statement for the times when they are asked to elaborate on the first statement, and a thirty-minute statement for those occasions when a speech is called for. The topic of the speech may differ from time to time and place to place, but the themes should be constant and repeated again and again.[3]

Superintendents cannot bring about change alone. Good leaders understand that they are leaders of leaders and that different leaders need different skills. It is not enough to delegate, one must also inspire. It is not enough to inspect, one must also provide direction. Great change leaders understand, moreover, that they cannot control change; they can only encourage it. They cannot manage change; they can only lead it. It is up to others much closer to the action to exercise control and to tactically manage the course that actions will take.

TO UNION LEADERS

- Distinguish between the use of power to stop bad things such as arbitrary dismissals and the abuse of due process and contract provisions from happening and the use of power to make good things happen. In many school districts, union leadership is the most stable leadership in the district. Make this count by leading schools into the twenty-first century rather than binding them to contract models that were successful in stopping bad things from happening fifty years ago.

- Recognize that schools are not the only bureaucracies in need of change. Unions too are bureaucracies. At the same time that they protect and extend the rights of employees, contracts tend to codify bureaucratic rules.

Those who have gained status in the union through successful leadership in an adversarial environment may well find such things as win-win negotiating threatening to them, just as threatening as cutting out central office waste can be to central office middle-level managers. Yet union leaders can benefit by becoming aware of the value of the steps mentioned here as they consider ways to support significant improvement efforts, especially when these efforts require fundamental changes in the way union leaders and management relate to each other.

Union leaders need to find ways to empower members to make critical decisions about conditions of work such as how many students will be accepted in a class and how long class periods in a given school can be, and at the same time preserve the collective power of the union to protect teachers' conditions of employment such as salaries, fringe benefits, and dismissal procedures. Union leaders need to recognize that for schools to improve, there must be considerably more flexibility than many master contracts now permit in the way time, people, space, and technology are used and deployed. What the master contract should provide is a mechanism for local school faculties to gain exceptions to the contract. Jefferson County, Kentucky (where teachers belong to the National Education Association), and Hammond,

Indiana (where teachers are members of the American Federation of Teachers), stand as exemplars of this approach to collective bargaining.

TO CENTRAL OFFICE STAFF: SUPERINTENDENT-LEVEL PERSONNEL, CURRICULUM SPECIALISTS, AND OTHERS NOT ACCOUNTABLE TO PRINCIPALS

• Understand that your most important job is to create and manage systems that will enable principals and teachers to concentrate on the core business of schools, the creation of intellectual activity that students find engaging and from which they learn. Only secondarily, if at all, should you see yourself as a supervisor. You are a capacity builder. Act like one.

• Use your position to enhance the status of teachers and principals and never detract from that status. You work for principals and teachers; they do not work for you. You depend for your livelihood on their doing their jobs well.

Many central office staff view their arrival at the central office as a promotion and see their jobs only as supervising and advising persons less experienced and skilled than they are. There will indeed always be some need for supervision and expert advice, but the greater need is for people with authority who know how to inspire others closer to the center of action to invent solutions to problems.

Central office staff can benefit by learning how to assess department and district capacity to support change. Given this assessment, they can determine how best to lead in the development and implementation of clear plans to make the school system and the community more adept at implementing change. They can also support the development of better schools by learning how to create coalitions around solutions to problems that have been identified and how to empower others to implement and refine these solutions.

TO PRINCIPALS

• Learn to see yourself as a member of the district-level team as well as the head of your own team at the building level. Recognize that your school is not the only system you need to consider; it is a part of a larger system. Other schools and other principals are not—or should not be—your competition. They are your allies and coinventors. Your competition lies elsewhere, especially in the newly emerging purveyors of education, entertainment, and edutainment that are even now capturing the hearts and minds of our children and youths, as I described in Part One.

• Remember that your primary tasks are to keep the entire school focused on the core business of the school, creating quality work for students, and to remove any barriers that distract teachers from this focus. You are as responsible for what teachers do in the classroom as are the teachers themselves. Good leaders do not exist outside the context of good followers, and good followers do not exist unless they have the potential to be good leaders. Developing that potential is what good leadership is all about.

Too many recent reform efforts encourage principals to see their schools as fiefdoms or feudal baronies that exist largely apart from the larger school system and the community whose support is needed if a school is to survive in the long run. Instead, principals will be more effective when they learn to use the district and the community, just as district-level officials will be more effective once they learn to be responsive to the needs of principals.

Principals will benefit as well from recognizing that some schools need to be given special status so that they can learn special things on behalf of all schools. For example, charter schools in which faculties agree to take on particularly thorny problems for which the district presently has no answers and then to share what they have learned with others are worth their weight in gold. Such charter schools belong to all the teachers and students in the district, not just to those who teach there and attend there. Charter schools are not competitors; they are the means by which we all may be able to beat the competition. Conversely, charter schools that serve only to relieve pressure brought to bear by special interest groups and charter schools that are not required to pay back the system's investment through new inventions and new solutions to persistent problems are not worth chartering.

Indeed, any school that is enjoying special success can contribute its knowledge to the system. The question to ask is, What are people in this school doing that we could and should be doing? If the answer is that they are serving children better prepared to learn from traditional academic methods and materials, forget the lesson. If, however, they have somehow learned to invent better work for the students they serve regardless of the students' ability to learn in traditional academic ways, then there is something to be learned from them.

TO TEACHERS

- Learn to care as much about the quality of the tasks you provide for students as you care about the quality of your own performance. Indeed, learn to evaluate your work by the extent to which students find it engaging and the extent to which students learn from it, as opposed to the extent to which students find you to be engaging and the extent to which students learn from you.

- Recognize that the task of inventing quality work for students and leading them to do it is best accomplished not by going it alone or even in a team but by pulling on all the resources available to you throughout the district. At the same time, become a resource to others as well. Recognize that "what if?" questions contain the prospect of solutions; "yes, but" statements preclude invention.

For the most part the view of the teacher as leader and inventor does not dominate either the thinking or the research in education. Indeed, it is commonplace to assume that teaching is the cause of learning and to argue that when learning has not occurred, teaching has not occurred. That is nonsense. What has not occurred is that students have not been brought to expend the effort needed to learn. Teaching occurred, but too few students cared or became engaged.

Teachers who view themselves as leaders understand that they are effective only to the extent that they are able to get students to do those things that result in learning. Sometimes those things involve listening to the instructor, and sometimes they involve activities such as writing, reading, and creating other intellectual products. As leaders, teachers are students of student motives, just as leaders in other arenas are students of the motives of those whom they intend to lead.

The cellular structure of schools[4] and the relative isolation of school faculties from each other and from the resources of the central office serve to make teaching a lonely and isolated business. The creation of collegial support structures and also support from those outside the school can offset this isolation, but this will happen only when teachers come to see the outside support as something to be welcomed rather than as a threat or an implicit criticism of their own competence and worth.

TO PARENTS

- Spend a little time each day talking with your children about school and how important it is to you and to them that they do well in school. Even if you cannot help your children with their schoolwork, you can inspire them to do that work, and you can affirm how important it is that they have completed it.

- Do your best to help teachers understand what motivates each child you have in school. Does he or she respond well to public approval for quality performance, or does such approval cause embarrassment? How does your child typically react when his or her performance falls short of expectations? Does your child enjoy novelty, or does she or he prefer the routine and predictable?

Too often schools expect more of parents than some parents can provide, and too often parents provide schools less support than the schools and teachers have the right to expect. It is well and good when parents join the PTA, attend parent-teacher conferences, and volunteer to participate in school events. It is even more important that parents evidence a personal interest in the success their child is having in school and that they take the time to see what their child is doing in school by reading materials written for school assignments and viewing student-produced videotapes and so on.

It is unreasonable to expect that teachers will have the detailed knowledge of an individual child's motivational makeup that an observant parent has. Yet once armed with the parent's knowledge, the teacher is often positioned to customize schoolwork so that the student is more likely to do it with enthusiasm. For example, the child who is embarrassed by public acclamation for a performance may respond better if the teacher sends a simple laudatory note to the parent that the parent reads to the child. Other children may need, indeed demand, all the public praise that can be mustered.

TO NONPARENTS

• Recognize that the future of our society depends on strong public support for education. Whether that support should take the
form of public schools or some form of private schools subsi-
dized by public dollars is, nowadays, a subject for debate. But
democracy cannot survive unless the public is willing to support
the education of all children, even when those children are not
one's own and look different from oneself.

• Know that the children of America need you almost as much as
they need their parents. They need you to ask them how they are
doing in school, to attend to occasions where they do well, to
celebrate with them, and to counsel them when they fall short.
These celebrations may take place in a church, a synagogue,
mosque, or any other place where concepts of duty, virtue, and
diligence can be discussed with ease; they can take the form of
public displays of exemplary student work in airports and in
shopping centers. At a much simpler level, nonparents might
make it a habit to express interest in how the children of colleagues and friends are doing in school and in what they are
doing.

The many Americans who do not have children in a public school,
whether they are grandparents, married persons with no children, sin-
gles, or parents with children in private schools, sometimes feel that
they have no investment in the public schools. This is not so. Looking
just at matters of self-interest, on a basic economic level, property values are often affected by the perceived quality of the schools. On a
larger level, in just a few years the children in school now will be creating the goods we use, supplying our medical care, running our financial system. It does no good to bash the public schools, even if your
children do not attend them. Bashing the local schools is somewhat
akin to being a Ford Motor employee who drives a Chevrolet. It cannot be prevented, but even from the point of view of the employee's
livelihood it is not to be desired.

Even those who have chosen private schools for their children, especially those who have chosen parochial schools, have an investment
in public education. If the public schools in the community are not
healthy, then even those children who are receiving a fine education
in the private and parochial schools will find few jobs where they grow

up. The quality of the local workforce will not be up to the standards required to do productive work in the twenty-first century. Without a quality workforce in the community, twenty-first century businesses will not be attracted, and those citizens who are most well educated will be most likely to move.

CONCLUSION

As an author and consultant I have always prided myself on never telling readers or clients what to do. Rather I have tried to help them discover what they need to do and then help them do it. In writing this chapter, I have stepped over the line I had drawn for myself. Nevertheless, recalling the questions I have been asked by many school leaders, it is my hope that these initial answers will fulfill a need and that just like more indirect forms of discussion they encourage readers to take a careful and honest look at the considerable contribution that each person could make to reforming schools so that they meet today's expectations for student learning.

CHAPTER ELEVEN

Epilogue
A Future for Public Education?

I magine that the year is 2020. How likely is it that we might see an article like this one morning in our on-line newspaper?

April 1, 2020

EDUCATION IN THE NEW MILLENNIUM

In the past thirty years, America's schools have seen dramatic shifts in attendance patterns. Only 40 percent of high school age students attend formally organized schools. About 10 percent have dropped out of school altogether. The other 50 percent either attend private schools (15 percent) or get their high school education through virtual high schools operated by colleges, universities, and private corporations.

These data from *The Condition of Education: 2020,* a report recently released by the Center for Education Statistics, also show that about 20 percent of primary school age students are home schooled and another 30 percent get their education through *educational cooperatives,* informal alliances among like-minded parents. These cooperatives employ private providers who deliver instructional content that reflects the parents' personal views and values. Such alliances are typically small. Most have ten or fewer students, and the schoolroom may be a family room or a garage, although some real-estate developers are now offering home buyers access to educational facilities, just as housing developments of the 1980s and 1990s offered recreation centers.

These cooperatives have their roots in the late 1990s and the first decade of this century.

First, many of the parents who wanted to home school their children discovered they could not afford to give up a second income to conduct this schooling, and some began to create informal support networks with other home schooling parents.

Informal cooperatives soon followed, formed first by religious conservatives who found the public schools too secular, but parents with other views quickly saw how specially tailored schools could ensure that their beliefs dominated in their children's instruction. Although competition between the job and home schooling is now easing thanks to increased telecommuting, cooperatives continue to grow because many parents believe they are in a better position to control what their children learn when the instructors are directly accountable to them and when they can directly control curriculum content.

Second, it was during the first decade of this century that *school vouchers* became commonplace. Initially, legislators intended parents to use these vouchers for tuition at private or proprietary schools. By 2010, they had combined the ideas of the school voucher and of the tax-free *education account* to create the *education vouchers* that parents are now using to pay for not only tuition but also hardware and software, access fees to interactive educational television providers, and tutors.

When vouchers were first introduced, private school enrollment surged, only to level off quickly as parents discovered that in the long run control always follows dollars. Moreover, some of the most prestigious private schools, especially religious schools, have never accepted vouchers, fearing this might threaten their autonomy and make them subject to state and federal government requirements. Even those private schools that initially found vouchers a boon soon discovered that many of their traditional parents were becoming concerned over the resulting changes in the student body and were seeking alternatives to school, not just alternative schools. These parents now are among those fueling the continuing growth of educational cooperatives.

Despite the increasing use of vouchers, resistance to increasing their value is strong. One reason for this, often suggested by legislators, is that many nonparent taxpayers see vouchers as just one more entitlement. Now that entitlements like Social Security are threatened, many taxpayers have little patience with expanding entitlements to people they believe may not know how to use such funds wisely, the least well educated and the poorest in American society, those once called the underclass. Senior citizens sometimes refer to vouchers as an "intergenerational wealth transfer" and see them as a symptom of younger Americans' apparent unwillingness to support benefits for seniors.

Although some 50 percent of primary school age children still attend public schools, these schools have also changed over the past few decades.

In taxpayers and legislators' quest for school accountability, most public schools are now directly managed and controlled at the state level. In 30 of the 51 states, superintendents and key executive staff in local school units (typically organized by region) are appointed by the state board of education. The primary function of the office of the superintendent is to monitor compliance with legislative directives. Local school boards today are mostly advisory boards rather than governing boards.

Much to the disappointment of initial advocates of charter schools, the charter school has become one means of transforming locally operated schools into state-operated schools. Because local boards of education were typically slow to grant charters in the 1980s and 1990s, chartering authority was often transferred to the state or to the state university system. After the charter school scandals of the first decade of the century, state governments typically responded by increasing charter school regulation and inspection. Today, charter schools are considered a part of the state system of schools and operate under much the same rules as other public schools. The freedom and flexibility sought by the founders of the charter school movement have been lost in the battle for accountability.

As education shifts to the private sector, rapid changes are also occurring in educational materials and in the costs of schooling.

Educational publishing houses that once concentrated on developing textbooks and other materials for schools are increasingly targeting the home schooling and educational cooperative markets. The homes of privately schooled children tend to be more technologically sophisticated than underfunded public school classrooms, and many materials first developed at the time it was thought public schools would be revived through the application of technology have now been modified for use in the home and the cooperative school.

Parents can obtain both printed materials and software that uphold their values and attitudes. Religious conservatives can purchase materials reflecting their values; secular humanists can purchase materials reflecting their values, and so on. These curricula are intentionally ethnocentric. Little in them encourages an empathetic understanding of cultures and groups other than those the parents represent and prefer. The terms *market niche* and *market segment* are increasingly a part of the lexicon of curriculum developers.

Gone are the days when curriculum developers strove to create a common curriculum or to promote a common culture. Today the quest is to develop materials acceptable to and easily embraced by the various subcultures that make up America. As one designer told us: "The only way to survive in this business is to recognize that different groups and factions have different curriculum needs. To create a curriculum aimed at a common culture is to fight the reality that in America there is increasing diversity and decreasing commonality in values. What most parents want is a curriculum that supports their own value set. They do not want a curriculum that encourages their children to explore alternatives to that set, except perhaps to see the errors in other sets of values and the superiority of the values the parents want their children to embrace."

When it comes to costs, the average per pupil expenditure for education has increased about 50 percent for privately schooled students since 2000 (an increase similar to the rise in medical costs during the last half of the twentieth century). Only some of this expense has been offset by vouchers. Most of the increase is being paid by private sources, including parents. Meanwhile, children attending public schools, where per-pupil expenditures are indexed to the worth of vouchers, are receiving less support than they were in the year 2000.

In the first half of the twentieth century, Americans had a great deal of faith in their schools and believed in the importance of public support for public education. In the last half of the twentieth century that confidence in public schools and concern for the preservation of public education eroded. Efforts to address the issues raised by critics of the public schools in that period produced limited results. Finally, beginning about 1990, conservative political leaders, journalists, and critics began to advance the notion that public education was beyond redemption. They argued for competition among schools and more educational choice for parents. Vouchers and charter schools were to be the means of reaching these goals. Now school competition and choice are accepted by most people. Every state has some form of voucher program. Every state allows charter schools. Whether these initiatives represent a new beginning for education in America remains to be seen.

    See the related story "Culture Wars of 1990s Become a Real Shoot-Out in 2020."

I believe it is highly unlikely that such a scenario would be a new beginning for schools, although the situation it describes is a real possibility. Charter schools are advocated as a way to escape school bureaucracy and thus increase teachers' flexibility in finding the best ways to educate students. Vouchers are gaining growing acceptance as a solution to perceived problems of school choice, given schools with, among other differences, widely varying results on standardized testing that are interpreted to mean that some schools perform better than others (and not that some schools have more students prepared to learn academic content than others). Shouldn't the poor have the same rights as the rich to choose the schools their children attend, either public or private? Why should affluent parents who place their children in private schools not receive the same subsidy for the education of their children as do the less affluent? So the questions of voucher advocates go.

But what is likely to be the ultimate longer-term outcome? Consider the two ways that vouchers might become available. Vouchers might be seen as simply an extension of the currently existing agreement between taxpayers and parents. Parents accept some degree of community control of the education of their children in exchange for taxpayer support for that education. If this is the direction vouchers take, it is almost certain to lead to some form of government regulation of private and parochial schools, whose leaders now claim the virtue of being largely free from "government interference." In the 1950s, when the debates about the role of the federal government in education were beginning to get very serious, the conservative mantra was that "with government dollars, comes government control." In the intervening years the federal government has gained a great deal of control over local schools with very little money (6 to 10 percent of the education budget comes from federal sources).

Those who see vouchers as a means of promoting freedom of choice and avoiding ham-fisted intervention by government bureaucrats will not find this first conception of vouchers a happy one. Leaders of traditional private schools and well-established parochial schools are most likely to resist any governmental controls on vouchers, arguing that the market will be the best regulator of performance.

It is likely, therefore, that vouchers will be dispensed on a model similar to that used for dispensing food stamps. Just as some commodities (cigarettes and liquor, for example) cannot be bought with food stamps, parents would not be able to buy some kinds of education with vouchers. For example, segregationist academies would likely be placed off limits as would cult schools (assuming a legal basis can be established for distinguishing cults from religious organizations).

Yet one consequence of employing this alternative is that those paying for the education of children will have even less control of the way their dollars are used than is now the case. In the short run, parents may gain something by using vouchers; in the long run, the worth of vouchers may diminish precisely because it has long been a tradition in America that there should be "no taxation without representation." As nonparent taxpayers see their taxes used primarily for private benefit rather than for avowed common interests, as they see school taxes becoming tuition taxes, public support for educational funding is almost certain to erode.

Under these circumstances, it will not be hard for politicians, prodded by the growing senior citizen population, to make the case that taxes for education are an intergenerational wealth transfer. With the relatively young increasingly unwilling to support entitlements like Social Security for the relatively old, the relatively old may become less willing to fund private education for the young, especially if that education supports values some senior citizens find alien or repugnant.

In sum, my concern about vouchers is that in the long run vouchers are not likely to do what proponents claim they will do, and the unintended consequences may be a further estrangement of the public from supporting education either public or private. The fact that, for the first time in American history, in many communities nonparents constitute more than 50 percent of taxpayers makes this a matter of real concern.

Charter schools are seen by some as a compromise between the present situation of highly centralized schools (whether centralized at the local or state level makes little difference) and the entitlement and free market ideas inherent in arguments for vouchers. The idea of the charter school is that the governmental education authority grants some group or organization the authority to constitute and conduct a school independent of government "interference" except for the specific provisions set forth in the charter agreement. Usually these provisions have to do with performance measures, financial accounting, and so on. As of the time this book is being written, thirty-eight states have some form of charter school legislation.

The most fundamental potential problem with charter schools is that unless their charters are carefully crafted, the schools are likely to become increasingly exclusionary. The majority of the community will have little or no direct contact with these schools nor will the community have a means of influencing what these schools teach.

In short, unless both voucher and charter school measures are implemented with care, they will further exacerbate a growing rift between the citizenry and the schools. They may provide nonparents with reasons, or excuses, to oppose providing public dollars for the education of America's children whether in public schools or in private schools. These possibilities should be considered in concert with the possibility of the kind of curricular niche marketing described in the scenario that opened this chapter (a possibility that the Internet and interactive-on-demand television and other technological advances smooth the way for).

Under such circumstances, there will, of course, still be public schools, but they are likely to be government schools, run primarily by the state and controlled by such bureaucratic forms of accountability as can be assessed with quick scoring tests that ensure some minimum level of academic skill but that do little to inspire or encourage excellence. These schools will likely be attended by the children of the poor and the relatively powerless. The result of all this might well be an academically well grounded but culturally oblivious elite, who have little understanding of or tolerance for those whose ideas and values conflict with their own, who are attempting to lead a mass comprising persons who have been trained rather than educated, molded rather than refined. This is a prescription for Bosnia in America. I, for one, find it frightening.

Of course there is an alternative. The public schools can succeed in reforming themselves. This book, representing over forty years of thought and effort in the field of school reform, offers some means for the schools to change their current pattern of unsustained, uncoordinated change for a continuous drive toward sustained and focused change.

Some of the things I recommend are little more than truisms. For example, anyone who has given the matter a moment's thought knows that children and young adults need, in addition to their parents, many adults who are significant to them. As society is evolving, however, it is becoming increasingly difficult for parents, to say nothing of nonparents, to respond productively to this need, and many young people are becoming increasingly estranged from the values and commitments that gave rise to public education in America in the first place, that is, the quest for what we have in common rather than the celebration of what divides us.

Some other things I recommend are under present circumstances virtually undoable. Few teachers would resist the idea of having more substantial interactions with colleagues, but the way time is organized in schools, such interactions are difficult to sustain. Most superintendents would love to be able to develop and deliver clear messages that tell those inside and outside schools where the school district should be headed or how it might get there. But, preoccupied with attending to the requests and complaints of multiple constituencies in the community and with managing real and threatened crises, they do not feel they have the time to do what would seem to be their most essential task.

If *restructuring* and *systemic change* do not mean changing the conditions that make it difficult or impossible to do what needs to be done to improve the schools, then the words have no meaning. If teachers do not have the time to engage in significant dialogue with colleagues, then it is necessary to reconfigure rules, roles, and relationships so that teachers do have this time and students do get more attention. If interactions between the superintendent and the board of education make it nearly impossible for the superintendent to attend to maintaining and coordinating continuous improvement and to communicating that direction, then the rules and relationships that govern interaction between the board and superintendents must be altered.

Such changes are unlikely to occur until school leaders arrive at a consensus about four questions:

- What is our business?
- Who are our customers?
- What products do we provide these customers?
- What improvements in existing products can we imagine, and what new products might we create?

This book was written to help all those concerned with our schools formulate realistic answers to these essential questions, answers that will lead to educating most students to a high level and educating all students to a greater extent than schools do now. It is time for leaders in education to stop accepting the fictions that dismiss criticism of the schools, to understand the changes in society that are creating the new and greater expectations many different elements in society have today for the education of children, to accept that some of the most important things in learning are under educators' control (namely, the tasks that students are given to do in order to learn), and to realize that the need for successful change has never been more urgent. Given the necessary leadership, our schools can achieve what they must achieve to survive.

Notes

Preface

1. See C. W. Mills, *The Sociological Imagination* (New York: Oxford University Press, 1959), pp. 3–24.

Chapter One

1. Rosabeth Moss Kanter calls such organizations "change adept." I will develop this idea more fully later, but I want to acknowledge even now my great debt to Kanter's formulation. See R. M. Kanter *On the Frontiers of Management* (Boston: Harvard Business School Press, 1977), especially chap. 1.
2. R. Hofstadter, *Anti-Intellectualism in American Life* (New York: Knopf, 1963).
3. R. M. Kanter, *Rosabeth Moss Kanter on the Frontiers of Management* (Boston: Harvard Business School Press, 1997), p. 209.
4. L. Rose and A. Gallup, "The 30th Annual Phi Delta Kappa/Gallup Poll of the Public's Attitudes Toward the Public Schools," *Phi Delta Kappan,* Sept. 1998, p. 47.
5. Rose and Gallup, "The 30th Annual Phi Delta Kappa/Gallup Poll," p. 47.
6. See, for example, D. Berliner and B. Biddle, *The Manufactured Crisis: Myths, Fraud and the Attack on America's Public Schools* (Reading, Mass.: Addison-Wesley, 1995).
7. National Commission on Excellence in Education, *A Nation at Risk* (Washington, D.C.: U.S. Government Printing Office, 1983).
8. See P. C. Schlechty, *Inventing Better Schools: An Action Plan for Educational Reform* (San Francisco: Jossey-Bass, 1997), for more details.
9. See Schlechty, *Inventing Better Schools.*
10. Rose and Gallup, "The 30th Annual Phi Delta Kappa/Gallup Poll," p. 43.
11. S. Farkas and J. Johnson, *Given the Circumstances: Teachers Talk About Public Education Today* (New York: Public Agenda Foundation, 1996).

12. Richard Hofstadter, *Anti-Intellectualism in American Life*, for example, maintains that Americans' dissatisfaction with their schools has a long history.

13. D. Cumming, "Panel Urged to Upgrade Tech Schools," *Atlanta Journal Constitution*, Oct. 15, 1999, p. 1.

14. P. F. Drucker, *Management: Tasks, Practices, Responsibilities* (New York: HarperCollins, 1974).

15. Herb Childress, in "Seventeen Reasons That Football Is Better Than High School," *Phi Delta Kappan*, Apr. 1998, pp. 616–619, illustrates the point I am discussing here. I elaborate my views later.

16. See Schlechty, *Inventing Better Schools*.

17. What I hope the reader will ponder here is the question, How might nonparents be involved in the life of schools in ways that will meet nonparents' needs and at the same time enhance the quality of the experiences provided to children and youth?

18. Rose and Gallup, "The 30th Annual Phi Delta Kappa/Gallup Poll," p. 53.

19. Rose and Gallup, "The 30th Annual Phi Delta Kappa/Gallup Poll," p. 55.

20. D. Matthews, *Is There a Public for Public Schools?* (Dayton, Ohio: Kettering Foundation Press, 1996).

21. George S. Counts was a prominent figure in the progressive era in education and a radical reformer. The question posed was the title of a pamphlet, "Dare the School Build a New Social Order," published by Counts in 1932 (New York).

22. See Schlechty, *Inventing Better Schools*.

23. P. Hersch, *A Tribe Apart: A Journey into the Heart of American Adolescence* (New York: Ballantine, 1998).

24. W. Waller, *The Sociology of Teaching* (New York: Wiley, 1967; originally published 1932), p. 10.

25. See J. S. Coleman, *The Adolescent Society: The Social Life of the Teenager and Its Impact on Education* (New York: Free Press, 1961).

26. Waller, *The Sociology of Teaching*, p. 33.

27. See, for example, Hersch, *A Tribe Apart*, especially chap. 2.

28. The best and most elaborate illustration of this master-apprentice model I have seen occurred years ago at Worthington High School in Worthington, Ohio, where I was teaching at that time. Charles Rouscoulp, who also taught there and who eventually published the book *Chalk Dust on My Shoulder* (Columbus, Ohio: Merrill, 1969), for years maintained the practice of giving his English composition classes excerpts from the draft of his book and asking for criticism, which he sometimes heeded in writing the final draft. A number of excellent writers came out of Rouscoulp's classes.

In addition, testimony from students and former students made it clear that he was one of the most admired teachers in a school district with many outstanding performers.

29. One potential consequence of the technological revolution is that more people may be able to carry out their employee duties at home. Should this happen, it would certainly reshape some of the problems discussed here.

30. Rose and Gallup, "The 30th Annual Phi Delta Kappa/Gallup Poll," p. 46.

31. J. Johnson and S. Farkas, in *Getting By: What American Teenagers Really Think About Their Schools* (New York: Public Agenda Foundation, 1997), offer some insights into teenagers' current opinions about schools.

32. A. Morita, *Made in Japan: Akio Morita and the Sony Corporation* (New York: Dutton, 1986), p. 14.

33. See R. Dreeben, *On What Is Learned in School* (Reading, Mass.: Addison-Wesley, 1968).

34. I am indebted for this phrase to Carl Bridenbaugh, who used it as the title of his presidential address to the American Historical Association in 1963 (see C. Bridenbaugh, "The Great Mutation," *American Historical Review,* 1963, pp. 315–331). In it, he argued that the world of 1962 had less in common with America at the beginning of the twentieth century than the world of the late 1900s had in common with fifth-century Athens. I am suggesting here that the great mutation that Bridenbaugh identified was just beginning, and it is yet to reach its resolution.

35. See, for example, D. Halberstam, *The Fifties* (New York: Villard Books, 1993).

Chapter Two

1. R. M. Kanter, "Introduction," in *Rosabeth Moss Kanter on the Frontiers of Management* (Boston: Harvard Business School Press, 1997), pp. 4–5. Used with permission of Harvard Business School Press.

2. See J. Bruner, *Toward a Theory of Instruction* (Cambridge, Mass.: Harvard University Press, 1966).

3. I. R. Weiss, *Report of the 1977 National Survey of Science, Mathematics and Social Studies Education,* Se-78-72 (Washington, D.C.: National Science Foundation, 1978). I participated as a consultant in Weiss's study.

4. P. C. Schlechty, *Inventing Better Schools: An Action Plan for Educational Reform* (San Francisco: Jossey-Bass, 1997), pp. 168–169.

5. See P. C. Schlechty, "Career Ladders: A Good Idea Going Awry," in T. J. Sergiovanni (ed.), *Schooling for Tomorrow* (Needham Heights, Mass.: Allyn & Bacon, 1989).

6. See P. C. Schlechty, "A Framework for Evaluating Induction into Teaching," *Journal of Teacher Education,* Jan.–Feb. 1985, pp. 37–41.

7. J. P. Kotter, *Leading Change* (Boston: Harvard Business School Press, 1996); see also M. G. Fullan, *The New Meaning of Educational Change* (2nd ed.) (New York: Teachers College Press, 1991).

8. The literature on change and innovation is replete with stories about *early adapters* and *late adapters.* It has been my observation that there are early and late resisters as well. Sometimes only a few persons will resist a structural change in its early stages. When the fact of the change is not well understood initially, many may continue to believe that like so many prior change efforts, "this, too, shall pass." As the change becomes more evident and its wide scope more fully understood, individuals begin to understand its implications for themselves and for their interest groups. If the negative implications seem more apparent than the gains, the number of resisters is likely to increase. This resistance may be compounded by the fact that by the time a structural change has reached this point, it is also likely to have gained enough momentum within the system that the resisters will feel the need to organize a counter movement. The goal of the guiding coalition should be to enlist the support of these potential powerful resisters before they feel the need to organize a counterrevolution.

9. Kanter, "Introduction," in *Rosabeth Moss Kanter on the Frontiers of Management.*

10. Kanter, "Introduction," in *Rosabeth Moss Kanter on the Frontiers of Management,* p. 129. Used with permission of Harvard Business School Press.

11. See M. Wheatley, *Leadership and the New Science: Learning About Organization from an Orderly Universe* (San Francisco: Berrett-Koehler, 1992).

12. L. Olson, "'Annenberg Challenge' Proves to Be Just That," *Education Week, 16*(39), June 25, 1997, p. 1.

13. J. Anderson, "Getting Better by Design," *Education Week, 16*(38), June 18, 1997, p. 48.

14. As I indicated earlier, my thinking about change-adept organizations owes much to the work of Rosabeth Moss Kanter, especially her formulation of the characteristics of change-adept organizations set forth in the introduction of her book *Rosabeth Moss Kanter on the Frontiers of Management.* Though my own formulation of these characteristics differs somewhat from Kanter's work, my debt will be obvious to those who have read what she has written.

15. See, for example, W. Bennis, *Why Leaders Can't Lead: The Unconscious Conspiracy Continues* (San Francisco: Jossey-Bass, 1989).

16. L. J. Perelman, *School's Out: A Radical New Formula for the Revitalization of America's Educational System* (New York: Avon, 1992).

17. A. M. Schlesinger, *The Disuniting of America: Reflections on a Multi-cultural Society* (New York: W. W. Norton, 1998).

18. P. F. Drucker, *Management: Tasks, Practices, Responsibilities* (New York: HarperCollins, 1974).

19. Kanter, "Introduction," in *Rosabeth Moss Kanter on the Frontiers of Management,* p. 135. Used with permission of Harvard Business School Press.

20. Those who style themselves *constructivists* should find the concept of knowledge work useful, because the construction of knowledge is a form of knowledge work, just as is the application of knowledge to tasks and problems.

Chapter Three

1. See T. Sizer and N. Sizer, "Grappling," *Phi Delta Kappan,* Nov. 1999, *81*(3), pp. 184–190, for a discussion of this concept.

2. D. Lortie, *Schoolteacher: A Sociological Study* (Chicago: University of Chicago Press, 1975).

3. The reader familiar with classic literature in sociology will recognize my debt to Robert K. Merton, who developed a typology similar to this one to help analyze modes of adaptation to norms. My usage here is very different from what Merton intended, but I feel obliged to acknowledge my indebtedness to him. See R. K. Merton, *Social Theory and Social Structure* (New York: Free Press, 1968).

4. This distinction reflects a typology suggested by Amitai Etzioni that I used many years ago as a means of distinguishing among types of student involvement in school. In this typology, the highest level is moral involvement, where the student buys into both the means and the ends of schooling. The next level is calculative involvement, where the student is prepared to comply in exchange for things he or she desires, which may or may not be officially intended. Alienative involvement (something of an oxymoron) requires coercion. Although I do not discuss it in detail here, I continue to believe this framework has some utility in assessing levels of student engagement. See P. C. Schlechty, *Teaching and Social Behavior: Toward an Organizational Theory of Instruction* (Needham Heights, Mass.: Allyn & Bacon, 1976), or better yet, A. Etzioni, *A Comparative Analysis of Complex Organizations: On Power, Involvement, and Their Correlates* (New York: Free Press, 1961).

5. C. Thomas, *The Louisville Courier-Journal,* Nov. 28, 1998, p. A9.

6. I am sympathetic to the view that the present emphasis on statewide standardized testing is often misguided and educationally unsound. In some instances the amount of time spent in testing and in teaching students how

to take tests is almost unconscionable. Yet the public does have the right and the need to know how well schools are doing at their job. In a climate where more and more people distrust all public institutions, "trust me" is not good enough. Educators must find ways to respond to the public demand for accountability while preserving the conditions in which learning can occur in schools. I address this subject in more detail later in this book.

7. R. J. Herrnstein and C. Murray, *The Bell Curve: Intelligence and Class Structure in American Life* (New York: Free Press, 1994).

8. See, for example, J. Kozol, *Savage Inequalities: Children in America's Schools* (New York: Crown, 1991).

9. See W. E. Deming, *Out of the Crisis* (Cambridge, Mass.: MIT Center for Advanced Engineering Study, 1986), for a full discussion of such issues of accountability.

Chapter Four

1. J. Coleman, *The Adolescent Society: The Social Life of the Teenager and Its Impact on Education* (New York: Free Press, 1961).

2. See W. E. Deming, *Out of the Crisis* (Cambridge, Mass.: MIT Center for Advanced Engineering Study, 1986).

3. For more detail in refuting this fear, see P. C. Schlechty, *Schools for the 21st Century: Leadership Imperatives for Educational Reform* (San Francisco: Jossey-Bass, 1990); *Inventing Better Schools: An Action Plan for Educational Reform* (San Francisco: Jossey-Bass, 1997).

4. P. Senge, *The Fifth Discipline: The Art and Practice of the Learning Organization* (New York: Doubleday, 1990).

5. D. Halberstam, *The Reckoning* (New York: Morrow, 1986).

6. T. J. Peters and R. H. Waterman Jr., *In Search of Excellence: Lessons from America's Best-Run Companies* (New York: HarperCollins, 1982) was the first best-seller in this genre.

7. In P. C. Schlechty, *Teaching and Social Behavior: Toward an Organizational Theory of Instruction* (Needham Heights, Mass.: Allyn & Bacon, 1976), I distinguished among the student as product, the student as client, and the student as member. As I now view the matter, the student as client is nothing more or less than a sanitized and "professionalized" view of the student as product. The student remains a person to be worked on, and the assumption is that those who are "working on him or her" have special skills that qualify them to do such work, that is, they are professionals in the sense that physicians are professionals. Also, I have come to the view that students in schools, like children in all societies, cannot be full-fledged members of

the organization precisely because they are children. This does not mean
that they cannot be honored, and it does not mean that they occupy a di-
minished place. Indeed, when they are seen as customers, the focus of all
school activity must be on them and the needs they bring to the school.
Moreover, what the idea of customer does that the idea of member does not
do is to remind us that students are volunteers whose commitments and
loyalties must be earned rather than demanded or commanded. It also requires us to redefine the purpose of schools and the products that schools
create in service to that purpose. See Schlechty, *Schools for the 21st Century*
and *Inventing Better Schools,* for further explication of these points.

8. See M. Tucker, *Standards for Our Schools: How to Set Them, Measure Them,
and Reach Them* (San Francisco: Jossey-Bass, 1998).

Chapter Five

1. Herb Childress, "Seventeen Reasons That Football Is Better Than High
School," *Phi Delta Kappan,* Apr. 1998, pp. 616–619, similarly presents a set
of lessons based on observation made in the athletic environment, another
competitor for students' attention.
2. See, for example, "At the Five-Year Mark: The Challenge of Being Essential,"
Horace, 6(1), November, 1989.

Chapter Six

1. P. B. Crosby, *Quality Is Free: The Art of Making Quality Certain* (New York:
McGraw-Hill, 1979), pp. 4–15.
2. I have read and found useful Tom Peters's book *The Pursuit of WOW: Every
Person's Guide to Topsy-Turvy Times* (New York: Vintage Books, 1994).
However, what I am referring to here is very different from what Peters is
referring to. Furthermore, I was using WOW to mean working on the work
before Peters wrote his excellent book.
3. This analogy was first suggested to me by Paul Hagerty, presently superintendent of the Seminole County Public Schools in Florida.
4. Any local effort that does not take these standards into account is subject to
criticism from the proponents of state-mandated standardized tests. Unless
they are prepared to offer an alternative convincing to the public, teachers
and administrators must find some way to accommodate the demand for
improved test scores. Maybe, just maybe, if students learn more and if what
they learn is important to them, test scores will go up. It is worth taking a

risk to find out, but in taking the risk, richness, texture, and grappling must be given as much value as are scope and sequence.

5. As the case of the Allentown bar illustrates, to insist on a standardized set of learning expectations is not to insist on standardized work for students. Indeed, it is customized work, work that responds to the motives of each student but that results in common learning, that is the goal.

6. T. Sizer and N. Sizer, "Grappling," *Phi Delta Kappan,* Nov. 1999, *81*(3), pp. 184–190.

7. The phrase *product focus* describes attention to the products of students in response to the work they are given. Students produce solutions to problems. They also produce insights into issues. Performances and exhibitions are student products as well. Product focus is not to be confused with the so-called project method, with which I am not enthralled.

8. R. J. Stiggins, "Assessment, Student Confidence, and School Success," Phi Delta Kappan, Nov. 1999, *81*(3), p. 195.

9. *New World Dictionary.* New York: The World Publishing Company, 1974.

10. R. Rosenthal and L. Jacobson, *Pygmalion in the Classroom* (Austin, Tex.: Holt, Rinehart and Winston, 1968).

Chapter Seven

1. L. B. Resnick and M. W. Hall, "Learning Organizations for Sustainable Education Reform," *Daedalus,* 1998, *127*(4), p. 97. This and other quotes from this source in this chapter are reprinted by permission of *Daedalus,* Journal of the American Academy of Arts and Sciences.

2. See Resnick and Hall, "Learning Organizations for Sustainable Education Reform," for a useful discussion that bears on this point.

3. I have been told that there is research that supports this point, but I have not yet been able to locate it. I can report that I have used this strategy in my own teaching and found it to be quite effective. It seems that one way to encourage a person to practice a skill or to develop an understanding is to communicate the importance of it to others. The Alcoholics Anonymous program is, in large part, based on such simple understandings.

4. See, for example, N. Kerwait, "Time on Task," A Research Review Report, no. 332. Paper presented at a meeting of the National Commission on Excellence in Education, Washington, D.C., November, 1982 (ED 228236).

5. Resnick and Hall, "Learning Organizations for Sustainable Education Reform."

6. Resnick and Hall, "Learning Organizations for Sustainable Education Reform," p. 97.

7. T. R. Sizer, *Horace's School: Redesigning the American High School* (Boston: Houghton Mifflin, 1992); see especially chap. 6.

8. P. Senge, *The Fifth Discipline: The Art and Practice of the Learning Organization* (New York: Doubleday, 1990).

9. C. E. Silberman, *Crisis in the Classroom: The Remaking of American Education* (New York: Random House, 1970).

10. For example, the outcomes-based approach to instruction grew out of a strongly behaviorist perspective, tracing back to the 1960s' fascination with behavioral objectives and management by objectives, and this did much to reinforce the view that outcomes-based education was value laden and that the values with which it was laden were antithetical to the values many parents wanted for their children.

11. W. Waller, *The Sociology of Teaching* (New York: Wiley, 1967; originally published 1932), p. 1.

12. See, for example, G. Moller and M. Katzenmeyer, *Every Teacher as a Leader* (San Francisco: Jossey-Bass, 1996).

13. *Critical friends* conversations are designed to promote collegial analysis of classroom problems. Although such improvement teams are being used more and more in the workplace, in the context of schools, they are still seen as innovative and sometimes threatening, as I discussed earlier in this chapter. Teachers typically are isolated from each other and seldom see each other work, and the critical friends idea directly assaults the norm of the closed classroom door.

14. R. M. Kanter, "Introduction," in *Rosabeth Moss Kanter on the Frontiers of Management* (Boston: Harvard Business School Press, 1997), p. 8.

Part Three

1. P. F. Drucker, *Managing in Turbulent Times* (New York: HarperCollins, 1980).

2. T. J. Peters, *Thriving on Chaos* (New York: Knopf, 1987).

Chapter Eight

1. R. W. Callahan, *Education and the Cult of Efficiency* (Chicago: University of Chicago Press, 1963).

2. It is well to keep in mind that change can have unanticipated *beneficial* consequences as well as unanticipated harmful consequences. When a change effort fails to produce intended results, leaders should determine that there

are no unseen benefits before they decide to abandon it. Similarly, even when a change effort succeeds in producing the intended results, leaders should ensure that any unintended negative consequences that also occur do not "cost" more than the beneficial consequences may be worth. Sociologists have long been concerned with such manifest and latent functions; see, for example, R. K. Merton, *Social Theory and Social Structure* (New York: Free Press, 1968).

3. See, for example, B. Joyce and B. Showers, "Synthesis of Research on Staff Development: A Framework for Future Study and a State-of-the Art Analysis," *Educational Leadership*, Nov. 1987, *45*(3), p. 77.

4. J. M. Burns, *Leadership* (New York: HarperCollins, 1978).

5. See T. J. Sergiovanni, *Leadership for the Schoolhouse: How Is It Different? Why Is It Important?* (San Francisco: Jossey-Bass, 1996).

6. M. Wheatley, *Lessons from the New Workplace* (videocassette) (Carlsbad, Calif.: CRM Films, 1992).

7. S. Farkas and J. Johnson, *Given the Circumstances: Teachers Talk About Public Education Today* (New York: Public Agenda Foundation, 1996).

8. In presentations, Tom Peters frequently comments on the minimal "inspirational value" of the statement, "We're no worse than anybody else." Behaving each spring like some business leaders behave, when test scores come out many school leaders utter some version of this phrase.

9. This sentence is an adaptation of John Dewey's classic definition of reflective thought (*How We Think* [Lexington, Mass.: Heath, 1910]). Those who aspire to lead change could do worse than read this classic work. Other relevant books that are also accessible to the nonspecialist reader (which most of us are) are P. L. Berger, *The Social Construction of Reality: A Treatise in the Sociology of Knowledge* (New York: Irvington, 1966); W. Waller, *The Sociology of Teaching* (New York: Wiley, 1967, originally published 1932); L. Cremin, *The Transformation of the School* (New York: Knopf, 1961); D. Lortie, *Schoolteacher: A Sociological Study* (Chicago: University of Chicago Press, 1975); D. Berliner and B. Biddle, *The Manufactured Crisis: Myths, Fraud and the Attack on America's Public Schools* (Reading, Mass.: Addison-Wesley, 1995); L. Bolman and T. Deal, *Reframing Organizations: Artistry, Choice, and Leadership* (San Francisco: Jossey-Bass, 1997); P. C. Schlechty, *Schools for the 21st Century: Leadership Imperatives for Educational Reform* (San Francisco: Jossey-Bass, 1990); P. C. Schlechty, *Inventing Better Schools: An Action Plan for Educational Reform* (San Francisco: Jossey-Bass, 1997); and four reports from Public Agenda: J. Johnson and J. Immerwahr, *First Things First: What Americans Expect from the Public Schools* (New York: Public Agenda Foundation, 1994); J. Johnson and

S. Farkas, *Assignment Incomplete: The Unfinished Business of Education Reform* (New York: Public Agenda Foundation, 1995); S. Farkas and J. Johnson, *Given the Circumstances: Teachers Talk About Public Education Today* (New York: Public Agenda Foundation, 1996); J. Johnson and S. Farkas, *Getting By: What American Teenagers Really Think About Their Schools* (New York: Public Agenda Foundation, 1997). For the person who wants a deeper understanding of the power of symbols and symbolic expressions, I recommend two classic works by E. Goffman, *The Presentation of Self in Everyday Life* (New York: Doubleday, 1959), and *Frame Analysis: An Essay on the Organization of Experience* (Cambridge, Mass.: Harvard University Press, 1974). Any leader or group of leaders that takes the time to read these books and to reflect on their meaning for what the leaders are about should be well prepared to inspire beliefs in others and to teach the great lessons that must be taught if our schools are to serve us well in the twenty-first century.

10. See Schlechty, *Inventing Better Schools,* and Chapter Nine in this volume for some suggestions for the kind of assessments leaders might want to conduct and ways to conduct them.

11. One of the most effective workshops I ever participated in was on total quality management and was provided to the senior staff of a large urban school district by a local business that was noted for its success in implementing a TQM program. The designers and providers of the workshop were two persons who, some years earlier, had dropped out of school in the district from which the trainees came—quite a reward for the providers and perhaps a bit of revenge thrown in.

12. See Lortie, *Schoolteacher.*

13. See, for example, H. Becker and B. Geer, *Boys in White: Student Culture in Medical School* (New Brunswick, N.J.: Transaction, 1977, originally published 1961); Lortie, *Schoolteacher.*

14. Wheatley, *Lessons from the New Workplace.*

Chapter Nine

1. R. E. Kelley, "In Praise of Followers," *Harvard Business Review,* Nov.–Dec. 1988, pp. 142–148.

2. J. P. Kotter, *Leading Change* (Boston: Harvard Business School Press, 1996).

3. I have already written extensively on the role of beliefs in shaping the change agenda. See, for example, P. C. Schlechty, *Schools for the 21st Century: Leadership Imperatives for Educational Reform* (San Francisco: Jossey-Bass, 1990)

and *Inventing Better Schools: An Action Plan for Educational Reform* (San Francisco: Jossey-Bass, 1997) for specific suggestions about how leaders can use the development of consensus around a set of beliefs and the creation of a common vision to build teams and orient action. Among the other useful materials available are two books I have found especially helpful: T. A. Kayser, *Building Team Power: How to Unleash the Collaborative Genius of Work Teams* (Burr Ridge, Ill.: Irwin, 1994) and M. Schrage, *No More Teams! Mastering the Dynamics of Creative Collaboration* (New York: Doubleday, 1995).

4. A. Etzioni, *A Comparative Analysis of Complex Organizations: On Power, Involvement, and Their Correlates* (New York: Free Press, 1961).

5. É. Durkheim, *The Rules of Sociological Method* (New York: Free Press, 1938).

6. See, for example, E. Fromm, *Escape From Freedom* (New York: Farrar & Rinehart, 1942); E. Hoffer, *The True Believer: Thoughts on the Nature of Mass Movements* (London: Secker & Warburg, 1952).

7. See Schlechty, *Inventing Better Schools,* chap. 12.

8. See Schlechty, *Inventing Better Schools,* for further discussion of this.

9. Schlechty, http://www.clsr.org/.

10. See, for example, W. Ury, *Getting Past No: Negotiating Your Way from Confrontation to Cooperation* (New York: Bantam, 1993).

11. See also R. A. Heifetz, *Leadership Without Easy Answers* (Cambridge, Mass.: Harvard University Press, Belknap Press, 1994).

12. P. Senge, *The Fifth Discipline: The Art and Practice of the Learning Organization* (New York: Doubleday, 1990); P. Drucker, *Management: Tasks, Practices, and Responsibilities* (New York: HarperCollins, 1974); A. S. Grove, *High Output Management* (New York: Random House, 1985).

13. M. Walton, *The Deming Management Method* (New York: Putnam, 1986).

Chapter Ten

1. See P. C. Schlechty, *Inventing Better Schools: An Action Plan for Educational Reform* (San Francisco: Jossey-Bass, 1997).

2. I and others have made serious suggestions in this regard; see Schlechty, *Inventing Better Schools,* chap. 13; Education Commission of the States, *Governing America's Schools: Changing the Rules* (Denver, Colo.: Education Commission of the States, 1999).

3. J. P. Kotter, *Leading Change* (Boston: Harvard Business School Press, 1996).

4. D. Lortie, *Schoolteacher: A Sociological Study* (Chicago: University of Chicago Press, 1975).

Index